Introduction to Public Speaking

FOUNTAINHEAD
PRESS

Our "green" initiatives include:

Electronic Products

We deliver products in nonpaper form whenever possible. This includes PDF downloadables, flash drives, and CDs.

Electronic Samples

We use a new electronic sampling system, called Xample. Instructor samples are sent via a personalized Web page that links to PDF downloads.

FSC Certified Printers

All of our printers are certified by the Forest Service Council which promotes environmentally and socially responsible management of the world's forests. This program allows consumer groups, individual consumers, and businesses to work together to promote responsible use of the world's forests as a renewable and sustainable resource.

Recycled Paper

Most of our products are printed on a minimum of 30% post consumer waste recycled paper.

Support of Green Causes

When we do print, we donate a portion of our revenue to Green causes. Listed below are a few of the organizations that have received donations from Fountainhead Press. We welcome your feedback and suggestions for contributions, as we are always searching for worthy initiatives.

Rainforest 2 Reef

Environmental Working Group

The Speaker's Primer by Joseph M. Valenzano III, Stephen W. Braden and Melissa A. Broeckelman-Post

Designer: Susan Moore

Books may be purchased for educational purposes.

For information, please call or write:

1-800-586-0330

Fountainhead Press
Southlake, TX 76092

Web site: www.fountainheadpress.com
E-mail: customerservice@fountainheadpress.com

First Edition

ISBN: 978-1-68036-307-4

Printed in the United States of America

Table of Contents

Key Terms • 167

Index • 173

1
Understanding Public Communication

The ability to use symbols, create meaning, and communicate ideas defines what it means to be human. To be sure, many different species communicate in their own way—dogs bark, snakes hiss, and some species of insects dance—but human beings are unique in our complex use of symbols to define ourselves and the world in which we live. Even more so, we influence people and move them to action through the creative and effective presentation of our ideas. Think about the different contexts in which we do this—contexts specific to the human world.

When we think of public speaking, the first context that comes to mind is politics. Public speaking is certainly an integral part of any democracy, and it remains one of the more commonly understood venues in which people deliver remarks to audiences. Debates, campaign events, presidential addresses, and a myriad of other situations provide politicians with opportunities to speak to audiences. However, the political realm is not the only one in which public speaking skills are a necessity.

In the private sector, where companies seek to convince consumers to purchase their goods or services, representatives are often called upon to deliver presentations designed to facilitate sales. Corporate executives also address their employees and investors periodically to inform them about the state of the company's finances and what the goals are for the coming quarter or year. In business, these modes of interaction involving speech have been influenced greatly in recent years by the development of electronic media such as Skype, Prezi, and even something as simple as conference calling. But the importance and utility of speech do not stop with politics and business—it even extends to our personal lives.

At some point in all our lives, we will attend a wedding and a funeral. We may also go to an anniversary celebration, awards ceremony, or some other function where we hear, and perhaps even deliver, speeches. Each of these situations requires us to know how to properly develop and deliver remarks to a specific audience in much the same way that political and business contexts demand we do. Quite simply, the use of symbols through speech is a central part of what it means to be human. In this handbook, we will help you learn how to create and convey effective presentations so that you can maximize your ability to deliver information, change minds, and influence audiences.

In this chapter, we provide a brief foundation of some important concepts related to understanding how the communication process works. This breakdown of the central components of communication is then followed by an explanation of how public speaking is different from casual conversation. Finally, we dispel some popular myths about public speaking so that you can move forward and learn how to deliver effective presentations.

Communication Models ✗ - 3 types

We use theories to explain most, if not all, human behaviors. The field of communication has several models that illustrate how communication functions between people. It is essential to understand how these models work because they inform the choices we make in preparing and performing a speech. In this section, we will cover three different models, each of which is a valid way of explaining communication in different contexts. First, we discuss the most basic model of the communication process, the linear model of communication. Then we explain the interactive model of communication, which complicates the linear model by introducing a few new variables to the communication process. Finally, we delve into the transactional model of communication, which is a bit more involved than the interactive model.

Linear Model of Communication (#1)

The first model developed to explain the communication process was the **linear model of communication** (see Figure 1.1). This model views communication as something that one person does to another. In this model, communication flows in one direction only, much like a river. The idea is very basic and at its most complicated contains seven elements.

FIGURE 1.1

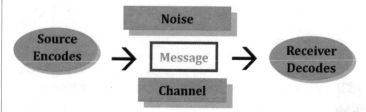

The first of these elements is the source, which in terms of public speaking is the speaker. The speaker is the person responsible for inventing the idea on which he or she intends to speak and crafting the message that conveys that idea to an audience. When the speaker converts the idea into words he or she is encoding it. This encoding process is simply taking an abstract notion and giving it meaning through the application of symbols. The end result of the encoding process is a message, which is the content or idea the source initially wanted to provide to the audience. This message is then delivered through a channel, which in the case of public speaking is the voice. A person's voice is the channel through which a source's encoded message travels to an audience in a presentation.

So far this sounds fairly simple, and you may be wondering how it could get confusing or how a person's message could be misinterpreted. Well, even in that simple initial stage of encoding and delivery through the channel, speakers can make poor word choices that do not accurately reflect the meaning of the source's idea. The speaker may also use words the audience does not understand when encoding the message. These are two small ways this seemingly easy process can get confusing. Problems, though, are not simply reserved to the source in the linear model, so let's take a look at how the linear model explains what happens after the message travels through the channel to its destination.

linear model of communication
theory that views communication as a one-way process in which a source conveys an encoded message through a channel to a receiver, who then decodes that message

source
the person responsible for inventing the idea on which he or she intends to speak and crafting that idea to an audience

encoding
taking an abstract notion and providing it meaning through the application of symbols

message
the content or idea that the source tries to convey to the audience

channel
the medium through which an encoded message is transmitted from a source to a receiver

When a message is sent, it is also received, and the audience, also called the receiver, processes those symbols. The processing done by the receiver is called decoding, which essentially takes the symbols used to encode the message and draws meaning from them. This is much like what some kids do with decoder rings in cereal boxes. To understand the message, you need the key to understand how it was encoded. In terms of public speaking, receivers need to understand the symbol system, or language, used by the speaker when sending the message.

receiver
the person or audience that a message is being transmitted to

As before, this may seem easy, but all of us have been in a situation when as the receiver of a message we did not exactly understand what was being said. This can occur in a classroom during a lecture, in a debate between two political candidates, and even in a casual conversation with a friend. We may be speaking the same language, but when we have different definitions of words we process them differently than the speaker might intend, resulting in confusion. What leads to the interruption or inaccurate decoding of a message sometimes comes not from a person's listening ability but from some other force.

decoding
the process of drawing meaning from the symbols that were used to encode a message

The other force that can impede the delivery and proper decoding of a message is called noise, and noise is the final component of the linear model of communication. Noise refers to anything that can change the message after the source encodes and sends it. There are a variety of different types of noise, some physical and some psychological, but all throw a wrench into the communication process. The chart in Table 1.1 shows the different types of noise speakers and audiences might encounter during a presentation.

noise
anything that can change the message after the source encodes and sends it

TABLE 1.1

Types of Noise	
Physical Noise	**Psychological Noise**
<ul><li>Other sounds</li><li>Visual barriers</li><li>Poor volume and projection</li><li>Distractions in the room</li><li>Hunger, tiredness, and other bodily limitations</li></ul>	<ul><li>Preoccupation with other thoughts</li><li>Emotional reaction to the topic</li><li>Prejudice or ill will toward the speaker</li><li>Unwillingness to listen</li><li>Resistance to the message</li></ul>

In looking at this model, it seems to adequately explain a basic form of communication, but we all know that the process is more involved, because receivers are not simply sponges that absorb information provided by a source. So, although usable, this model provides an incomplete explanation of how communication functions between people. It was not long after the model was developed that it was rethought and extended to include a more active role for receivers. Next, we go over the changes that were made in the more thorough interactive model of communication.

Interactive Model of Communication (#2)

The interactive model of communication (see Figure 1.2) expands our understanding of the communication process by taking into account that messages flow back and forth from the receiver. Whereas the linear model of communication views the communication process as complete when the receiver decodes the sender's message, the interactive model does not; here we will see the sender and receiver are both responsible for encoding and decoding messages.

interactive model of communication
communication theory that views communication as a two-way process that includes feedback and the environment

FIGURE 1.2

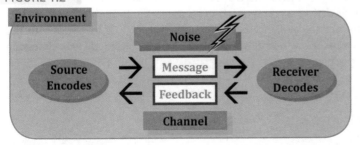

feedback
the receiver's response to a message that is sent to the sender

The main way in which the interactive model is different from the linear model is in the concept of feedback. Feedback occurs after the receiver decodes the sender's message and is essentially the receiver's response to the message. This new message then flows linearly back to the sender, who becomes the receiver of the feedback to the original message. To better conceptualize this process, think about a telephone call or a text message.

When you say something or write a message on one end and send it to the receiver, the receiver processes your message and responds either verbally or nonverbally. You then receive that response, thus completing the communication process. The introduction of feedback creates a fuller picture of what happens when two or more people interact.

environment
the context in which the communication process takes place

A second aspect added in the interactive model of communication is that of environment. The environment provides a deeper understanding of context than noise did in the linear model. In fact, noise is part of the environment, but not the whole thing. The environment is the context, which includes a plethora of different things that both help and hinder the communication process. See Table 1.2 for a few aspects of the environment that both senders and receivers should consider when encoding and decoding messages.

TABLE 1.2

Environmental Elements		
• Beliefs	• Participants	• Physical setting
• Context	• Relationships	• Values
• History		

Although it provides a better picture of how communication works, even the interactive model is not perfect. One of the major missing components in this useful model is the idea that receivers and senders do not wait to provide feedback. Next, we will look at perhaps the richest explanation of the communication process, the transactional model.

Transactional Model of Communication (#3)

Although more illustrative of how the mechanics of the communication process works, the interactive model of communication did not take into account one very important aspect of how we communicate: the fact that both encoders and decoders send and receive messages simultaneously, and both parties use the same channel. The transactional model of communication (see Figure 1.3) is a far more complete explanation of communication because it recognizes that communication is constant and thus we play the roles of sender and receiver simultaneously in just about every interaction.

transactional model of communication
the theory that views communication as a constant process in which all parties simultaneously play the roles of sender and receiver

FIGURE 1.3

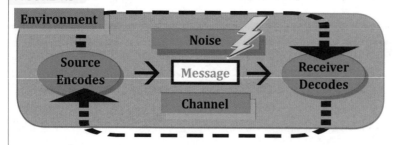

This model is particularly useful when explaining the dynamic context of face-to-face communication, such as what occurs when we have a conversation or deliver a presentation to an audience. In both of these scenarios the sender is also reacting in real time to how the audience is receiving the message. If the sender notices confused looks, perhaps he or she then asks a question to find out what needs to be clarified. This change in remarks is a direct result of feedback from the audience.

The transactional model of communication helps us understand that things never go as planned, and so we constantly adapt to feedback. This dynamic model which explains how communication functions most accurately reflects public speaking as a process. Now that we have a model for appreciating the complexity of the speech process, let's get a picture of how not all speech is the same by differentiating speech from casual conversation.

Conversation Versus Speech

All speaking situations, and thus all forms of speech, are not equal, although there are similarities among contexts. Informal conversations and speech have several such overlaps but also some significant differences. When we understand some of these similarities and differences it can place public speaking in a new, less threatening light (see Table 1.3).

TABLE 1.3

Similarities and Differences in Conversation and Speech	
Similarities	Differences
<ul><li>Audience-centered</li><li>Attention to feedback</li><li>Goal-driven</li><li>Logic is required</li><li>Stories for effect</li></ul>	<ul><li>Language choices</li><li>Speeches require more organization</li><li>Use of notes</li><li>No interruptions</li><li>Delivery style</li><li>Physical arrangement</li></ul>

We all know how to talk to each other, and rarely does a day go by when we don't have a casual conversation with someone. Certain aspects of those interactions also color public speaking situations. First, both conversations and speeches are audience-centered. By this we mean that we pay attention to the audience when making choices regarding our speech. In conversations as well as speeches there are certain topics we address only with particular people or groups. We also pay attention to the feedback we receive from the receivers in both situations so we know how to respond. Both conversation and speech are activities centered upon the audience.

A second quality shared by conversation and speech is that both are goal-driven activities. We seek to accomplish something, whether it is conveying information or changing the audience's mind, whenever we either have a casual conversation with someone or deliver more formal remarks. These goals differ with each event and interaction, but there is always something we want to achieve. A third area of overlap related to the achievement of goals is that in both conversation and public speaking we need to organize our thoughts logically in order for the receiver to understand what we are saying. Finally, in both situations we want to tell stories to our audiences for maximum effect. In short, conversation and public speaking both seek the same outcome in an organized way that does not bore people. This is not to say that there are not differences between the two communication practices.

One significant difference between the two relates to the language choices we make. Conversations tend to be colloquial and relaxed, while public speaking requires more formal language. For instance, in public speaking contexts speakers should not swear or use slang terms, but in conversations these things may very well happen.

There are a few other notable differences between public speaking and conversation. One of those pertains to the structure of the remarks. Although both conversations and speeches present information in a logical manner, speeches are more clearly organized and less prone to tangents than conversations, and note cards or outlines are often employed to help speakers stay on track. Additionally, whereas we all know people who interrupt a conversation, such interruptions are not the norm during formal presentations.

A final area of difference can be seen in delivery. Conversations often occur in very small intimate settings that do not require people to raise their voices; however, when giving a speech you must make sure everyone in the audience can hear you. Physical delivery is also different in that when giving a speech we should avoid distracting mannerisms and verbal pauses, while these things often feature prominently in conversations. During a conversation, people are usually sitting or standing together so that every person can see the others' faces, but during a speech, the speaker usually stands at the front of the room facing a seated audience that is looking only at the speaker.

Now that we understand how communication works, and how public speaking is not all that different from conversation, let's cover some common misconceptions regarding public speaking that many people hold.

Public Speaking Myths

It is no secret that people communicate with varying degrees of skill. Some people are adept at interpersonal conversation, while some are more comfortable communicating in groups. When it comes to public speaking and formal presentations, some people naturally feel more comfortable, even enjoy the experience, while others fear it more than they do death. That fear, like many others, is irrational and indicates that someone has bought into several myths regarding public speaking. In fact, as with interpersonal and small group communication, with training and practice anyone can deliver a competent speech. In this section, we will cover those myths that keep people from developing their public speaking skills—and as the first myth indicates, public speaking is a skill, not a talent.

Myth #1
Public Speaking Is a Talent, Not a Skill

Good speakers are made, not born, and they are made through hours of practice and preparation. Like any skill or complicated task, public speaking takes time to develop because of the many components involved. Thankfully, many ways exist to hone this skill and become a competent public speaker.

People can start improving their speaking skills by taking a public speaking course and reading and studying texts such as this one. These courses are available at colleges and universities around the country, as well as more informally through organizations such as Toastmasters. One course, though, is not a silver bullet and will simply provide you with the tools you need to improve. The real work comes when you practice with the tools provided to you.

Another way to develop your speaking skills is by watching and listening to good speakers. Many people learn well through modeling, and there is no shortage of good speakers or speeches for you to read and watch. This exposure to good practices will help spark ideas and provide samples upon which you can reflect as you work to improve your speaking.

Finally, there is no substitute for preparation and experience. Taking as much time as necessary to develop your speech, practicing, and editing it will pay off. Additionally, the more speeches you deliver, the better you will be because you will become more comfortable with the context and more familiar with your own speech patterns. Don't shy away from chances to give presentations but rather embrace them as opportunities to hone your skills.

Myth #2
Speech Is Easy; We Do It All the Time

As we have shown, communicating is a natural human activity. As children, we begin trying to speak very early in life, and because we have been speaking for so long we think it is easy to do. But just because we do it all the time doesn't mean we do it correctly or as well as we could. We are all guilty of having said something at an inappropriate moment or of not being prepared to answer a question or deliver remarks. Presentations are not something that can be prepared the night before and then flawlessly delivered. They are, in fact, the opposite.

Choosing the right words to convey ideas to an audience takes thought, and thought takes time. It takes even more time to organize your thoughts into a coherent presentation, and so waiting until the last minute is simply not an option. Finally, we may be comfortable with speaking in conversation, but presentations to attentive audiences in a formal setting are an entirely different matter. This is why it takes time and practice to speak well.

There is a big difference between speaking well and delivering a good, effective speech. Just because we have been doing something for a while does not mean that we do it well.

Myth #3
There Is No "Right Way" to Deliver a Speech

Many people believe that there is no correct way to give a speech and that all ways of delivering a speech are equally acceptable and effective. If that were the case, we would not have great speeches or speakers, because they would all be equally good. There is a proper way to construct and deliver a speech, and to be a competent presenter you need to learn what is and is not effective.

To say there is a "right" way of delivering a speech does not mean there is not more than one way to approach a speech topic. There are untold ways in which a topic could be covered by a speaker; however, the principles of organization, delivery, language, and style apply to how the treatment of that topic is conveyed. In this book, we will show you these guiding principles for effective speech and illustrate that the idea that all speeches are equally good is simply not correct.

Summary

In this chapter we introduced you to some foundational ideas regarding communication and public speaking. We explained the three models of communication: linear, interactive, and transactional. We then showed how conversation and public speaking share certain similarities and differences. Finally, we dispelled a few myths people hold about public speaking. This overview of some foundational concepts related to public speaking will help provide a clearer understanding of how to develop effective public presentations.

Key Terms

channel 2
decoding 3
encoding 2
environment 4
feedback 4
interactive model of communication 3
linear model of communication 2
message 2
noise 3
receiver 3
source 2
transactional model of communication 4

In COMM 1000/1003

There are a number of myths surrounding this course. Let's address these myths here:

1. **This course is an easy A.** Even though this is an entry level course, the principles of delivery, organization and time along with the preparation time required to be an effective public speaker are not always easy. While the concepts of this course are not difficult to understand, putting these concepts into practice can pose challenges. The course is not difficult if you come to class and keep up with all assignments. On the flip side, it should not be viewed as an easy A.

2. **I'll never have to deliver a speech like this outside of this class.** The concepts taught in this class are only the beginning. You will likely find yourself referring back to what you learned in this class throughout your college career when giving presentations in other classes or for organizations you belong to. Over and over we run into individuals—in town, on airplanes, at conventions, etc.—that

tell us how much they valued having to take public speaking in college. Most admit they didn't take it serious enough at the time, and would have paid much better attention had they known how often public speaking would be required of them.

3. **It is impossible to do well on the final exam.** The final exam in this course is cumulative and covers a lot of content. However, keeping up with the readings and truly understanding the concepts taught in this course beyond knowing the basic definitions outlined in the text, ensures you will do well on the final. Well doesn't always mean an A, but a B is considered good and a C is considered average. These are all acceptable grades and can be achieved if time and effort is put into learning (not just memorizing) as you progress throughout the semester.

2
Speech Anxiety

Many people have fears and anxieties about a variety of issues. Some people fear animals, others shiver at the thought of entering open spaces, some go rigid when they see spiders, and yet others are afraid of tight spaces. Fears are a part of being human, and either we must find a way to manage our fears, or they will manage us. In this chapter, we examine a common fear that grips people from all walks of life: the fear of delivering a speech. Most communication scholars label this anxiety communication apprehension. There has been a plethora of research and testing done in the communication discipline over the last forty years, and coping methods of varying degrees of success have been developed to help alleviate the anxiety produced by the mere prospect of public speaking.

We have many anxieties, and some of these manifest as a phobia, or "a persistent, irrational fear of a specific object, activity, or situation that leads to a compelling desire to avoid."[1] Phobias are more than discomfort or anxiety; they are an intense activation of the base instinct to avoid a threat. For instance, those with arachnophobia, the fear of spiders, will run at the sight of a spider or leap onto a couch just to avoid contact with the small creature. Phobias are, in many instances, irrational responses to something that should not be perceived as a significant threat.

There are a great many phobias, and Table 2.1 provides a list of those that often rank in the top ten fears people have. These phobias impact our lives, often in negative ways. They may prevent us from doing things we want to do, sometimes including advancing our own careers, because a fear makes us incapable of completing a task. In this respect, it is not hard to imagine how a fear of public speaking, or communication apprehension, can impede our ability to get a promotion, complete a sale, or excel in a classroom. In this chapter, we will focus on apprehension in a public speaking

phobia
a persistent, irrational fear of a specific object, activity, or situation that leads to a compelling desire to avoid

1 Dictionary.com, http://dictionary.reference.com/browse/phobia. (Accessed January 31, 2012).
2 http://www.phobia-fear-release.com/list-of-the-top-ten-phobias.htm.

situation. We will provide an overview of communication apprehension, go over the physical effects induced by this condition, and finally present some ways in which you can cope with anxiety in public speaking situations.

TABLE 2.1

Top Ten Phobias/Fears

1. Arachnophobia: fear of spiders
2. Social phobia: fear of being evaluated
3. Aerophobia: fear of flying
4. Agoraphobia: fear of not being able to escape
5. Claustrophobia: fear of being trapped in a small space
6. Acrophobia: fear of heights
7. Emetophobia: fear of vomit
8. Carcinophobia: fear of cancer
9. Brontophobia: fear of thunderstorms
10. Necrophobia: fear of death

www.phobia-fear-release.com/list-of-the-top-ten-phobias.html[2]

Communication Apprehension

communication apprehension
the fear or anxiety associated with real or anticipated communication with another or others

Anxiety caused by the prospect of public speaking is often referred to as communication apprehension, which provides a more accurate depiction of this fear. Communication apprehension is defined as "the fear or anxiety associated with real or anticipated communication with another or others."[3] This is a broader definition than simply calling it a "fear of public speaking" for two reasons. First, communication apprehension is not specific to public speaking; rather it can manifest in a variety of different speaking contexts, including one-on-one interactions. Second, "fear" is an absolute term, whereas apprehension is best understood on a linear scale (see Figure 2.1): On one end, we are not reluctant to communicate at all, and on the other we are always reluctant and fearful to communicate with others. Neither is ever truly the case, but rather we all experience communication apprehension in varying degrees.

FIGURE 2.1

comfortable   apprehensive

There have been numerous studies regarding communication apprehension and its effects on people. Those who experience higher degrees of communication apprehension are less satisfied with their abilities to express themselves and are not as assertive in interactions with others.[4] One would think that, as a result of this, those with high communication apprehension would begin working on presentations in advance, but the opposite is actually typically true. People with high communication apprehension often procrastinate because they do not believe they will succeed.[5] This is an example of the self-fulfilling prophecy, which is convincing yourself that something is going to happen before it does, thus leading to the occurrence of what you originally expected.

self-fulfilling prophecy
convincing yourself that something is going to happen before it does, thus leading to the occurrence of what you originally expected

The self-fulfilling prophecy can be negative or positive. If you convince yourself that you will fail a calculus examination, then, with that mind-set, you likely will. However, convincing yourself that you will do well in an upcoming soccer game, although certainly not a guarantee, will enhance your chances of success. These preconceived notions have a powerful effect on people, and later we will suggest some ways to help ensure that you have a positive vision of delivering your speech.

One important step in understanding your level of communication apprehension is identifying to what degree you are anxious about interacting with others. Professor James McCroskey developed a survey instrument that

3 McCroskey, J. C. (1977). Oral communication apprehension: A review of recent research. *Human Communication Research, 4,* 78–96.
4 Ayres, J., & Heuett, B. L. (1997). The relationship between visual imagery and public speaking apprehension. *Communication Reports (1),* 87–94.
5 Behnke, R., & Sawyer, C. (1999). Public speaking procrastination as a correlate of public speaking communication apprehension and self-perceived public speaking competence. *Communication Research Reports,* 40–47.

helps individuals measure their level of communication apprehension. The PRCA-24, the latest version of this scale, can be very helpful in identifying your own degree of communication apprehension. See the sample of the PRCA-24 on the next page.

Learning about yourself is just one step in managing communication apprehension; you must also understand what the fear physically does to you. Many people believe they know the answer to this, but what we are about to tell you may surprise you and help you find ways to overcome your fear.

Physical Effects of Communication Apprehension

Anxieties begin in the brain with thoughts and perceptions about things around us that we believe threaten us. Once they emerge in our thoughts, anxieties then physically manifest themselves, and to some people this is more distressing than the mental duress. In fact, the physical dimensions of anxiety are what we naturally focus on when we feel fear or trepidation toward some external stimulus.

Suppose you are batting in a fast-pitch softball game with two outs in the bottom of the ninth inning; the bases are loaded, there are two outs, and your team is down by three runs. You go to the batter's box, your stomach is churning, you are perspiring, and there are butterflies in your stomach. You are aware of all these physiological feelings, but how much do the fans in the stands actually see? The answer is that they see very little, and often none, of your anxiety—even the physical effects. The same principle is true of giving a speech to a live audience. You may have the same feelings as the batter, but the audience sees little, if any, of the effects of the anxiety. For speakers who are self-conscious about their appearance while delivering the speech, this should afford some comfort, because the bottom line is this: no one sees your anxiety or apprehension.

To further illustrate the invisibility of anxiety let's take a look at some of the common physical reactions that occur when we are anxious or stressed. One physical effect of anxiety is a rise in blood pressure. This is not necessarily a bad thing, as it can give you energy, nor is it anything an audience will notice and correctly attribute to fear on your part. Higher blood pressure in these situations sends signals to the brain that it needs to pay heightened attention to your surroundings—not a bad thing. Blood pressure is also something that is internal, and thus not likely to be noticed by people around you. Of course, it can cause your face to flush red, but this can be explained away as a result of the heat in a room, not your anxiety over a public speaking situation.

In addition to higher blood pressure, some people also experience shortness of breath when they are anxious, and in speaking situations this can negatively affect the delivery of the speech. Shortness of breath, however, can also be explained by myriad other causes. Perhaps you are coming down with or recovering from a cold; you may suffer from asthma; there may be something in the air to which you are allergic. All of these are plausible explanations to which other people, or you, can attribute the shortness of breath.

A third physical effect of stress and anxiety is called galvanic skin tightening. Your skin, like any organ, responds to stimuli and stress. Specifically, your skin tightens when you are anxious, nervous, or stressed. Obviously we ourselves do not even feel this happening, so it stands to reason that the audience cannot see it either. Interestingly enough, this particular response to anxiety is used as an indicator of deception on lie detector tests and is virtually impossible to fake. For our purposes, though, it is enough to know that this physical effect of fear is not noticeable to the human eye—it is related to one of the most common physical reactions to anxiety, though, which we will discuss next.

The tightening of our skin tends to make us sweat as well, and perspiration is the final physical manifestation of anxiety we will discuss. Apprehension can cause us to perspire, but that doesn't mean the people around us believe we sweat because of anxiety; there are multiple factors that may make us perspire. Many other variables that play a role in our sweating are part of our external environment, such as sunshine, a room that has elevated temperature, or a very crowded, small conference room. You also may have just concluded a workout and taken a hot shower, which can also make you sweat for a period of time. These variables are all outside speakers' power to change, but may make them perspire nonetheless. In these situations, it is important to understand two things: the audience does not automatically correlate perspiration with fear, and, more importantly, the audience members are in the same conditions you are in and so are probably dealing with the same physical responses.

Personal Report of Communication Apprehension

This instrument is composed of twenty-four statements concerning feelings about communicating with others. Please indicate the degree to which each statement applies to you by marking whether you: Strongly Disagree = 1; Disagree = 2; are Neutral = 3; Agree = 4; Strongly Agree = 5

_____1. I dislike participating in group discussions.
_____2. Generally, I am comfortable while participating in group discussions.
_____3. I am tense and nervous while participating in group discussions.
_____4. I like to get involved in group discussions.
_____5. Engaging in a group discussion with new people makes me tense and nervous.
_____6. I am calm and relaxed while participating in group discussions.
_____7. Generally, I am nervous when I have to participate in a meeting.
_____8. Usually, I am comfortable when I have to participate in a meeting.
_____9. I am very calm and relaxed when I am called upon to express an opinion at a meeting.
_____10. I am afraid to express myself at meetings.

SCORING:
Group Discussion: 18 – (scores for items 2, 4, & 6) + (scores for items 1,3, & 5)
Meetings: 18 – (scores for items 8, 9, & 12) + (scores for items 7, 10, & 11)
Interpersonal: 18 – (scores for items 14, 16, & 17) + (scores for items 13, 15, & 18)
Public Speaking: 18 – (scores for items 19, 21, & 23) + (scores for items 20, 22, & 24)

Group Discussion Score: _____
Interpersonal Score: _____
Meetings Score: _____
Public Speaking Score: _____
To obtain your total score for the PRCA, simply add your sub-scores together. _____

Scores can range from 24–120. Scores below 51 represent people who have very low CA. Scores between 51 and 80 represent people with average CA. Scores above 80 represent people who have high levels of trait CA.

To see the entire report, go to: http://www.jamescmccroskey.com/measures/prca24.htm

There is no doubt that stress and anxiety, particularly in public speaking settings, can elicit physical reactions from each of us, from heightened blood pressure to perspiration. There is also no doubt that audiences do not automatically correlate the physical responses to the anxiety we may be feeling—that is unless we tell them the two are related! The more you focus on your physical responses, the more likely you are to experience even more anxiety. It is far better to just let the body do what it does and not focus on it. After all, if you pay attention to your physical response to anxiety, your audience will do so as well.

So, we now know that everyone experiences communication apprehension to some degree or another and that our bodies react to the stress produced by anxiety in these situations in ways that are virtually invisible to the audience. Both of these facts should provide some comfort when you prepare a presentation, but there is more we can do to manage our anxiety than simply understanding the situation. In the final section of this chapter, we will go over a few things to assist you with managing both the mental and physical manifestations of anxiety.

Combating Communication Apprehension

Our bodies' reactions to stress may be outside our direct control, but there are several ways we can mitigate the potential damage that anxiety can cause. In this section we will provide several simple tips for preparing a presentation that will help reduce communication anxiety.

Practice, Practice, and Practice

We mentioned earlier that people with high communication apprehension are more likely to procrastinate preparing a speech, despite the fact that they should be spending more time getting ready so they can overcome their fear. So it stands to reason that the first suggestion we have for coping with communication anxiety is to practice your presentation as much as possible for as long as you can.

At first, practice giving the speech alone so that you become more comfortable with what you plan to say. Once you have a final version of your speech prepared and you have practiced it alone, add a mirror to the practice equation. Practicing in front of a mirror can increase your comfort and allow you to see what you look like when delivering the speech. Practicing in front of a mirror is not enough, though, as it does not accurately simulate the situation in which you will be presenting. So, after taking advantage of the mirror, add some actual people to create an audience. Make sure these are people you know and with whom you are comfortable, such as friends and family. Ask them for honest feedback and make some adjustments. This practice regimen helps simulate the experience of delivering your remarks to an actual audience, but there is something else to try to simulate when practicing. We will cover practice more extensively in Chapter 19.

In addition to an audience, whenever possible you should try to have a few practice sessions in the environment within which you will be speaking. If it's a boardroom, then practice at a dining room or kitchen table; if it's a large conference room, see if you can get access to it in advance; if it's a classroom, try to go when there is not a class occupying the space. It is as important to become comfortable and to practice within the environment in which you will speak as it is to simulate the audience to whom you will speak. Practicing with both of these things in mind will help alleviate some apprehension about delivering your talk.

Employ Relaxation Techniques

Practicing remarks in advance is the best suggestion we can offer, but often times you will not be afforded much notice before giving a presentation, thus limiting the amount you can feasibly practice. Such short-term presentations only serve to heighten our apprehension about public speaking, so they require more immediate methods for reducing stress and tension. One such method is to learn to use relaxation techniques before presentations. This is very useful in situations in which you have little time to prepare and practice but can also be helpful when you have had time to practice.

There are a variety of relaxation techniques that can help calm nerves, lower blood pressure, and help you focus before giving a talk. Some require a little more time than others, but all are helpful in a pinch. Simply taking a few minutes to stretch your back, shoulders, and legs will help unleash some pent-up tension in your muscles and allow you to feel and look more comfortable in front of an audience. Remember, public speaking is a physical activity in much the same way jogging and weightlifting are, so it stands to reason that we should prepare for giving speeches in a way similar to how we prepare for workouts.

For some people with high communication apprehension, it might also be beneficial to engage in more structured and consistent stretching exercises. In these instances, joining a Yoga or Pilates class might help train you in more varied methods of relaxation and stretching. It also might provide the opportunity for you to go to a class before or even after a presentation to help reduce tension and relax.

A third relaxation technique is deep breathing, and of all the relaxation techniques we have discussed this one takes the least amount of time. There is a lot to be said for closing your eyes and taking a few deep breaths before beginning a presentation. This helps improve the flow of oxygen in your blood, reduces blood pressure,

Communication Apprehension

Sarah was not looking forward to taking a public speaking class. She remembered the time that she had to give a speech in her history class and was afraid she would have to relive that speech all over again. On that day, Sarah had been so anxious about giving her speech that she waited until the day before to prepare, didn't sleep at all, and did not even eat breakfast before she went to class. Throughout the morning she couldn't concentrate on anything except the fear of standing up in front of the class to speak. By the time Sarah got to her history class she was sweating, having trouble breathing, and worrying that she would forget everything. While she was speaking, Sarah kept tripping over her words, forgot several things she wanted to say, and could feel her face flushing as she struggled to get back on track.

This time, Sarah decided to do things a little differently. As soon as her instructor handed out the first speech assignment, she began doing research and creating an outline, even though she knew she would not need to give her speech for a couple more weeks. She practiced her speech in a mirror several times and then asked several of her friends to listen and provide feedback as she practiced a few more times. Each time she practiced her speech, Sarah could feel her fear subsiding and she became more and more confident. The night before her speech, Sarah felt ready to give her speech, so she went to bed early, and before she fell asleep she spent some time visualizing herself giving her speech successfully. The next morning, Sarah still felt a few butterflies in her stomach and could feel her palms sweating, but she tried to keep her focus on her speech and on her audience. Though she still made a few mistakes, Sarah could see her audience nodding in support, and when her speech was over she felt like she had done a great job and was even starting to look forward to the next speech assignment.

Breathing Exercises

4-7-8 Breathing

This exercise also uses belly breathing to help you relax. You can do this exercise either sitting or lying down.

1. To start, put one hand on your belly and the other on your chest.
2. Take a deep, slow breath from your belly and silently count to 4 as you breathe in.
3. Hold your breath and silently count from 1 to 7.
4. Breathe out completely as you silently count from 1 to 8. Try to get all the air out of your lungs by the time you reach 8.
5. Repeat several times or until you feel calm.

Breath Counting

Sit in a comfortable position with your spine straight and head inclined slightly forward. Gently close your eyes and take a few deep breaths. Then let the breath come naturally without trying to influence it. Ideally it will be quiet and slow, but depth and rhythm may vary.

1. To begin the exercise, count "one" to yourself as you exhale.
2. The next time you exhale, count "two," and so on up to "five."
3. Then begin a new cycle, counting "one" on the next exhalation.

Never count higher than "five" and count only when you exhale. You will know your attention has wandered when you find yourself up to "8," "12," even "19." Try to do 10 minutes of this form of meditation.

and focuses your thoughts. There are various forms of deep breathing exercises in which you can engage, and all are helpful in reducing anxiety before speaking situations.

TABLE 2.2

What Should I Eat Before I Give My Speech?		
	Poor Choice	**Better Choice**
Breakfast	Sugary cereal and white toast with jam	Oatmeal with fruit, nuts, and a glass of milk
	Pancakes or waffles with maple syrup	Scrambled eggs and whole wheat toast
Lunch	Fettuccini alfredo	Grilled chicken with steamed vegetables and brown rice
	Large burger and fries	Turkey, Swiss, lettuce, and tomato sandwich on whole grain bread
Snack	Cookies or candy bar	Fruit and yogurt
	Potato chips and energy drink	String cheese and whole wheat crackers

Finally, it is imperative that when speaking you feel your best, and so you should always get a good night's sleep before your presentation and make sure you are not hungry. When it comes to sleep, you may feel the need to stay up late the night before a talk to practice as much as you can, but if this keeps you from being well rested the next day then the efforts will be counterproductive. In terms of food, be careful not to be hungry when you talk, but also not to be so full as to want to take a nap. Before you speak, have a nutritious meal that includes a healthy balance of complex carbohydrates, proteins, and fats that will be digested slowly, and try to avoid simple carbohydrates and refined sugars that will give you a burst of energy followed by a crash as your blood sugar levels spike and then fall quickly. You should also avoid eating heavy meals that might make you drowsy (see Table 2.2).

Visualize Success

Those with high communication apprehension, envision giving a speech as a torturous experience, and they see all the possible ways they can fail or make mistakes. Like the self-fulfilling prophecy, this often leads to that result, thus perpetuating the cycle of communication apprehension. No amount of practice or relaxation techniques can change the way we envision the speaking experience, so this third way to reduce anxiety aims to combat the negative mental picture we might have of delivering a presentation.

The best time to visualize success is following a practice session; however, it works just about any time you want to do it. After you have practiced your speech a few times and feel more comfortable with it, get in a relaxed position on your bed, the sofa, or a recliner. One thing that is required is for you to be alone, with no distraction. Visualization requires concentration, and so it is important that you do not listen to music, watch television, e-mail, text, or use Facebook or Twitter when trying to do this. Close your eyes and see yourself giving the speech from beginning to end. Visualize your confidence, pride, and good delivery. Concentrate on visualizing what you have control over instead of focusing on audience reactions. Focusing on audience reactions might lead to a letdown if the visualized responses do not occur when you deliver the speech. Visualizing success can work, just like the self-fulfilling prophecy.

Dialogue with the Audience

One of the scariest aspects of public speaking is the perception that you speak to an audience of many people, all of whom are focused on you. One way to reduce the anxiety this situation creates is to change the way we understand the public speaking context. Instead of viewing it as a presentation to a large group, treat it like multiple simultaneous dialogues or conversations. That is to say, instead of presenting to a class of thirty, you are holding thirty conversations at the same time. We all have conversations daily, and so this may help you reduce the anxiety that a group of people may induce.

This dialogic approach can be extended as well if you want to create actual give-and-take with the audience. This can work, especially if the audience is small and well mannered. Before letting audience members join in the discussion, make sure you have a strong grasp of the makeup of your audience and their feelings toward you and the ideas you plan to advocate. One final word of caution regarding dialoguing with an audience: if someone asks a question to which you do not know the answer, be honest and tell the audience you do not know, but that you appreciate the question and will find out and get back to them if you can.

Systematic Desensitization

Each of the suggestions we have made thus far pertains to specific speech situations, and although applicable every time you deliver a speech, in isolation they can have little impact on your overall apprehension toward public speaking. This is where the approach called systematic desensitization comes in. Systematic desensitization is the process in which a person is slowly introduced to a fear and each time he or she overcomes the fear the intensity decreases. So, in the case of a fear of heights, a person might go to the second floor of a building until he or she is comfortable there, then the third, and so on. This gradually desensitizes a person to the cause of their anxiety.

systematic desensitization
the process whereby a person is slowly introduced to a fear such that each time he or she overcomes the fear the intensity is decreased

This approach can be applied to help overcome a fear of public speaking. First deliver a speech to one person until you are comfortable, then add a person you do not know, and soon you will be speaking to larger and larger groups. This slow immersion can only happen over a long period of time, but it is also tremendously effective at assisting people in overcoming their fear. It can also be applied to practice sessions before a single speech to help speakers slowly get used to the audience they will soon encounter. Ultimately, managing our communication apprehension involves a combination of each of these strategies but also requires persistent, consistent, and dedicated practice.

Summary

In this chapter we defined speech anxiety, which is more broadly labeled communication apprehension. We then covered the physical effects of the anxiety and explained that, although we might believe we know what causes it, the audience does not necessarily know. Finally, we provided several ways to help manage communication apprehension, but emphasized that practice and repeated public speaking experiences were key to managing apprehension.

Key Terms

communication apprehension   9
phobias   9
self-fulfilling prophecy   10
systematic desensitization   15

In COMM 1000/1003

Many individuals have irrational fears about public speaking. It's easy to project a "worst-case" scenario and run with that in your mind. However, that will get you nowhere in terms of dealing with the normal feelings of anxiety that go along with public speaking. So, in an effort to name some of these fears, and maybe have a good life, here's a list of things students have said in the past.

Worst-Case Scenario (i.e., I would just die if I _____.)

- Vomited

- Fainted

- Ran out of the room screaming

- Forgot to zip my pants

- Tripped on my way to the podium

- Stumble over every word

- Forget my entire speech

Chapter Objectives
- Understand the importance of ethical speech
- Recognize the ethical responsibilities of a speaker
- Appreciate the ethical obligations of audience members

3
Speaking and Ethics

Communication, and in particular speech, is a very powerful tool. It can be used to enhance the public good, or it can be wielded in a way that manipulates and harms people. Like any tool, the operators involved need to understand how to apply the device to achieve maximum benefit from it. Instruction manuals are easy to identify for things like drills, Blu-Ray disc players, and even cars, but for good speech there is no such manual. Instead, good speakers follow good ethical principles, and those principles constitute the "instruction manual" for speech making.

In this chapter, we will broadly define ethics and discuss why speech must be governed by sound ethical principles. We will then lay out the basic ethical responsibilities of speakers and audiences, both of whom play a role in speech making and meaning construction. Before we explain why ethics are important to the practice of speech, however, we must provide you with a definition of ethics. Ethics involve morals and the specific moral choices to be made by a person. It is, for all intents and purposes, a way for people to make good, sound choices for themselves and their community. Since we build communities through communication with others, ethical speech is at the core of a healthy community, and we must be careful about what we say and how we interact with others.

ethics
involve morals and the specific moral choices to be made by a person

Public Messages Cannot Be Taken Back

Once we say something we cannot take it back. In that way it is much like shooting a bullet from a gun, because you cannot "un-say" the words, just as you can't "un-fire" a gun. Think of an interpersonal situation in which a couple is dating and one partner is angry at the other. In a moment of frustration one shouts out, "I hate you!" to the other person. The sender of that message may begin to regret the words and apologize, noting that anger and emotional pain caused the outburst. The offended party can accept the apology and forgive the person, but the words were said and an apology in this situation can't fully undo the damage. Words matter because they leave an indelible mark on a relationship.

We all know words can inflict significant damage in an interpersonal relationship, but they can do even more damage in a public speaking setting. Even though public speaking may seem like a less intimate setting, saying something unethical or offensive can be more damaging than in an interpersonal setting. Whereas much of interpersonal communication is spontaneous, public speaking is more planned and formal, so the audience often attributes careful thought to the speaker in a public speaking setting. That is to say, they believe you say what you mean. Of course, in interpersonal settings, especially those with people who know you, such a slip can be explained away as just that, a "slip." In speeches it is harder to say you "slipped" when you had time to prepare your comments.

The damage done when we say something unethical or offensive is not just to the listener. Yes, the audience may take offense, walk out, and suffer discomfort at hearing your comments, but you also are harmed when this happens. Your credibility as a speaker takes the brunt of this damage, and you may not be invited to speak again, depending upon what you said. Knowing that communication is irreversible, and thus permanent, as well as acknowledging the lasting impact our words have on ourselves and others is an important step toward becoming an ethical speaker.

Our words also let the audience into our minds, allowing them to see how we see the world. Our word choices reflect our impressions of our environment and carry with them significant meaning for ourselves and others. The words we use reveal what we feel about everything from the audience to our political views and reflect our personal values and beliefs. In this way, our messages to audiences in public speaking settings impact how the audience sees us and will have an impact on the effectiveness of our messages. If the audience does not understand or agree with our worldview, it can increase the challenges we face in a public speaking setting.

In today's mediated environment this is especially crucial. Many people upload commentaries, speeches, presentations, and even casual blogs to the Internet via YouTube and other online Web sites. We may not think that what we say will hurt anyone, because there is no one in front of us when we videotape these comments and post them. The truth is that once we send our videos into the digital world they can reach many people, even those we don't know. For that reason alone it is especially crucial that we pay careful attention to our words and what we say; once we send them into cyberspace, they will never disappear and may go viral.

Ethical Responsibilities of Speakers

As the originator of a message in a public speaking situation, the speaker is bound by several ethical responsibilities. These obligations begin at the start of the speech making process, then progress through the research stage, and culminate with the delivery of the presentation itself. It is important to be attuned to the moral issues that arise throughout the development of your remarks, because doing so will help you keep the best interests of your audience in mind. In this section, we briefly cover the ethical responsibilities of speakers from the planning of a presentation, to researching the topic, all the way through the delivery of the speech.

The Ethics of Choosing a Topic

In many instances, speakers know the broad topic on which they will present, but even in these instances it is important to maintain a focus on ethics when narrowing the topic. This means that speakers must choose topics and messages they firmly believe are in the best interests of their audience. Choosing self-serving messages or crafting topics in a way that is designed to manipulate an audience is a perversion of a speaker's responsibilities. As the creator of the message, you own what you say and so you should take care to keep others in mind when you decide what you will say. Remember, words cannot be taken back.

Personal duties that we all have for balancing ethical responsibilites when choosing a topic

- A duty to ourselves to do the best we possibly can

- A duty to our families to provide for them by keeping our jobs

- A duty to the audience and the greater public to seek the common good

- A duty to our employers to achieve results

When choosing or narrowing the topic of a presentation, we often find ourselves balancing various ethical responsibilities that sometimes compete with one another. We have a duty to ourselves to do the best we possibly can, a duty to our families to provide for them by keeping our jobs, a duty to the audience and the greater public to seek the common good, and a duty to our employers to achieve results. It is not hard to envision a situation in which these duties conflict and present us with an ethical dilemma. When it comes to message construction and meaning making through speeches and statements, how do we maintain our ethical principles when the situation is not so clear? This is the hard work we must do before we even decide what to say to someone, but once we know what we will say and how we will balance our ethical obligations, our requirement to do what is right does not stop.

The Ethics of Research

The ethical requirements of speech making are not restricted to keeping the audience in mind when we choose a topic; they also come into play in research and speech development. In almost every instance in which you will be called upon to deliver a speech, you will need to incorporate some degree of evidence that you researched. In a business meeting, it could entail explaining sales figures; in a design presentation it could be the history of the site upon which you plan to build; and in a class it will most likely be scholarly research on a topic. In each instance, however, you must keep the interests of the audience in mind, properly evaluate the evidence you choose to cite, and properly attribute the source of that information.

Thanks to technology, we have vast amounts of information at our fingertips. This is both good and bad. Good because we can easily conduct research from our desks, but potentially hazardous because the Internet is rife with biased and fabricated information. For that reason, it is essential we know how to properly evaluate information we find before we decide to use it in a presentation or report. As researchers, we need to discern the true from the false and facts from opinions. Facts are bits of information that can be verified and substantiated. They can be qualitative, as in historical events or testimony, or quantitative, as in polling results and the outcomes of scientific experiments. Opinions, on the other hand, vary from person to person and from group to group and are not as reliable as facts because they are often biased. Identifying the difference between opinions and facts will help you enhance your credibility. That credibility can be greatly diminished if the audience realizes you are citing a biased source.

When evaluating a source, there are several questions you should ask yourself to help determine whether the source can be trusted.

1. **Will this person benefit from getting me to believe that this information is true?** A source who is being paid as a spokesperson for a company trying to sell you something or trying to win your vote is biased. Sometimes biased sources are accurate, but they are often misleading, and as an ethical communicator, you have a responsibility to do additional research and find a more credible source.

2. **Is this person an expert in this area or in a position to know this information?** Individuals who have special training and experience related to the information they are sharing are more reliable sources than those who do not. For example, a cardiologist is a better source than an auto mechanic for information on how to keep your heart healthy, but an auto mechanic is a better source than your family doctor for learning how to change the oil in your car.

3. **Are the claims made by this source substantiated by other credible sources?** If you have a single source that makes a claim, but find ten other reliable sources that say the opposite is true, it is likely that the ten sources that agree are accurate. For example, if you find one source that says you can lose weight by eating three pizzas every day, but find many other sources that say you must limit your calories and exercise in order to lose weight, it is probably not true that eating large quantities of pizza will help you lose weight.

4. **Is this source recent enough to be relevant?** If you are speaking about a current topic, you should use the most recent sources you can find. For example, an article written twenty years ago is not a good source to learn about the most energy-efficient cars available today. However, if you are giving a speech about an important figure in the Civil War, a source that is twenty years old might be acceptable.

plagiarism

taking the intellectual achievements of another person and presenting them as one's own

global plagiarism

taking an entire piece of work and saying that it is your own

incremental plagiarism

using part of someone else's work and not citing it as a source

patchwork plagiarism

taking ideas from more than one piece of work and putting them together into a new piece of work, and then presenting them as original work without giving due credit to the sources

patchworking

taking original source material and changing a few words in it, but not enough to consider it a paraphrase, all the while not citing the original source material

Biased sources and opinions are not the only pitfalls of which researchers must be aware, and their use is not even the most grievous mistake a speaker can make. Plagiarism is perhaps the greatest offense a speaker can commit because it takes advantage of both the audience and the actual source of the information. When speakers plagiarize, they steal the intellectual achievements of another person and present them as their own, thus deceiving the audience into believing the speakers were responsible for more than they actually were. Like many crimes, plagiarism comes in many forms, so let's take a moment and describe what these various forms look like.

The first type of plagiarism is global plagiarism, which is taking an entire piece of work and saying it is your own. Suppose a roommate gave a speech in a class different from your class and you took that speech and put your name on it. That would be an example of global plagiarism. Many consider it the worst kind of academic dishonesty. In these cases, speakers do no original work and act as if they did. They have robbed the source of the credit deserved for creating the speech and tricked the audience into believing they themselves are a reliable source of information.

The second type of plagiarism is incremental plagiarism, which involves using part of someone else's work and not citing it as a source. An example of incremental plagiarism would be copying a few sentences from someone else's speech or paper and putting them directly into your speech without citing the source or using quotation marks. Despite the fact that in this case the work is not stolen in its entirety, it is clearly still an incident of dishonesty. This type of plagiarism is a bit more common than global plagiarism, but it is just as unethical because of the way it treats the source and the audience.

The last type of plagiarism we will address is patchwork plagiarism. Patchwork plagiarism takes ideas from more than one piece of work and presents them as original work without giving due credit to the sources. This is perhaps the most common form of plagiarism, but just because more people do it does not make it right. It is deceitful and unethical in that it still robs others of the credit they deserve for work they conducted, and it falsely inflates the credibility of the speaker.

Patchworking is a process that closely resembles patchwork plagiarism. When writers or researchers employ patchworking they take original sentences or work from another source, changing a few words in it and not citing the source. The changes are minimal and do not really change the idea presented in the original source, and without any attribution to the source material this remains plagiarism. It is sometimes evidence of a poor attempt at paraphrasing, but may also be a deliberate attempt to deceive an audience. In both instances, however, it is an unethical practice and speakers and writers need to avoid it.

As we have mentioned when discussing each of these types of plagiarism, it is important to cite sources in your written work. It is also essential that when speaking we verbally attribute those sources, because failure to do so also constitutes plagiarism. Having the sources in your outline or manuscript is not enough; you must mention them to your audience as well.

When delivering a speech, you must note where the work came from by mentioning the author or publication in which you found the information. Ideally, your verbal citation should include as many of the following four pieces of information as possible for your source: (1) the name of the publication, (2) the date the source was published, (3) the author of the work and/or name of the person who is providing the information used in the source, and (4) the credentials of the source. It is best to cite your source first and then give the information, not the other way around. Citing the source after sharing the information is awkward and can hurt the flow of your speech, but citing the source before sharing the information can heighten audience attention and help the audience sense the importance of the information you are sharing. For example, in a speech you might cite your source by saying, "According to the February 10, 2012, issue of *Time,* Dr. Gary Landreth, a scientist at Case Western Reserve University, has discovered that a drug called bexarotene can reverse Alzheimer's disease in mice."

Thus far we have discussed the ethical requirements of a speaker when choosing and researching a speech topic. There is one more area in which speakers have an ethical requirement, and that is when they actually deliver the speech. In the next section, we will provide some general guidelines for ethical speech delivery.

The Ethics of Language and Delivery

Even if you prepare a topic with the best interests of the audience in mind and research the topic appropriately and thoroughly, there are still ethical pitfalls of which you must be aware when you actually deliver the speech. These ethical responsibilities primarily involve the language you choose to use when describing ideas, people, or things to an audience. Let's look at some general guidelines that will help you make good choices regarding the language and delivery of your presentations.

Maintain Composure. Every time we speak to someone, whether individually or in group settings, we must pay the person the same respect we hope he or she will give us. Sometimes our audience agrees with us, which makes conversation and discussion easier in many ways. Other times some or even all of an audience will disagree with what we are saying, but that doesn't allow us to suspend civility and respect for them. In fact, it makes it even more important to be respectful and civil. There are also times when an audience will be neutral toward you and your topic, but respect is important in these instances as well.

Regardless of how the audience feels toward you or your topic, always show them respect. Knowingly insulting or offending an audience, even a single audience member, will get you nowhere. You may not like a particular person or his or her position, but purposely injecting unneeded negativity into the situation will damage your credibility and destroy any chance of conveying your message successfully. Sometimes it is hard to maintain your composure if someone is heckling or being rude when you are speaking, but even in these instances you should keep a moderate tone of voice. People always respond to your tone before your message, so staying moderate and calm will help diffuse the situation and enhance your credibility because you will be seen as reasonable.

Beyond keeping a moderate tone, you also owe it to yourself and your audience to be polite and professional. Losing your patience or temper will eliminate any chance of reaching an audience, and you could even lose the respect of those people who support you. This does not mean you cannot call the hecklers out on their behavior, but you must do so in a civil way. This involves first describing their behavior and then asking them to hold their comments and concerns until after you have finished speaking. Unfortunately, there are occasions when this technique does not work, but you still cannot allow yourself to get agitated and focus on the heckler. This is not what the rest of the audience came for, and you should not give one person more attention than everyone else in the room. Explaining this may also help the situation. Additionally, members of the audience may come to your aid if you appear reasonable in dealing with the heckler (see Table 3.1).

TABLE 3.1

Some Rules for Civility[1]	
Pay attention	Respect others' opinions
Speak kindly	Listen
Don't speak ill of others	Mind your body
Assert yourself	Respect other people's time
Don't shift responsibility and blame	Acknowledge others

Describe People with Respect. As speakers, we often like to use colorful language to describe ideas, places, and even people. We must be careful, however, in choosing how we describe others so we don't risk offending our audience by not treating others as people. When we use images of animals or objects to refer to people in a negative way we are dehumanizing the people, that is, making them appear to be less than human. This insults and demeans people by depriving them of being the very thing that they are: human beings.

---

1 These ten rules are taken from a larger list in the book. Forni, P. M. (2002). *Choosing Civility: The twenty-five rules of considerate conduct.* New York, NY: St. Martin's Press.

Using dehumanizing language to describe people is very tempting when we do not agree with them or if we are in conflict with them over something. In fact, such a technique is very common in presidential war rhetoric. It makes it more likely other people will see the person being dehumanized as an animal and not a person, thus making it less likely the target audience will respect the person. In war, such imagery actually makes it easier for people to engage in violent behaviors against an enemy they do not view as being human.

Furthermore, it is important to use gender-inclusive language when describing roles so you are not using language to inadvertently exclude a particular group. The titles of many professional roles have changed to reflect the inclusion of both men and women in those professions, and as a speaker you should respect others by using inclusive language. Table 3.2 provides several examples of gender-inclusive language.

TABLE 3.2

Gender-Inclusive Language	
Inappropriate	**Appropriate**
Policeman	Police officer
Mailman	Mail carrier
Stewardess	Flight attendant
Mankind	Humankind

Language, as we will discuss later, is a very powerful tool. Being an ethical speaker requires you to respect your audience's humanity even when you do not agree with them. Such respect will help foster a more effective dialogue over differences, instead of a combat rooted in insults.

Avoid Profanity. Profanity is a common part of everyday language. We see it in movies, hear it on television, laugh at it when it is used by comedians, and even use it to describe everyday situations and frustrations. Despite its common usage, profanity has no place in a public presentation and should be avoided. Sure, a few audience members might be amused if you drop the occasional curse word, but it is likely most people will not be impressed. In fact, it damages your credibility when you choose to inject profanity into your speech because people see it as a linguistic tool of a weak mind. It simply does not make you seem intelligent.

Not only does profanity damage your credibility as a speaker, but it also insults the intelligence of your audience. Even when you use a swear word to try to elicit a laugh from your audience you are essentially saying two things:

1. You do not know how to tell a joke or make your audience laugh without swearing, and
2. You think the audience cannot understand humor, and by extension your speech, if it doesn't involve profanity.

This is not to say there will never be a moment when profanity is acceptable. In fact, if you are quoting someone who used profanity you might need to repeat the terms. This is acceptable with the caveat that you make the audience aware that you are quoting someone. You should let them know before quoting the term that what you are about to say may offend some in the audience. Doing this should be rare and should only be done when not saying the word or words would eliminate the effect or reason for including them.

Balance Simplicity and Complexity. Acting ethically when delivering a speech also requires that you make an honest attempt to speak to your audience on their level. What this means is that you take care not to oversimplify or overcomplicate things for your audience. To ensure you understand what your audience knows about a subject or concept you should review any audience analysis data available. This will enable you to approach topics with a clearer idea of what the audience knows and what they do not.

If you walk into a speech expecting that your audience knows nothing about the subject on which you are speaking, then you run a high risk of insulting their intelligence and losing their attention during the presentation. For example, if an engineer delivers remarks to a group of mechanics on the model for a new engine design and begins with a detailed description of why cars need engines, the speaker will have lost the audience and will likely be perceived as condescending. On the other hand, if you expect your audience to know things they do not know, it will result in negative audience perceptions as well. Take the case of the engineer and change the audience to a group of middle school students. If the engineer uses technical terms that middle schoolers do not know, then he will lose the audience, and they will also see the engineer as arrogant and ineffective. For this reason, knowing your audience and making an attempt to meet them on their intellectual level is essential for ethical speaking. No one likes to be made to feel unintelligent.

Balance Emotion and Logic. Oftentimes when we feel passionate about an issue or idea we inject that enthusiasm into our speech. Additionally, we try and "push" people to agree with us by using emotional stories. These elements of an appeal definitely have their place, but capitalizing on emotion to move an audience denies them the opportunity to sift and weigh the evidence for themselves and come to their own decisions on the matter. As speakers, we need to respect the ability of our audience to make an informed decision for themselves and not fear that they might disagree with our position. To that end, we must balance emotion with logic, for emotional appeals can be very influential with an audience.

Emotions are a powerful force in our lives, and some of the strongest emotions are negative. Consider anger, rage, jealousy, hatred, and envy. These are powerful forces that have been manipulated by speakers time and again throughout history to get audiences to act in ways they normally would not if they were also provided accurate evidence. Look no further than the case of Adolf Hitler, whose words capitalized on a downtrodden German populace by igniting anger in them toward a specific group of people. This resulted in one of the most inhumane periods in human history: the Holocaust.

The power of emotions does not solely lie in negative feelings; positive emotions can also be powerful. Some of these are love, pride, joy, and gratitude. Think of commercials calling on you to donate to Doctors Without Borders, a charity that finances medical assistance in impoverished countries. The appeal focuses on activating your love, or even sympathy, for the plight of other humans in order to get you to donate to their cause. This is a positive emotion you feel, and an equally positive cause, but creating an appeal based on emotion alone denies the audience the opportunity to properly evaluate the organization and its mission.

Although humans are emotional beings and emotions can be used successfully, especially in a persuasive speech, relying upon them alone constitutes unethical behavior. If people make decisions based primarily on emotion, then they might make decisions that lack logic and reasoning. Audiences make better decisions, and speakers make better cases for their argument, when emotions are tied to logic. So, when developing your speech, incorporate appeals to emotions in tandem with the logic and evidence you use.

Up until now we have focused our attention on the ethical requirements of speakers, but they are not the only ones with such obligations. In the next section, we discuss the ethical dimensions of being a good audience member.

Ethics as an Audience Member

Even though the spotlight remains on a speaker during a presentation, there are still ethical responsibilities to which audience members are beholden. Too often in today's smartphone-dominated world audience members do things such as text message, check e-mails, or even do work during someone else's presentation. These types of behaviors are not innocuous and innocent, but rather are rude and unethical. Speakers put a lot of work into their presentations, and audience members have the responsibility to listen attentively and respectfully.

Be a Responsible Audience Member

Keep an Open Mind. Audience members should always approach a speech or presentation as an opportunity to learn something new. If you do this and keep an open mind to what the speaker is saying, you are giving the speaker the respect his or her work and effort deserve. There might be ideas in the speech about which you disagree, but there might also be ideas in the speech with which you agree. Being ethical and responsible audience members means that we should give the speaker the benefit of the doubt and hold our own biases in check so we can concentrate on the message. It is entirely possible that the speaker might change our opinion on something, but even if we do not ultimately change our opinion, we have allowed the speaker the opportunity to present ideas to us. It is, after all, what we would want if the situation were reversed.

Do Not Heckle. Too often we see people attending political meetings who interrupt speakers and yell at them in the middle of their presentations. Just because we disagree with speakers does not give us the right to attack them and interrupt their remarks. Heckling is particularly nasty when the interrupter tries to demean the speaker. The end result of heckling is an uncomfortable environment for everyone else, and hecklers actually call negative attention to themselves. A heckler's disruptions can upset and throw off the speaker, and heckling can upset and interfere with the message reception of the other audience members. Just as you have ethical responsibilities to the speaker, you have ethical responsibilities to your fellow audience members. If the speaker or the message upsets you so much you feel warranted to engage in heckling, you should remove yourself from the environment and let the event continue instead of disturbing it for everyone else. Hecklers often wrongly assume that everyone else in the audience agrees with them, and they have thus prejudged not only the speaker but also their fellow audience members.

Pay Attention. It is true that we will find some speakers and their topics boring, but our lack of interest doesn't mean we can do something else during the presentation. We might think speakers can't see us holding our cell phones, searching the Internet, or sending a text, but they almost always notice, and it distracts them. Such behavior tells speakers that you think they are boring and unimportant and can damage the speakers' confidence in an already challenging situation.

There are nonverbal behaviors that audience members engage in that distract the speaker and the audience. For example, putting your head down on the desk, slouching in your seat, and closing your eyes are all disrespectful to a speaker. A speaker could infer a lot of different things from these behaviors, such as laziness, indifference, and even contempt. That said, these nonverbal behaviors are not the worst things an audience member can do; the worst is when members of the audience start talking to each other during a presentation. It is a simple rule not to engage in side conversations when someone else is speaking.

Summary

In your public speaking class you have the ethical obligation to pay attention to all speakers, just as you would want your classmates to do when you're speaking. Giving a speech is hard for many people, as we covered in the last chapter, and your attention can actually give them support and strength while they are speaking and can improve their performance. No one likes to be ignored or mocked when they are speaking, so we should all be respectful audience members when someone is delivering remarks.

In this chapter, we discussed the concept of ethics and how it applies to public speaking. We explained that messages cannot be retrieved once spoken, and we covered the ethical responsibilities of a speaker throughout the speech preparation and delivery process. Finally, we covered the ethical obligations of audience members. Ethics are important in all walks of life and are certainly an important element in the communication process.

Key Terms

ethics   17
global plagiarism   20
incremental plagiarism   20
patchwork plagiarism   20
patchworking   20
plagiarism   20

In COMM 1000/1003

Students sometimes deliver speeches which border on being unethical. The use of clear language, strong sources, and a willingness to address the ethical implications of the topic are important. Here is a list of speeches that could have gone VERY wrong, but because the students were aware of how close they were to crossing a line, they made sure they had solid research and were extremely careful in how they approached the topic.

1. Hazing should be allowed.

2. Prisoners should grow their own food.

3. All drugs should become legal.

4. Dealing drugs is a way to make money in college.

5. Nothing is wrong with polygamy.

- This chapter will unpack the different dimensions along which cultural differences can be explained

- This chapter will identify different categories of cultural difference.

- This chapter will provide students with suggestions for using dialogue to help understand intercultural communication

4
Culture and Diversity

We live in an increasingly global society, and understanding how this impacts your communication with others is incredibly important. Now, more than ever, speakers encounter diverse audiences, work with a variety of different colleagues, and live in communities with people who are different than them in some ways. Appreciating the backgrounds and the experiences of others helps us become more effective communicators because we become sensitive and respectful toward others when we speak, making it more likely that they will listen to what we have to say.

In this chapter, we explain how culture and diversity impact our communication with others. First, we define culture and unpack the different dimensions of it. We then provide some detail on specific categories of backgrounds that create and influence the diverse audiences we encounter when we communicate in almost any context. Finally, we offer some concrete suggestions for enhancing your ability to interact successfully with diverse groups of people in a variety of situations.

Understanding Culture

According to the Oxford English Dictionary, **culture** is "the distinctive ideas, customs, social behavior, products, or way of life of a particular nation, society, people, or period."[1] Geert Hofstede, one of the first social psychologists to study culture, defines culture as "the collective programming of the mind distinguishing the members of one group or category of people from another. The 'category' can refer to nations, regions within or across nations, ethnicities, religions, occupations, organizations, or the genders."[2] No matter which definition you prefer, culture is a complicated powerful component of human development and life. It influences our self-concept, our priorities, our personality and how we communicate with one another.

culture
the distinctive ideas, customs, social behavior, products, or way of life of a particular nation, society, people, or period

1 Culture. (n.D.). In *Oxford English Dictionary online.* Retrieved from http://www.oxforddictionaries.com/us/definition/american_english/culture
2 Hofstede, G., & Hofstede, G. J. (2013). Culture. http://www.geerthofstede.nl/culture.

co-culture

groups that are impacted by a variety of smaller specific cultures that intersect in our lives

Culture, however, is not so simple as to say a person belongs in, or is affected by, only one culture; the fact is, we belong and are impacted by a variety of smaller specific cultures that intersect in our lives. These smaller groups, called co-cultures, exist within and alongside larger cultural groups, allowing individuals to simultaneously belong to several cultures and co-cultures.

Let's look at an example to illustrate how cultures work and collide in our lives. Darius grew up in a Russian-American family and is a practicing Roman Catholic. Darius happens to be quite proud of his ethnic heritage, and also makes sure he goes to mass every Sunday. That said, he does not speak Russian, nor does he agree with all the Church's teachings. Nevertheless, many of the customs and beliefs of both groups inform Darius' perspective on the world around him. Many of his friends in the neighborhood he lives in are Russian, and he belongs to the Knights of Columbus as well, but none of his Russian neighborhood friends are affiliated with that organization. Darius belongs to both cultures, which constitute co-cultures within the larger American or Western culture.

One type of culture that is particularly influential is national culture. The specific traditions of a national culture vary greatly between countries, but their national cultures can all be understood through six consistent dimensions. Hofstede identified these six dimensions that help us understand differences in national cultures:

- **High vs. Low Power Distance**: Cultures with high power distance have high levels of inequality in power distribution in organizations, families, and other institutions; whereas cultures with low power distance have less inequality. This is best understood through where power lies in social structures, as democratic countries typically have low power distance because everyone has an equal share in decisions, while high power distance is best characterized by monarchies and dictatorships where only a few have access to power and others are removed from decision making.

- **High vs. Low Uncertainty Avoidance**: Cultures with high uncertainty avoidance have a low tolerance for ambiguity and minimize the possibility of uncomfortable, unstructured situations by enforcing strict rules, safety measures, and a belief in absolute Truth. Cultures with low uncertainty avoidance have fewer rules, take risks and are tolerant of change.

- **Individualism vs. Collectivism**: Individualistic societies have loose ties between individuals and expect each person to look out for him/herself and their immediate family. Collectivist cultures have strong ties between individuals, strong communal bonds, and often live in extended families that are deeply loyal to the group.

- **Masculinity vs. Femininity**: Masculinity and femininity refer to the distribution of emotional roles between the genders and the difference in the values of men and women. In masculine cultures, men are typically highly assertive and competitive, and women are somewhat assertive and competitive. In feminine cultures, men and women are both much more modest and caring.

- **Long-Term vs. Short-Term Orientation**: Cultures with long-term orientation are pragmatic and focus on future rewards, with an emphasis on saving, persistence, and adaptation. Cultures with short-term orientation focus on the present and past and emphasize national pride, tradition, social obligations, and saving "face" in the here and now.

- **Indulgence versus Restraint**: Indulgent cultures freely allow gratification of desires that allow individuals to enjoy life and have fun. Restrained cultures have strict social norms and discourage acting simply out of want.

low-context cultures

the language used in an interaction, in which very little emphasis is placed on the nonverbal communication, environment, and situation

It is easy to see how different nations and countries can differ along these spectrums. It is important to note, though, that Hofstede felt these dimensions fell along a continuum, and do not exist as simply "either-or." For example, a culture is not either collectivistic or individualistic, but falls somewhere in between each on a line.

In addition to the six dimensions of culture identified by Hofstede, Edward T. Hall explains that most national cultures can also be identified by how much importance is placed on nonverbal cues. In low-context cultures, such as the United States and Germany, meaning is derived mostly from the language used in an interaction, and very little emphasis is placed on the nonverbal communication, environment, and situation. In high-context cultures, such as Korea and Saudi Arabia, a great deal of meaning is derived from the nonverbal expressions, environment, and situation in which the communication is taking place, and less emphasis is placed on the words.

These seven different dimensions of culture allow us to begin to understand the complexity of different cultures. This understanding can enhance our ability to interact with people by helping us see how they might differ from us in terms of values along these continuums. Next we will explore some different cultural categories in addition to nationality, beginning with race and ethnicity.

Race and Ethnicity

A common cultural marker happens to also be a demographic category we find on college and job applications, census data, and other types of reports. Race refers to a set of physical characteristics shared by a group of people, such as skin color, body type, facial structure, and hair color. These physical characteristics are genetically inherited and reflect adaptations to the geographic region in which someone's ancestors previously lived. However, there is no biological difference between races in other characteristics, such as intelligence, athleticism, or other abilities. Due in large part to the fact these characteristics developed in particular groups in specific regions, those groups created a culture themselves because of the fact they lived in close proximity to each other. The common physical characteristics helped individuals identify with each other, and eventually for communities together.

Another cultural marker that developed due to the close proximity of people is ethnicity, but ethnicity should not be confused with race. Ethnicity refers to a group of people who identify with each other based on a common experience, which might include geographic or national origin, ancestry, history, cultural and social norms, religion, race, language, ideology, food, dress, or other factors. Ethnicity can sometimes (but not always) be related to national heritage. At times, violent conflicts and disputes evolve out of differences in ethnic heritage and values between two or more groups. The results of these conflicts can sometimes create new national boundaries, such as when the former Yugoslavia split into the nations that exist today. At other times, several ethnic groups might co-exist in the same nation. In fact, Tufts professor Colin Woodard[3] argues that the United States is really made up of eleven nations, each of which has a different history, ancestry, and set of deep-seated attitudes.

A recent example of ethnic tension can be seen in the Crimea region of the Ukraine, where Russian speaking citizens of Ukraine sought support from the Russian Federation when the political situation in the country became unstable. Ukrainian nationals in Crimea disagreed with this approach and an international crisis which has yet to be resolved ensued.

Ethnic heritage can also be a source of reinforcement for individual identity through cultural celebrations. In major American cities twice a year Italian Americans celebrate the Feast of San Genarro, a food festival central to their culture. A number of cities also have areas designated Little Italy, Little China, and so on where people who share that ethnic heritage settled. These areas offer a great opportunity to explore some of the ethnic differences between people in fun, interesting, and if you like food, tasty ways.

Sex, Gender, and Sexual Orientation

Another set of significant cultural categories refers to one's physical, psychological and romantic definitions of their identity. To properly appreciate how these aspects of a person's self-concept relate to culture, we must first differentiate between the ways we define our sexuality. According to the American Psychological Society[4], sex refers to one's biological classification as male, female, or intersex (having both male and female physical characteristics) based on one's reproductive organs and chromosomes. Sex is an objective way of identifying the group to which a person belongs based on biology. Often, job applications and college applications ask for this information but are prohibited from using it to make job hiring decisions.

high-context cultures
language in which a great deal of meaning is derived from the nonverbal expressions, environment, and situation in which the communication is taking place, and less emphasis is placed on the words

race
a set of physical characteristics shared by a group of people, such as skin color, body type, facial structure, and hair color

ethnicity
a group of people who identify with each other based on a common experience, which might include geographic or national origin, ancestry, history, cultural and social norms, religion, race, language, ideology, food, dress, or other factors

sex
refers to one's biological classification as male, female, or intersex based on one's reproductive organs and chromosomes

3 Woodard, C. (2013, Fall). Up in arms. *Tufts Magazine.* Medford, MA: Tufts University. http://www.tufts.edu/alumni/magazine/fall2013/features/up-in-arms.html
4 American Psychological Association (2014). Practice guidelines for LGB clients. Retrieved from http://www.apa.org/pi/lgbt/resources/guidelines.aspx?item=2.

gender
a social construction that includes the all of the beliefs, attitudes, actions and roles associated with being masculine or feminine

sexual orientation
the sex and gender to whom a person is romantically and sexually attracted to

Sex is also often incorrectly used as a synonym for gender, which is quite different. Gender is a social construction that includes the all of the beliefs, attitudes, actions and roles associated with being masculine or feminine. One's biological sex does inform one's gender identity, but gender is more than a simple reflection of physical characteristics. Gender includes one's psychological sense of self as being male or female regardless of their physical biology. Gender also includes the societal expectations for behaviors, attitudes, and roles filled by feminine or masculine minded individuals. It is important to note that these expectations vary by the larger culture in which one exists. Where biology defines our sex, psychology creates our gender identity.

In addition to the physical and psychological aspects of our sexuality, there is an emotional and romantic dimension as well. A person's sexual orientation refers to the sex and gender to whom a person is romantically and sexually attracted to. Sexual orientation includes many categories along a continuum. The three most common categories include: being attracted to members of the opposite sex (heterosexual), members of the same sex (gay or lesbian), or members of both sexes (bisexual). The declaration and enactment of sexual orientation is both an intensely personal decision and, for some people, a public declaration of belonging to a group.

This public declaration of belonging to a group presents us with an example of how sexual orientation can be construed as a culture. Many cities across the globe hold Gay Pride Parades which, in effect, are public celebrations of LGBTQ culture. These parades reinforce ties between individuals who identify with this culture and help serve to promote their beliefs, attitudes and values.

Age

We do not often think of age as a cultural marker, but it definitely operates as one such in any society. While none of us will be the same age for the rest of our lives, age is not a permanent characteristic, a person's age may tell you something about their life experiences, as well as some possible attitudes and beliefs they may hold. Let's look at a few examples of different generational cultures in the United States[5]:

- The GI Generation: also sometimes referred to as the Greatest Generation, this is the generation that fought during World War II.

- The Silent Generation: too young to fight in World War II, but came into adulthood during the rise of the middle class and the relatively prosperous time that followed.

- The Baby Boomers: the children of the GI generation, grew up with Woodstock and the Vietnam war, tended to focus on careers and set high expectations for their children.

- Generation X: graduated from high school in the 80s and 90s.

- The Millennials: graduated high school after 2000, tended to be very protected by their parents and had high expectations set for them.

The generation that each person lives in shapes their experiences, expectations, and attitudes toward others. Not everyone from a specific generation acts and believes the same way, but people always identify with the times in which they grew up. As these different generational groupings illustrate, age, as a cultural group, is not as simple as labeling someone "old" and "young," or "elderly" and "middle-aged." Those labels are defined purely by a number and fail to recognize the importance of the experiences each person lives through and how those experiences inform a person's generational culture.

Physical and Cognitive Diversity

Age, ethnicity, race and sexuality are not the only ways in which we are different. In fact, unless you have an identical twin, you are probably the only person who looks exactly like you, acts like you and thinks like you. When you consider that there are now over seven billion people on earth, there is inevitably a great deal of physical diversity among humans. However, our differences go beyond appearances to include abilities. Some people have especially high levels of specific physical abilities (for instance, Usain Bolt holds world records in

---

5 Howe, N., & Strauss, W. (2000). *Millennials rising: The next great generation*. New York: Vintage.

both the 100 and 200 meter dashes), while others have lower levels of specific physical abilities (for example, Helen Keller could not see or hear). These differences make us no better or worse than someone else, but rather add to the richness of the human experience.

At some point, most, if not all, of us will experience some type of physical or cognitive impairment. Some of these are permanent while others are temporary; some are due to genetics, others still an illness or accident. For example, some people are born blind, while others may develop blindness due to macular degeneration or an accident. Others still may temporarily lose their sight temporarily after surgery as well. This is important to note because not all people with the same impairment are the same, they just may simply share a limitation or different level of ability. Furthermore, these differences also do not define the person, but rather are a part of them, just as is their age, ethnicity, and race.

Likewise, there is great diversity in our cognitive abilities and preferences. There is a broad range in IQ, learning styles and preferences, interests, memory, and experience among people. Many cognitive challenges such as dyslexia, ADHD, Alzheimer's, or memory loss are not immediately apparent when we meet someone. Like the physical impairments we discussed a moment ago, some people live with these challenges for their entire life while others might experience them for a shorter period of time. For example, medication or a concussion, for example, can temporarily impact a person's short-term memory, as can a concussion, while the effects of Alzheimer's are permanent.

Ideological Diversity

Thus far, we have primarily focused on physical differences between people, but the diversity of thought is just as important. Often the debate over this emerges in politics where people hold different ideas on policy and effective governance. These views are the result of a commitment to an ideology, or set of ideas, beliefs, and ideals that form our worldview and provide a basis for action. Ideology forms the basis for political beliefs and is heavily influenced by both the family and society in which we grow up. As Colin Woodard showed when defining the Eleven Nations in the US,[6] there is a great deal of ideological diversity even within the United States, and that ideological diversity expands even more when we consider the entire globe. That said, let's focus a bit on ideological diversity in the United States specifically.

ideology
set of ideas, beliefs, and ideals that form our worldview and provide a basis for action

Religious Diversity

One final area of difference that both creates its own cultural norms and also enhances diversity in America is religion. There are numerous faiths practiced in the United States. Despite the prevalence of the Abrahamic faiths (Judaism, Christianity, and Islam), each contributes to the fabric of our culture in their own way. In 2009, the US Census Bureau issued a statistical breakdown of the religious affiliations of people in the United States. In it they found a tremendous amount of diversity, including within Christian faiths. For instance, the report lumped 30 different denominations of Christianity under one group; each of these faiths has different religious perspectives, practices, and beliefs. The report also included a note to the growing number of Muslim, Wiccan, Buddhist, and even non-religious persons in the US.[7]

The growth of non-religious and unaffiliated but spiritual people requires some discussion. It is a mistake to assume the beliefs of someone based on their specific affiliation, just as it is unwise to assume someone has no faith or belief in morality/spirituality because they are unaffiliated with a religious group. Many people still hold these beliefs privately, and should not be discounted or counted simply based on the religious groups with whom they identify. Understanding and appreciating these differences, while not necessarily agreeing with them, is essential for developing a respectful community in which to live.

---

6 Woodard, C. (2013, Fall). Up in arms. *Tufts Magazine*. Medford, MA: Tufts University. http://www.tufts.edu/alumni/magazine/fall2013/features/up-in-arms.html

7 U.S. Census Bureau. (2009). Self-described religious identification of adult population: 1990 to 2008. 2010 statistical abstract. Retrieved December 18, 2009, from http://www.census.gov/compendia/statab/2010/tables/10s0075.pdf

Religious groups also play important roles in local, state, and national communities. They often do good work on behalf of the community in which their members live and help to promote charitable endeavors across the world. Churches, synagogues, mosques, and temples all also practice their own culture by providing members opportunities to connect with each other and share stories and experiences. These efforts build their religious culture, but also help to contribute to the larger communal culture as well.

Communication, Culture, Diversity, and Dialogue

As a speaker and listener, it is important for you to understand, acknowledge, and appreciate the diversity that cultural differences provide our society. The differences in language, experiences, values, beliefs, and perspectives can enrich our lives in many ways, but also first requires communication grounded in the purpose of understanding others rather than trying to convince them of anything. It requires us to be perceptive of both the context in which we find ourselves, as well as the way that context might be different for someone else. In this final section, we provide three tips to help enhance your ability to use communication to understand and respect differences between people, and then discuss the concept and practice of dialogue as a vehicle to promote understanding.

- **Make the message accessible.** As a speaker, it is important to consider the range of abilities in your audience and to adapt your presentation where possible to help the entire audience understand what you are saying. For instance, you might need to add captions to film clips, avoid combining red and green on slides so that those with colorblindness can read your text, and include signposts and transitions that make it easy for your audience to follow along if their attention wavers for a few moments. Using microphones, handouts, and other assistive methods may help people better follow your message, regardless of any limitations or challenges they may have.

- **Don't highlight differences in others.** Though you might think that acknowledging the different abilities or backgrounds of others makes you seem like you understand them or are trying to help them, they may take issue with this. It calls them out in front of others and specifically heightens the differences they may not want others to know. So, act no differently and whenever possible, if you need to make an make accommodations of sorts, do so in a way that everyone shares in it so as not to segregate your audience.

- **Avoid "ist" language.** This is the type of language that demeans, ignores, inappropriately calls attention to, or disrespects members of a separate culture or group. This includes ageist, racist, and sexist language that does not respect the humanity of other people. This type of language depicts the other group as a passive object and not an active subject, thus making them seem less than the group of the person making the statement.

dialogue

speaking in a way that encourages others to listen and listening in a way that encourages others to speak

In addition to these tips, a commitment to ethical communication is central to respecting diversity. This ethical commitment is made real through the practice of dialogue, or speaking in a way that encourages others to listen and listening in a way that encourages others to speak.[8] In addition, dialogue is communication where the goal of both the speaker and the listener is to understand, not necessarily agree with, the other. Dialogue is key to respecting diversity because it encourages us to understand, though not always agree with, the experiences, perspectives, practices, and beliefs of others.

ethnocentric

believing your group's perspective is the only correct one and thus judging others based on their conformity to your way of doing things

Dialogue is not easy, and requires a variety of different skills. First, it involves listening with an open mind and not pre-judging other individuals based on incomplete information or stereotypes. To do this we must also engage in the dialogue through asking clarifying questions to make sure we understand what the other person is saying before making a decision regarding their statements. These questions should not come in the form of interruptions, but rather after individuals are done speaking. Dialogue also asks us to respect the inherent humanity of the other person in the interaction, and not devalue them or their experiences because they may be different. In short, avoid being ethnocentric, or believing your group's perspective is the only correct one and thus judging others based on their conformity to your way of doing things.

8 Griffin, Em. *A First Look at Communication Theory, 8th edition.* (2012) New York: McGraw-Hill Companies, Inc.

Dialogue allows us to appreciate cultural differences in a respectful way, thus keeping those aspects of diversity that improve our lives and communities. As you can see, communication is the core of a robust, vibrant, and interesting community that values diversity in appearance, action and thought.

Summary

In this chapter we discussed the relationship between culture, communication, and diversity. We first explained the theoretical underpinnings of culture and explored the various dimensions all national cultures share to some extent. We then discussed several categories of difference that are both their own cultural groups and contribute to a diverse society. We also offered some suggestions for how to effectively engage in understanding and appreciating difference through communication, specifically by practicing dialogue.

Key Terms

co-cultures 28
culture 27
dialogue 32
ethnicity 29
ethnocentric 32
gender 30
high-context cultures 29
ideology 31
low-context cultures 28
race 29
sex 29
sexual orientation 30

In COMM 1000/1003

It is worthwhile to consider presenting speeches on topics that reflect different cultural backgrounds. Students that have diverse experiences are strongly encouraged to present their ideas and experiences to the class. Here are two examples.

1. An informative speech on the difference in Christmas in Mexico vs. America

2. An informative speech on a particular cuisine popular in other parts of the world

- Identify appropriate speech topics

- Help develop appropriately narrowed topics

- Determine specific purpose for speeches

5
Topic Selection

The first and perhaps most important task in the speech-making process is to select your topic. In some situations this can be difficult, and in others it is easy because the topic has already been provided. Determining what to speak about is also called the process of invention because it involves the creation of not only your topic, but also what you plan to say about it. Topic selection is a creative process that allows you to identify what you want your audience to understand by sharing with them how you understand the topic.

In this chapter, we will provide guidelines to help you develop your speech topics. This process begins broadly, with establishing the general purpose of your speech. Once this is clearly laid out, you will begin to narrow that purpose to a specific topic. When you have a more concrete topic you will then narrow your purpose even further by stating what it is you want to specifically say about that topic. Let's begin by discussing how we figure out the general purpose of a speech.

General Purpose Statements

Every speech begins with a general idea. This general idea covers what you want to do with your presentation. Do you want to inform an audience? Persuade them? Perhaps celebrate some accomplishment? Each of these is a very broad and general purpose, but it helps you begin to identify what you might say in your speech. For that reason, it is important to start by clearly writing your general purpose statement.

A **general purpose statement** is brief, usually only a few short words. It describes the type or category of speech you will prepare and deliver. There are three types of general purpose statements: those for informative speeches, persuasive speeches, and commemorative speeches. As you develop your speech, this general purpose can help guide what you choose to say and how you deliver it to the audience.

general purpose statement

a brief statement representing what you aim to do with the speech; there are three types

35

An informative speech gives the audience information but does not try to convince an audience to do or believe something. Think about instructors' lectures as speeches with the general purpose "to inform." In fact, the general purpose statement for any informative speech is "to inform," "to describe," or "to demonstrate." Notice how these general purposes would be helpful if you found yourself veering off and making a case for the audience to agree with, rather than staying true to informing, describing, or demonstrating something.

A persuasive speech has a much different general purpose than an informative speech. Persuasive speeches are intended to change or to reinforce the audience's attitudes, actions, beliefs, or values. These speeches might try to convince the audience to take a particular position on an issue or to induce the audience to take a course of action. Clearly, the general purpose moves beyond informing, describing, and demonstrating. A persuasive speech's general purpose statement is "to persuade" or "to convince." Again, as with an informative speechs' general purpose statement, these can help you stay on track when writing the body of your speech.

A commemorative speech is generally a speech of celebration, honoring someone, or presenting or accepting an award, such as a wedding toast or a funeral eulogy. Here the purpose is not to simply describe something, as in an informative speech, nor is it to try to convince someone of something, as in a persuasive speech. The general purpose of a commemorative speech is "to honor," "to commemorate," or "to celebrate." Each of these phrases gives a different tone to the speech than that of a persuasive or informative speech.

After you decide on the general purpose statement, you should begin to narrow your topic. This next step is crucial because topics that are too broad will lack substance. For example, an informative speech on the Olympics is extremely broad and could include any number of items. A speech that encapsulates all aspects of the Olympics would take weeks to deliver, and even then it is unlikely that all of it would be covered. There have been books and documentaries about one specific Olympic event, just one sport, or even just one athlete. So, with that in mind and with your general purpose clear, it is time to begin focusing your topic.

Choosing Your Topic

Once you know what your general purpose is, the next step is to choose something more concrete upon which to speak. Topics can be chosen in a variety of different ways, depending upon your situation. In many cases, the occasion will determine your topic other times you might be asked to speak about something on which you have knowledge or experience. In still other cases, you might decide you want to speak about something that piques your curiosity, sometimes you want to learn about and share with your audience. This last situation may be the case in most classrooms, but when you are speaking as part of your career you often do not get this opportunity.

In many professional situations in business the occasion will dictate your topic. For instance, salesmen try to sell particular products, thus limiting their ability to create a topic from their own interests. CEOs will provide input on the company to stockholders and employees, again dictated by the situation in which they find themselves. Accountants need to prepare updates on financial information for presentations to colleagues. In each instance the meeting situation dictates the topic to the speaker.

Despite the overwhelming influence of meeting types on selecting a topic, there are times when you might be called upon to speak based on your knowledge or expertise. This situation is most common in the fields of science and engineering, in which people who possess expert knowledge are often asked to explain those concepts to an audience with general knowledge. Think about doctors and medical researchers who try to explain cancer, heart disease, and other health risks to patients and advocacy groups, or engineers who need to describe structural changes to bridges and buildings. Experts from medical fields are sometimes called upon as expert witnesses in court cases. In each of these scenarios people from STEM and healthcare professions give presentations in which their topics flow from their area of expertise.

There are also times when your topic is something that interests you, but it is not very familiar to you. When this happens you teach yourself about your topic through your research, and then you teach it to the audience. This opportunity is rare in the professional world but very common in the classroom, where you are encouraged to explore ideas and topics that you are curious about. In education, instructors sometimes develop seminars and courses designed around ideas they want to study. These chances, though rare, are something you should take advantage of because they give you the opportunity to expand your knowledge.

Whichever of these approaches you choose for selecting a topic, it is imperative for you to narrow that topic to something that can be reasonably explored and covered in the amount of time you have for the presentation. In the next section of this chapter, we will discuss how to narrow a topic to a focus that fits your time.

Narrowing the Topic

The amount of time you may have to narrow your topic will vary, but in most instances classes allow more time than the professional world for generating presentations, and so give you more time to narrow your topic. Classroom settings mirror professional situations when it comes to time for speeches; there are time constraints and your professor will likely give you minimum and maximum time limits for your speech. Many professors will penalize your grade for violating the time target, much like going over the time limit will result in a negative experience in the professional world. This is why it is important to develop skills for quickly narrowing the topic of your speech. One of the most common methods for doing so is to brainstorm.

brainstorm
to create a list of possible topics and keep adding to this list as you think of new ideas

Brainstorming involves generating ideas and listing them as they come to mind. The process of narrowing your topic begins with writing down as many ideas as you can come up with regarding a specific topic. In true brainstorming, the strength lies in the spontaneous generation of ideas; initially, every idea is accepted. These ideas can be broad, narrow, specific, or general, because at this point it doesn't matter what they are. The list is then organized from general or broad, to narrow and specific categories under the broader labels. This helps organize your ideas into a more coherent model for coverage of topics.

In addition to, or perhaps even in conjunction with, brainstorming there is another tool you can use to help narrow and focus your topic: a concept map. A concept map, also known as a mind map, is a visual representation of the potential areas you could cover in your speech. This more visual model illustrates relationships between the ideas you generated as part of brainstorming. In a concept map, you circle topics that have certain things in common and draw a line connecting them to another group of ideas to which they relate. This visual representation makes it easier for you to understand your topic, and eventually helps you organize your ideas into an outline for your speech. Another strategy you can use is to analyze your ideas and choose those that are most important or interesting.

concept map
also known as a mind map, is a visual representation of the potential areas that you could cover in your speech

Once you develop your concept map and have a better idea of what you plan to talk about, you need to begin considering what aspects of the topic fit in the time you have to deliver the speech. There are three ways to go about making choices about what to cut and what to leave in the speech. You can choose to cover the most important elements of the topic, you can choose the most interesting or fascinating aspects of the topic, or you can combine the important with the interesting.

A topic will likely have several elements, but it is unlikely they will be equally necessary for the audience to know. For example, suppose you chose to deliver a speech on the AIDS virus to your class. You brainstormed the topic and generated the following potential topics: history of the virus, biology of the virus, affected populations, government treatment programs, famous people with AIDS, and medical treatments for the disease. Any one of these is too large for you to speak on to your class, so you then decide to brainstorm more and come up with Magic Johnson, Arthur Ashe, Mary Fisher, AZT, blood transfusions, homosexual community, and dirty needles. Now you are starting to see some links between broader and more specific ideas for your presentation.

This particular speech cannot cover all of these points, so you need to choose what to cover. You can elect to cover what you deem the most important elements of the topic, you can include the most interesting points about it in your presentation, or you can combine both. Looking at our example, the most important elements might be how the disease is transmitted and what segments of the population are most at risk. On the other hand, it might be more interesting to the audience to hear about famous individuals who contracted the disease, such as Mary Fisher, Magic Johnson, and Arthur Ashe. Finally, you could decide that the best way to go would be to combine parts of both and talk about at-risk populations and then choose one figure to talk about as a cautionary tale in your speech. Whatever route you choose, you have successfully employed brainstorming and concept mapping to appropriately narrow your speech's topic.

Knowing the elements of your speech topic is half the battle, and it was only made possible with a clear general purpose statement and time spent generating ideas for what to cover in the speech. Now that you have a narrow enough topic, some subpoints related to the topic, and a rough idea of how these all fit together, it is time to clearly articulate a specific purpose statement. In the next section of this chapter, we will discuss what this is and how you can effectively create one for your presentations.

Determining the Specific Purpose

specific purpose statement

a narrower version of the general purpose statement that identifies what you will talk about, what you will say about it, and what you hope the audience will take away from the speech

The specific purpose statement is derived from both the general purpose and the topic of your speech. It is a far more concise statement than the general purpose and serves as a guide as you go forward developing your speech. Specific purpose statements are composed of one declarative sentence that notes what you will talk about, how you will talk about it, and what you want the audience to walk away with at the end of the speech. Look at your specific purpose as an umbrella; everything you do in your speech should fit under this umbrella. You might discover some interesting information, but if it doesn't fall under the specific purpose, then it probably should not be included in your speech. To include this information might be interesting to the audience, but it will also confuse them and detract from the central idea you wish to communicate. The specific purpose should have a sharp focus.

Let's look at an example of a specific purpose:

> "My speech will inform my audience that the process of hosting a dinner party requires a focus on detail that begins with determining when the party will occur, who will be invited, and what will be served."

As you can see, this specific purpose statement provides a sharp and clear focus for the speech. It indicates the general pupose of the speech (to inform), the topic of the speech (hosting dinner parties), and the main points you will cover (timing, invitations, and menu). This is clearly an informative presentation, but it also has a very sharp focus, making it easy for the audience to follow what you plan to say.

Specific purpose statements for persuasive speeches are equally clear. Look at the following example:

> "My speech will convince my audience that Tiger Woods is the greatest PGA golfer of all time due to his short, middle, and long game, plus his ability to handle pressure, and the sheer number of tournaments he has won."

Again, all three of the purposes mentioned above are accomplished. The central argument is clear (Tiger Woods is the greatest golfer ever), and the main points that support that claim also are indicated. This allows the audience to prepare to hear this information and think about how it connects to the central argument you make.

In commemorative speeches, the specific purpose statement is different from the two previous examples we have discussed. Here is a commemorative speech specific purpose statement:

> "My speech will commemorate the occasion of Independence Day, a day when we celebrate the founding of our country, the principles that gave this country birth, and our development as a nation."

Here we notice the general purpose of celebration, the topic (Independence Day), and the main ideas that are to be celebrated in the speech. In each of these three examples, you see how specific purpose statements help ground speeches in a central idea, prevent you as the speaker from going off on tangents, and provide the audience with a sense of how the speech will unfold.

The specific purpose guides you in developing your speech and also serves as the foundation for creating your thesis statement. The thesis statement, which is the core idea you wish to communicate to your audience, comes from rewording the specific purpose statement so that it makes sense to an audience. Let's examine how we would retool the specific purpose statements from above so they work as thesis statements.

Informative speech specific purpose statement: My speech will inform my audience that the process of hosting a dinner party requires a focus on detail that begins with determining when the party will occur, who will be invited, and what will be served.

Informative speech thesis statement: Hosting a dinner party requires a focus on detail that begins with determining when the party will occur, who will be invited, and what will be served.

As you can see, all three of the elements of the specific purpose statement are there, but the thesis statement is constructed to make sense to your audience. The topic and structure of the statement changed very little in this example, except that the first few words of the specific purpose statement were eliminated. Let's see what happens when we use the persuasive speech specific purpose statement.

Persuasive speech specific purpose statement: My speech will convince my audience that Tiger Woods is the greatest PGA golfer of all time due to his short, middle, and long game, plus his ability to handle pressure, and the sheer number of tournaments he has won.

Healthcare Help

Healthcare providers often give workshops to teach first aid or to teach people how to live well with a new health condition. For example, you might be invited to talk with a high school health class about nutrition, teach a roadside emergency class as part of a driver's ed class, teach a workshop about living with diabetes, or teach a birthing class. When teaching these sessions, keep these things in mind:

- Be relevant. If you get to choose your topic, think about what is most important for your audience to know in their current situation.
- Don't overwhelm your audience with more information than they can take in at once.
- Keep solutions simple. Focus on things your audience can do to make the biggest difference.
- If you are breaking your presentation into points based on the steps in a treatment, make them easy to remember. For example, you might remind your audience they just need to remember CAB (Chest compressions, Airway, Breathing) to do CPR, or to use RICE (Rest, Ice, Compression, Elevation) when treating common injuries.

Persuasive speech thesis statement: Tiger Woods is the greatest PGA golfer of all time due to his short, middle, and long game, plus his ability to handle pressure, and the sheer number of tournaments he has won.

The same minor changes result in creating a clear thesis statement. Dropping a few words is all it takes to change one to the other. Let's see if the same holds true for commemorative speech specific purpose statements.

Commemorative speech specific purpose statement: My speech will commemorate the occasion of Independence Day, a day when we celebrate the founding of our country, the principles that gave this country birth, and our development as a nation.

Commemorative speech thesis statement: Today we celebrate Independence Day, a day that marks the founding of our country, celebrates the principles that gave this country birth, and marvels at our development as a nation.

Here the specific purpose statement and the thesis statement have more differences than a few simple words, but the essence of the idea is still the same. The changes only helped make the statement more appealing to the ear, rather than the eye; after all, the audience is hearing the statement, not reading it.

General Guidelines for Specific Purpose Statements

There are several things to keep in mind when creating the specific purpose statement. First, ensure that it is one statement. A specific purpose is just that: a statement, not a paragraph or an essay. The one statement summary approach helps you stay focused and not put too much information in the speech. That said, just because it is a single statement does not mean it cannot have clauses embedded within it; in fact, if you look at the prior examples, there are several clauses in each specific purpose statement. These clauses also help keep you focused. Ultimately, if you have more than one sentence, you are trying to do too much in that speech, and it will confuse both the audience and you.

It is also important that this single statement be declarative in nature. This means that the sentence makes a statement and clearly says something. Go back and review the statements we used as examples and you will find that all of them are direct, easy to understand, and declare something that will be done. This declaration weds you to the topic, and the supporting structure you state will support your comments about that topic. Your specific purpose statement is essentially a declaration of intent to the audience regarding what you will say.

Finally, understand that the specific purpose statement is not a rigid law by which you must abide but an evolutionary element of your speech. It can change based upon how you find the rest of your speech is coming together. In the end, the specific purpose statement must reflect how all the ideas fit together in your speech, but it can be adjusted as you craft the body of your speech.

Summary

Choosing and narrowing a topic can be a daunting task, even when the topic is provided to you in advance. It is a creative part of the speech-making process, and you must find a way to harness your creativity. In this chapter, we discussed how we invent or generate topics based upon identifying the general purpose of your presentation. We also discussed how to use brainstorming and concept mapping when developing ideas you think you might wish to include in your remarks. Finally, we showed you how to combine your general purpose and ideas generated through brainstorming to create a clear and concise specific purpose statement.

Key Terms

brainstorm   37
concept map   37
general purpose statement   35
specific purpose statement   38

In COMM 1000/1003

There are certain topics that we don't allow students to speak on. While some of these topics are seen as controversial—or hot-button issues—that has nothing to do with why they are on the list of banned topics. The reason the topics below are banned is because these are easy go-to topics that are often overused. These topics tend to be ill-received by an audience because they are bored. They've already heard all there is to hear on the topic.

Here is the list of banned topics:

- Abortion

- Gun Control

- Death Penalty

- Euthanasia (doctor-assisted suicides/right to die)

- Organ/Blood Donation

- Exercise

- Legalization of Marijuana

- Introduce aspects of what it means to be information literate

- Provide details of where to research specific types of information

- Detail tips for how to keep track of information gathered through research

6
Research and Preparation

Once you identify your topic, the next step in developing your speech is researching the information you plan to use in your presentation. In all but a few cases, speeches require some degree of research, which helps you appear credible and will increase your ability to impact the audience. The information you gather must relate to your topic and to your central idea, and, perhaps most importantly, be data the audience will respect.

On one hand, research has become easier today thanks to the Internet, which provides people with access to vast stores of data. On the other hand, technology has made it much harder to differentiate between good, credible information and false data or even opinions. The sheer amount of information available today makes the search for relevant and credible evidence more challenging. In this chapter, we address research and information used in speech construction. We will first explain information literacy and then detail the general types of information you might encounter when researching. Next we will discuss some places you might go to search for different types of information. Finally, we will cover the importance of keeping track of the information you find and plan to use in your speech.

Information Literacy

Media, friends, and family deluge us with new information every day. Websites, blogs, videos, advertisements, commercials, banners, billboards, radio programs, and e-mail constantly present us with new information. Navigating through this colossal amount of visual and verbal stimuli makes it essential for us to become critical consumers of information in our daily lives. The same skills are also necessary when looking for information when preparing a speech. For this reason, we need to familiarize ourselves with what it means to be information literate; the more clearly we understand information and how it works, the better we will be at crafting coherent arguments and evaluating the arguments of others. In this section, we detail the various skills necessary to become information literate.

Characteristics of Information Literacy

There are five characteristics of information literacy.

1. **Know why you want certain information for the speech.** You may want the information to catch the audience's attention, to provide background facts, or to make an argument and try to persuade an audience. What you wish to achieve helps you determine where you will go to get the material to help you create your speech.

2. **Know where to get the information you seek.** Today we can sit with our computer, tablet, or mobile phone and access much more information than we need, and this can make it difficult on a researcher, especially a novice. The Internet, however, is not the only place one can go to gather relevant information, and sometimes it is not even the best source to consult. Most university and college libraries contain expansive databases covering information and data from scholarly journals to trade journals, encyclopedias, legal databases, popular magazines, legal references, and daily newspapers from around the world. Always remember, though, that print materials and interviews are also possible avenues for gathering evidence to use in your speech.

3. **Know how to assess the quality of the information you have found.** Simply stumbling upon information does not mean you should use it—even if, on the surface, it seems to fit what you plan to say. It is essential that you learn how to evaluate what you find for two important things: accuracy and bias. Accuracy is the correctness of the information, and it is important that you cross-check the information. Failing to check for accuracy or knowingly presenting inaccurate information to an audience is unethical because this material could unduly influence the decisions and actions of those listening. If the other sources you find contradict the information you were hoping to use, especially if they are more recent or reliable, it is likely the information is not accurate. Additionally, if the audience does not trust or respect your sources, your credibility will likely be negatively impacted. You also must be sure to determine any potential biases in the information you find. Bias is an unfair preference or distortion of information, and to collect and use biased information is just as unethical as using inaccurate information, because it denies the audience the ability to evaluate the information on its own merits. Thus, assessing collected information for accuracy and bias is a key component of becoming an information-literate researcher, speaker, and audience member.

4. **Create new knowledge.** One of the chief aims of research is to pull together information from various sources in order to create a coherent explanation of how those pieces of data fit together. This process creates new knowledge for the audience because they see something in a different, more complex light through your efforts to make connections between sources of information. This synthesis of ideas is one of the most important aspects of information literacy and is highly respected in academia and the professional world. Information literacy does not mean you know a lot of information but rather that you know how a lot of information fits together and can explain those connections to others.

5. **Be accountable for your use of information.** You are responsible for the things you say, and just as you should respect authorship and not misrepresent yourself in a paper, you should also not misrepresent yourself or someone else when you speak. You need to be honest with your audience about what you know, what you think, and what you do not know. It is important to not make broad claims when you speak that you cannot back up with the information you collected in your research. Make sure your audience also knows where they can go to get that information if they wish to locate it. Essentially, accountability in information use means you take ownership of what you say and respect the ownership of what others have said.

As you can tell, being information literate is not as simple as it sounds. It involves developing your research skills and your analytical abilities, as well as adhering to ethical standards as you look for and use evidence. Being information literate allows you to judge information for quality and thus use good evidence to construct stronger, more effective speeches. These standards for assessing quality of information apply to each of the general categories of data you might find in your research. In the next section, we elaborate on those different types of information.

bias
an unfair preference or distortion of information

Types of Information

When conducting research you will find information that fits into one of three broad categories: background information, unique information, and evidentiary information. Identifying what type of information you find is one of the core characteristics of a strong researcher.

Background Information

In many speeches, you will need to provide the context for your speech. This may involve providing the audience with the who, what, when, where, why, and how relevant to your topic. Background is often the first type of information you encounter when researching a topic with which you are unfamiliar, and finding it will help you refine your topic and could be useful when explaining the topic to your audience.

Unique Information

Another type of information you will encounter when researching is data that is unique. It could be statistics, quotations, or stories about people and events that are not common knowledge but are nonetheless fascinating. This information can be valuable in capturing and maintaining the interest of your audience. Unique information gives your topic a personality by adding colorful facts, stories, or brief anecdotes, and it can also heighten audience appreciation and interest in the evidence you provide.

Evidentiary Information

This type of information is the core of your speech and is what you set out looking for when researching a topic. It is information that lends direct support to your thesis and the main points of your speech. Evidence can come in the form of statistics, testimony, examples, or a myriad of other materials that directly support the claims you make in your speech. What constitutes evidence varies depending on the topic of the speech, but for all intents and purposes evidence is the guts of your speech. For example, businessmen trying to sell a product may use data on cost or performance, or even testimonials from current or prior users of the product. The key element is its central relationship to the topic.

Knowing what types of information exist and how to evaluate them is essential for any researcher. Another important aspect of successful research, which we will discuss next, is knowing where to go to get the information you need.

Places to Research

As we mentioned earlier, technology has made information more readily available than it was in the past. This means that there are a great many more places for you to look to find research on your topics. In this section, we will discuss three sources of information you can take advantage of when researching: libraries, the Internet, and people. Each of these has its uses and can provide different types of informa-

Practical Politics

If you are working in politics, you will need to spend a lot of time doing research that will prepare you for the situations you will face both during the campaign and after you or the candidate for whom you are working is in office. For example, here are a few things that you will need to have someone on your political team research thoroughly:

- The issues: Make sure you have the most accurate information about every issue that you will deal with. When you are in a position to make decisions that will affect others in significant ways you have a responsibility to make sure your decisions are well informed and are in the best long-term interest of your constituents and society as a whole. Be prepared to defend your statements and decisions!
- The voters: Who are they? What issues are most important to them? What information do they have?
- Your opponents: What are their policy proposals? Where do they stand on important issues? What are their voting records?
- Yourself: Someone on your team should conduct research to find out what your opponents might discover about you during their research. This will give you the opportunity to correct any factual errors and be prepared to answer questions that will undoubtedly arise about your past.

tion. Be aware, however, that both your topic choice and the outcome you desire will help determine where you should go to find your information.

Libraries

Libraries today do not operate anything like they did ten years ago, let alone centuries ago. For instance, not that many years ago library patrons used physical card catalogues to search by author or subject, and learning the Dewey Decimal System was an important component of high school curricula. Today we can access research tools at our fingertips through computer databases and digital catalogues. This allows libraries to store even more information.

Although they vary in size and mission, most higher education libraries subscribe to electronic databases that contain an overwhelming number of books, encyclopedias, journals, and periodicals. EBSCOhost, for example, is an online system that can connect you to databases and indices for specific disciplines, providing easy, quick access to years of research. This search engine also provides source citations, abstracts, and many full-text copies of articles you can print, just as if the original source were right in front of you. When researching through this database and others, you can restrict your search to collect only entries that are available in full text or in peer-reviewed publications.

Higher education libraries almost universally have access to search engines that comb through subscriptions to hundreds of journals with thousands of articles in the social sciences, humanities, hard sciences, education, engineering, law, and other disciplines. Many of these resources are in full text, in either HTML or PDF format, making it easy to download copies of the material you need or want to your flash drive or desktop so you can open and read them later.

There are a great many databases that can help you refine your search to specific disciplines. One such search engine is ERIC, which focuses on education. There are military and government databases, legal databases, and science databases. One jewel to take particular note of is LexisNexis. This search engine combs through newspaper and magazine articles from around the globe and pulls up a news article or Op-Ed piece in a local newspaper miles away from where you are located. All of these search engines provide you with easy access to troves of information and include tools to help you find what you are looking for.

With all of this information located in different places, research can easily get frustrating. For that reason, when doing library work, seek out the librarians who work at your particular library before you get too irritated. They are trained in searching for material and know the library better than you do. You will also find that if you are polite to them these dedicated professionals will, in all likelihood, save you time and emotional energy. Take advantage of this tremendous resource when seeking information on specific topics.

The Internet

In addition to searching the stacks of information available both on library shelves and in the databases to which they subscribe, you can also search the Internet for information. There is a caveat: not all Web sites are created equal. Some are self-created and contain blogs that often consist of opinions, and thus are not a good source of scientific or factual data. One of the first steps in evaluating Web sites involves looking at the type of domain they exist on.

There are several form designations at or near the end of the Web address, and these are the domains of the specific Web site (see Figure 6.1). The most reliable of these domains is .gov. It is the most reliable because the sites are government run and have a mechanism for verification. The next most reliable is .edu, which means a site is hosted and managed by an educational institution, and as a result the source is very easy to identify, thus making the biases easy to see as well. The next most trustworthy is .com. This denotes a for-profit entity that makes money off of its Web site. Careful scrutiny is needed here as these sites generally contain biases, in that the company posts information that is accurate but places it in a positive light. The information may be accurate, but it may also be presented in a biased manner. This means that the information here might be usable, but you should proceed cautiously. The next level of domains is .org. The .org designation is used by nonprofit and noneducation groups and organizations. Like companies, these groups often have agendas, and so information

STEM Spotlight

Before you begin to develop a solution to an engineering problem, you will need to take time to go through the discovery process, which requires many of the same skills and steps you use when developing a speech. When you go through the initial discovery process, you will need to be prepared to do the following:

- Understand the problem
- Identify the requirements for the solution
- Understand the policies and obstacles that might limit your options
- Learn about the context in which the solution will be enacted
- Identify what other solutions have and have not been successful in other contexts

found here may well be accurate but biased. The most unreliable domains on the Web are .net. These Web sites do not have clear ownership and authorship; anyone can create a .net and post information on it. They are not monitored by entities, such as the FTC, that pay attention to companies, and so their information may be inaccurate as well as biased. Carefully examining the domain name will help you better identify useful information.

FIGURE 6.1

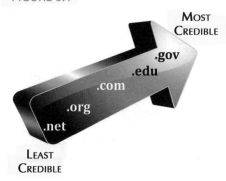

One of the most common places novice researchers go for information on the Web is an online encyclopedia, but this could be a very hazardous practice. Wikipedia, perhaps the most universally known online encyclopedia, is a dangerous source. Some of the pages on Wikipedia are well researched and written by experts, and you can usually identify these pages by the long list of peer-reviewed sources included in the reference page. However, anyone can upload or edit information on Wikipedia, even changing entries that were originally well researched, calling anything found on the site into question. Information found there might be accurate, but it also might be fabricated, posted out of malice, or even uploaded as a joke. Be sure to check with your instructor before you use Wikipedia as a source. Generally speaking, Wikipedia is a good place to find background information before you begin your research, but you should rely on other sources for supporting materials when developing your speech.

One final tip regarding searching for information online relates to the use of proper search terms. Search terms are the keywords that you type into the search engine to help locate material. Understand that Google does a keyword search of the Web when you use it to find information. This means that it will call up every Web site that contains the word or phrase you put in the search, resulting in a mountain of hits. One helpful way to minimize this pile of information and to focus it more succinctly around your topic is to use Boolean operators such as "and," "but," and "or" when typing in terms. As always, evaluate the returns using the Web site domain system we explained earlier.

People

People you know or whom you seek out can be great sources, but this depends upon the topic and your speech goals. One way to gather information from others is through interviews. Interviews can be conducted in face-to-face meetings, over the telephone, through e-mail, or even using technology such as Skype. It is often best to use a method in which you can see the other person during the interview so you can read the respondent's non-verbal communication, but this is not always possible. Using technology to see the other party in a discussion is becoming more and more commonplace in business, families, and even education with online distance courses, and it makes gathering information in a setting where you can see the person's nonverbal reactions much easier.

Boolean operator
using words such as "and," "but," and "or" when typing in search terms to focus the results

Regardless of what medium you use to conduct the interview, it is important to record what happens and what is said so you can relay accurate information in your speech. Make sure you have the respondent's consent when interviewing, as doing so without his or her knowledge would be unethical. Surreptitiously taping even a lecture without the instructor's knowledge is a grievous violation of someone's trust, and information gathered in this manner should not be used in a speech.

When you decide to conduct an interview to gather information for your speech, there are certain steps you should follow to make sure you get the most out of this tactic. First decide which type of interview testimony you want to collect. The two kinds of testimony are peer testimony and expert testimony. Peer testimony is provided by a nonexpert who gives an opinion or story regarding a particular topic. An expert, on the other hand, is someone with credibility and professional experience directly relevant to the topic you plan to discuss. It is distinctly possible that you might use one, the other, or both types of interviews for the same topic.

Suppose, for example, you wanted to present a speech about the Great Depression. There are many sources of recorded economic, political, and social information available, but an interview with someone who lived through the Great Depression's hardships would be an excellent source. Another possible source would be someone who had researched the topic and written extensively about the Great Depression in books, newspapers, or journals. Both interviews would provide good information for your speech, and you might use one, the other, or both in your final presentation.

After you find someone willing to be interviewed, you must prepare carefully for the interview. First decide exactly what you want to learn from the interview. Then you need to compile a list of questions to ask in order to get at that information. Before the interview begins ask the person how much time he or she has for your questions. During the interview, do not be afraid to deviate from your list of questions if the interviewee brings up an interesting topic. Much like when exploring information in the library or online, what you find out through a person's answers may change the focus of your research, and that is not a bad thing. After all, interviewing and researching are about going where the information takes you.

When you finish the interview, be sure to thank the person you interviewed. You should also send a follow-up thank you e-mail or card. These simple courtesies are professional, might help you if you need to speak to the person again, and are a good habit to form. Later, when transcribing your notes, make sure to clarify statements the person made if you are unsure what was said or what the person meant.

Interviews are not the only source of information people can provide; you can also sometimes gain access to personal correspondence. Personal correspondence includes e-mails people send to one another, collections of letters, and personal diaries or journals. Many libraries contain collections of these types of correspondences that may be available to you. These correspondences are generally considered rich data, as they are usually written from a personal perspective and reflect the feelings, opinions, and beliefs of the writers themselves. These primary documents can provide speeches with a degree of color that other information just cannot provide.

Whether you conduct an interview, find an article in a journal or magazine, or use a Web site from a company, it is imperative that you track where you gathered your information. In the next section, we will provide some tips on doing just that and supply some examples of common bibliographical techniques used to document sources.

Documenting Your Research

Documenting sources is an important element of any paper or presentation. One of the key differences between documenting sources in speeches and in papers is that you only need to document sources once in written papers, but twice in speeches, because the sources need to be cited in the outline or manuscript as well as verbally attributed when referencing them during the speech.

One of the most frustrating things about research is also one of the most avoidable. You will never be more irritated than when you reach the end of your preparation and realize that you need to go back and document all the places you found your information. To avoid this time-consuming concern it is important to develop a way

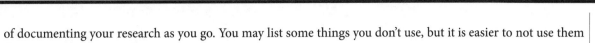
of documenting your research as you go. You may list some things you don't use, but it is easier to not use them than to repeat your search.

Ways to keep track of your research sources:
- Place notes on each piece of information you collect that lists the proper bibliographical citation for that piece of data. Then later, when you are finishing your speech bibliography, go back and get the notes for the information you used and log it into your bibliography.

- Keep a notebook in which you log all your information and where you found it. This is a bit more detailed, in that you are annotating the bibliographical citations so you know what information came from which source, and can be instrumental in making decisions about what to include in your speech and what to leave out. As with the notes, once the speech is complete go through the notebook and create the bibliography from those sources that you used.

- Keep an ongoing bibliography in the document itself. Each time you encounter information you plan to use, log it into your running bibliography so that you have it already recorded. Then, when the speech is finished, go through the bibliography and delete the sources you did not use. This simple task will save tons of time when you are preparing your speech and will ensure that you are making ethical use of the information you collected.

Generally speaking, there are three style manuals used to document sources. In English and some disciplines within the humanities, the preferred style manual is published by the Modern Language Association (MLA). In the social sciences and hard sciences, the preferred style manual is produced by the American Psychological Association (APA). Finally, in a few select humanities disciplines and in some areas of business, the footnote-heavy *Chicago Manual of Style* (CMS) is preferred.

American Psychological Association Style Guide (APA)

APA, the style favored by the social and natural sciences, is different from MLA style in several respects. For instance, although both MLA and APA require in-text parenthetical citations, the format in APA differs from that of MLA. Here are some examples of APA parenthetical citation styles:

- *One author, not directly quoted:* In the United States, having a standardized time became important when the railroad made faster travel possible (Gleick, 1999).

- *Multiple author, not directly quoted:* Entertainment programs can also educate viewers about social issues (Singhal & Rogers, 2003).

- *Author in text, directly quoted:* Gleick noted, "With the century ending, some towns and cities resisted the onslaught of precise and standardized railroad time" (1999, p. 44).

- *Web site with author, not directly quoted:* This is the first year that people living in the U.S. will watch more movies online than on DVDs (Pepitone, March 22, 2012).

- *Web site with no author, not directly quoted:* The first blood donation programs began during World War II ("Red Cross blood program," March 22, 2012).

- *Web site with author, directly quoted:* "That's a 135% year-over-year increase for online video" (Pepitone, March 22, 2012, para. 4).

There are several things to note here as well. First, if a work has more than six authors, you should use the last name of the first author and then the phrase "et al." to refer to the rest of the authors. When using the author's name in the sentence, you only need to put the year in the parentheses, or the year and page number if the material is directly quoted. Last, when the author is listed as "Anonymous," reference it by using the word "anonymous" followed by the date in the parenthetical citation.

APA, like MLA, calls for a list of all sources used in the speech to appear at the end. However, their list is called a "Reference List" and not a "Works Cited" page as it is in MLA. Like the other style manuals, the list is organized alphabetically. Let's look at how entries for some common sources are formatted in APA:

Magazine/Newspaper Article with Single Author:

Smith, J. (2010, November 8). Form and style. *The Detroit Free Press,* A8.

- Magazine articles only require the month, and not the specific date of publication, so they would appear (2004, November) in the above example.

Magazine/Newspaper Article with Multiple Authors:

Smith, J., Billbrook, S. O., & Cooper, M. (2008, January 2). Form and style. *Dayton Daily News,* A9.

Magazine/Newspaper Article with No Author:

The form is not right. (1994, March 18). *The Sacramento Bee,* A14.

Journal Article:

Smith, J. (2004). Bibliographies can be fun. *Canadian Journal of Communication, 17* (3), 88–124.

- Include the issue number only if the journal is paginated by issue.

Chapter in an Edited Volume:

Smith, J.A., & Lyle, G. (2008). "Bibliographies are difficult to master." In *Fun with citations* (Eds. H. Johnson, C. Levi, and J. Jones), p. 101–121. New York, NY: Routledge.

Book:

Jones, P. (2010). *Correctly tracking sources.* Chicago, IL: University of Chicago Press.

Web site:

Simpson, H. (2002, October 12). A letter to John Smith. Retrieved on: January 12, 2004. http://www.xgtsfjm-nouiyh.com/jstr/htm/070908.

A Letter to the Editor in a Newspaper:

Smith, J. (2010, July 17). People like food [Letter to the editor]. *Miami Herald,* p. A9.

Government Reports:

S. Rep. No. 207-294, at 9 (2006).

Pay close attention to the capitalization and punctuation schemes in APA, as they can be tricky. Notice, for example, that only the first word of article and book titles are capitalized, while the others remain in lowercase. Also note that the full name of the author is not listed; the first name is initialed only.

Oral Citations

In addition to listing and citing sources within your outline or manuscript, you also need to verbally attribute sources when speaking to your audience. Verbal attribution does not mean that you read off the entire bibliographical reference, or even tell the audience the page on which you found the information, but it does mean that you let the audience know the information came from someone other than you. This is important, as it is an ethical practice that also builds credibility with your audience. Ideally, your oral citation should include (1) the author or person who was the source of information for the article, (2) that person's credentials, (3) the name of the publication, and (4) the date that the source was published. However, you won't always have all four of these pieces of information, so you should share as many of these details as you can to let your audience know where you found the information. Here are several ways in which you could adequately attribute source material during a speech:

> According to Dr. Sanjay Gupta on June 15, 2009, on cnn.com, people who receive e-mail reminders with health tips are more likely to make healthy choices throughout the day.

> According to a recent Gallup Poll, increasing numbers of Americans are worried about the housing market.

> In his 2003 book *Lamb*, Christopher Moore offers an account of Jesus from the perspective of his fictional childhood best friend, Biff.

> Some people, such as *Washington Post* columnist George Will, argue that baseball should not add another wild card team to its playoff structure.

> The 9/11 Commission Report recommended a series of changes in government policy to respond to the threat of modern terrorism.

All of these statements verbally attribute information gleaned through research to their sources. These statements help increase credibility and also let the audience know where they can find the information you used.

Summary

Solid research on your topic is the backbone of a strong speech. Conducting good research was the focus of this chapter, and we introduced you to the five characteristics of information literacy so that you can understand what it takes to gather quality information on your topic. We also explained the different types of information you will encounter in your research, as well as where you can go to locate such information. Finally, we detailed the importance of documenting and attributing the sources you use and briefly explained the three major style manuals used in academics and the business world.

Key Terms

bias   42
Boolean operators   45

In COMM 1000/1003

The RBD Library here on campus is going to be your best resource when it comes to researching your topics for your speeches. And most of that research can be done from the comfort of your own dorm/apartment. There is even a specific page dedicated to helping you think about databases and websites to use for your research in this class. Go to http://libguides.auburn.edu/c.php?g=518952&p=3549584

- Learn basic methods for analyzing an audience before a speech

- Understand how audience analysis continues during a speech

- Familiarize yourself with ways to gather audience information

7
Audience Analysis

Speaking may seem like an act conducted by an individual, but it actually cannot be done without others. The audience is just as important in the speech process as the speaker. This chapter focuses on how to analyze the audience as a speaker so you can craft messages that work with the specific groups to whom you speak. We will first talk about some basic audience analysis methods that can take place before a presentation. Next we will explain how analyzing the audience does not stop with the start of your talk but rather continues during the entire presentation. Finally, we will discuss different ways to gather audience information using some common interpersonal and social scientific methods.

Before the Speech

The amount of time you have with your audience before a speech can vary quite a bit. For instance, you might be delivering a quarterly update on sales figures to your supervisor, in which case you roughly know when you will be asked to speak with your team. On the other hand, you might be asked to develop a presentation on plans for a new engineering project to three different investment companies with only a few days' advance notice. In each of these scenarios the phrase "before the speech" means something very different. In the first situation, you have a great deal of time to consider your audience, analyze them for relevant information, and ultimately make adjustments. In the latter you have precious little time and even less information on your potential audiences. In both situations, there are methods for gathering information on your audience before you give your presentation. In this section, we will discuss direct observation and the collection of demographic data.

Direct Observation

One tool for audience analysis is your perception of the situation in the moment. Through direct observation you can collect a great deal of information on your audience. Let's

When preparing for a sales presentation, work to identify what the customer needs (also sometimes called "identifying their pain") so that you don't waste everyone's time trying to sell a solution that won't fix the problem. Find out what the client cares about BEFORE you walk into the meeting and take some time early in your first meeting to make sure that you fully understand the problem. Here are a few ways to find out about your client:

■ Look at the client's Web site. Find out what the company does and look for key terms or a mission statement that sums up the company's values.
■ If you have an opportunity to do so, talk to someone within your client's company to find out about its goals and concerns.
■ Search for news articles to find out whether anything has happened at the company recently that caught the media's attention (positive or negative).
■ Try to find newsletters, white papers, research reports, and any other documents that might be available that will help you find out what your client has been working on recently.
■ Talk to others in your own company who have worked with this client in the past.

look at a few things you might observe and how they could quickly be incorporated into your presentation.

First, if the speech is at a company's office or complex you can examine the walls for photos, slogans, and materials that are prominently displayed. Companies post information about upcoming events as well, and this data can be easily added to your speech in the form of an off-hand reference. Acknowledging the company and the importance of its information demonstrates that you pay attention to detail.

In addition to environmental cues, you can get a fairly accurate read on how many people will be in attendance for the presentation and who they might be. It is not difficult to take a quick mental count of people in the room as you move about before the meeting or presentation. You can also tell who the people are by examining name badges, paying attention to introductions, and watching where people sit and how they dress. All of these behaviors can provide you with important data you might be able to use in your talk.

Finally, through direct observation you can get a feel for the emotional disposition of the audience toward you and your talk. Look at facial cues, eye movement, whether people have notepads, or if they seem excited. This information can give you a heads-up on what to expect when you begin your speech. If the audience looks bored, tired, or disengaged, you may need to begin with great energy or come up with something early in the speech to cause them to want to listen to what you have to say. On the other hand, if they seem interested, tap into that excitement from the beginning.

Demographics

Collect simple demographic data on your audience to help provide a picture of to whom you will be speaking. Demographics are categories of definable characteristics of groups of people, such as age, race, religion, socioeconomic status, education level, and sexual orientation. It is not hard to imagine how such data might be useful to a speaker.

demographics
categories of definable characteristics of groups of people, such as age, race, religion, socioeconomic status, education level, and sexual orientation

Demographic data is commonly collected by a variety of institutions. Political candidates make use of this data to know which segment of the audience to target and which message to present to that audience. The same commercials do not air in Oregon as do in Ohio, for example, where different issues matter more to particular demographic groups that reside there. Demographics allow candidates to tailor one message for one group of potential voters and another for a different section of the audience. Elected officials also use demographic data via polling to assess how the public feels about policies that have been passed or policies that are being presented in Congress.

Marketers use demographics to evaluate particular strategies about sales. For example, a marketing team for a luxury car manufacturer could analyze Census Bureau demographic data and determine whom they would like to target. Since they are more likely to target those living in high income zip codes, they will consult the Census Bureau information to find out where those zip codes are located. The Census Bureau report also provides information on religious practices, ethnic origins, and other such data. The one caveat to using Census Bureau data is that it is only collected every ten years, so be sure to get the most current and relevant information from them.

Demographic data is used in education by teachers as well as administrators. Administrators need to track performance by demographic groups and report it to their accrediting agencies. Students and professors frequently look around on the first day of class and note the number of females versus males, the age of students, and perhaps even ethnic or racial breakdowns of those present. This is in some ways an automatic reflex and illustrates how direct observation can also be used to gather demographic information about an audience.

In the United States some demographic categories are protected by federal government laws. For example, protected categories include age, race, gender, sexual orientation, religion, and disability. The law forbids treating people differently because they belong to a particular group within one of these categories. This illustrates the power of demographic categories and data, and the information and policies they shape in society. Knowing the reach and influence of demographics can be helpful to speakers who gather data about their audience ahead of time and make specific adjustments to their messages so they are more likely to resonate with that particular audience. Ultimately, demographic information can show differences in values, beliefs, and opinions among people—and it is there where the true power of this information resides.

People in different segments of demographic categories have different experiences, and these experiences shape their values and beliefs in different ways. For example, an 18-year-old freshman in college is going to see the world very differently from her great grandmother. They have different goals, expectations, voting and purchasing behaviors, and even different needs. Race also can serve as an indicator of different cultural experiences, beliefs, and expectations. This becomes especially insightful information when paired with geography, because it becomes possible to see how strong ethnic or racial identities can be in specific communities.

Gender also imparts information on expectations, beliefs, values, and behaviors. Research reveals that women and men communicate differently, especially in interpersonal and group communication settings—invaluable data for a speaker addressing a group predominantly consisting of one or the other sex.

Sexual orientation, religion, and disability/impairment can also mean differences between groups and individuals in those categories. But there are still other demographics that matter. Education has been shown to alter a person's views and attitudes about political and social issues. Vocation can also play a factor, as can things such as where a person lives and with whom he or she associates. Socioeconomic status can influence behaviors, in particular purchasing behaviors in the marketplace. All of this information can be invaluable to a speaker who has the time to make use of it in advance of a presentation.

Methods of Analysis during the Speech

The process and usefulness of audience analysis does not end as you begin your speech. In fact, perhaps the most helpful form of audience analysis occurs during the presentation as you observe and adapt to how the audience receives your message. In this section, we will discuss two elements involved in conducting audience analysis during the speech, including the continuing role of direct observation and polling the audience.

Direct Observation

As we mentioned when covering audience analysis before the speech, there is no more valuable tool than your own ability to observe the audience. During a speech, it is more likely that a speaker will react to nonverbal cues from an audience than to anything else. Generally, nonverbal behaviors tell how the audience is truly reacting to the message. This is because nonverbals are very hard to control, and so audience members tend to let them go, especially when they are not the one in the so-called spotlight. These actions are spontaneous and more accurate indicators of how audience members are receiving your message. If the speaker notices certain things about the audience, he or she then has an opportunity to take advantage of that information, often without the audience even knowing it.

You might notice that your audience is increasingly more engaged with you and your topic as the speech continues. Certain indicators of this may be head nods, smiles, raised eyebrows, clapping, or even cheering. This is, of course, a positive sign and means you are on the right track with what you are saying. This does not mean you should rest, however, because in their enthusiasm is an opportunity for more emotional connections between them, you, and your topic. You can increase the tone of your voice, use hand gestures more emphatically to make a point, or even reference someone in the crowd or some action taking place. These observations will solidify your identification with the audience and enhance the success of your speech.

TABLE 7.1

Strategies for Gaining Audience Interest	Tendencies that Lose Audience Interest
• Make eye contact • Vary tone, pitch, and pace • Use gestures to make a point • Use pauses effectively • Refer to someone in the crowd • Involve your audience (e.g., polling)	• Poor delivery skills • Not varying your tone, pitch, or pace throughout your speech • Reading your speech • Talking about things that are not relevant to your audience

Another powerful indicator of audience engagement is eye contact. First, as the speaker you should make as much eye contact with the audience as possible. The audience also should be making eye contact with you throughout your speech. This indicates respect and interest in you and/or your topic. If they are not making eye contact, then consider changing the energy of the delivery or the cadence and rhythm of your voice to get their attention and bring them back to the content of your presentation (see Table 7.1).

Lack of eye contact, however, is just one way an audience can indicate a lack of interest in your speech. The audience may show a decreased level of interest in a variety of ways, including shifting in their seats, talking to neighbors, reading, sleeping, or even leaving the room. Another key indicator is if you notice members of the audience looking at their watches or cell phones. This can mean they are impatient and want the speech to end. All these behaviors should communicate to you that the time has come to put some energy into your delivery to help refocus the audience's attention and try to get them engaged with the speech (see Table 7.2).

As you can see, direct observation of audience behaviors is a powerful tool for audience analysis that speakers can take advantage of and use to help deliver a successful presentation. It is not, though, the only strategy for audience analysis in their toolkit.

TABLE 7.2

Signals of Audience Engagement	Signals of Audience Disengagement
• Head nods • Smiles • Raised eyebrows • Clapping or cheering • Eye contact	• Shifting in their seats • Talking to neighbors • Reading • Sleeping • Leaving the room • Looking at watches or cell phones

Polling the Audience

Direct observation is something any speaker can do in virtually any situation; however, other strategies, such as polling the audience, may not be feasible in certain circumstances. Nevertheless, it is important to understand how to employ this useful technique for gathering information about an audience during a speech. This type of polling is considered informal, because it does not follow the rules of the scientific process, but its results are very helpful to any speaker. There are also different moments when you might consider polling the audience.

The first moment when you might poll the audience is during the introduction of your speech. In fact, this could be a creative attention getter. Not only do you get immediate feedback, but it is also a good way to get the audience engaged by asking them to respond and thus invest themselves in the outcome their answer produces. Even if the audience does not verbally or physically respond, they will likely mentally consider the question. Whether they answer or not, polling them has produced both data and attention. Generally, the best way to poll is by asking a question, or series of questions, and requesting that the audience members raise their hands if they agree or disagree with your statement. This can help introduce a topic and give you information about what parts of your topic might be the most relevant to cover.

The other instance when polling the audience can come in handy is during the speech when you cover something complex or difficult. This approach allows you to determine if the audience understands the points you are making. If they are following along, then continue as planned, but if they are not, slow down and readjust your coverage of the material so the audience can understand it. It is acceptable, as the speaker, to query them if you have any concerns about their comprehension of the issue, and the information you gather from this analysis holds tremendous value.

There is one important caveat to polling the audience to gather information: you cannot control the outcome of your question. Things could go as planned, and that is always a good thing, but they also might not. The audience members could turn to each other to discuss your question, thus taking their attention away from you as the speaker. They also might not answer the way you expect them to, and this may rattle your nerves because you are not prepared for their answer. To this end, be sure your questions are purposeful and get at the information you want to gather. Do not ignore what you receive from the audience but rather find the most effective way to use it in your presentation.

Other Ways of Gathering Audience Information

Although we have focused on a few audience analysis methods, there are several others which you can employ, depending upon the time you have to prepare your speech. Some of these methods include talking to a contact person, conducting a statistically valid survey of potential audience members before the presentation, and interviewing people who might attend your talk. As you can imagine, each of these is dependent on quite a few variables but nevertheless can provide you with valid and vital information as you prepare to speak.

Contact Persons

In many instances in which you deliver remarks to people outside your organization there is a contact person responsible for making arrangements regarding your presentation. This could be the person who manages the event at which you are speaking, the person who invited you to deliver a sales presentation, or simply a colleague at another company. If the speech is at a neutral site, such as a hotel conference room, then this contact person likely reserved the room where you will speak, arranged the seating style, and is in charge of the audiovisual equipment. This contact person should be able to give you some insights into the makeup of the audience and the environment in which you are speaking. If audience members are required to reserve seats in advance, you might even be able to get a list of potential attendees. If the list is not available, the contact person should be able to provide their background, their values, and possibly even their disposition toward the event at which you will be speaking. No matter what the situation, it can only help to have a healthy dialogue with your contact person regarding the event and the audience.

Scientific Surveys

Previously, we mentioned polling the audience, and we told you it was not scientifically rigorous. Of course, scientifically rigorous polling is not possible during a speech; however, if you have enough advance time you can accurately survey your potential audience. These surveys help to gather demographic data as well as people's feelings toward particular issues or topics. To do this you need to develop Likert scale questions that help people numerically gauge their feelings regarding a specific idea or object.

Likert scales provide a statement to which people circle a number indicating the strength with which they agree or disagree. Individuals must choose only one answer to each statement. Likert scales vary in terms of the ranges from which they ask people to make a selection, but generally they go from either 1 to 5 or 1 to 7, with

Teacher Tips

Polling the audience (your students) is one way to determine if your students understand the lesson and are ready to move on to the next subject. Checking for understanding is also sometimes called formative assessment and can include any strategy that allows you to find out what students know so you can use that information to adapt your teaching. Here are several ways you can check for understanding:

- Give a quiz.
- Ask direct questions about the content.
- Ask students to give examples that illustrate the concepts (in words, drawings, or role plays).
- Give students examples and ask them to identify the concept.
- Do a think-pair-share. Ask students to think about and write down their answers to a question, then talk about their answers in pairs, and then call on several groups to share their answers with the rest of the class.

While getting answers from a few students is helpful, you can more effectively assess your students' understanding by getting responses from all of your students at once. In any class, you can ask students to raise their hands to indicate which answer they think is correct, but if the resources are available you should also consider using technology such as clickers or PollEverywhere. As a bonus, these strategies help keep your students engaged and interested throughout your class!

Healthcare Help

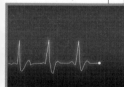

Patient questionnaires (e.g., the forms that everyone must fill out during a first visit to a new doctor or dentist, at a blood drive, etc.) are a survey method for quickly obtaining information about individual patients as well as aggregate data about all of the patients in your practice. To make sure that you get the most accurate information possible and that your patients are comfortable answering the questions honestly, keep these tips in mind when writing your questions:

- Make your questions as straightforward as possible.
- Choose a font and format that are easy to read, yet allow the patient to maintain some degree of privacy from nearby wandering eyes.
- Use familiar, everyday language your patients will understand.
- Choose neutral language that does not imply that a positive or negative value judgment is associated with particular answers.
- Questions should be comprehensive and relevant to your medical specialty.

the middle number representing a neutral opinion. This allows a researcher to see how strongly the population being measured feels regarding an issue. As you can tell, such information would be invaluable for a speaker in advance of a presentation.

An audience's answers to these questions can often be broken down by demographic category, thanks in large part to the inclusion of such questions on the survey. The larger the audience, the more segmented the data becomes when broken into demographic groups. For instance, the Nielson rating system, which is used to measure television audiences, breaks down surveyed populations according to demographic categories and provides advertisers with information regarding which programs they should advertise during.

Scientific surveys are not restricted to gathering demographic data or asking Likert scale questions; they can also contain open-ended questions that ask audience members to use their own words in response to a question. Open-ended questions allow audience members the opportunity to provide their reasons for feeling a certain way or their impressions of a specific idea or object. How they describe these things also tells you what is important and what might resonate with them. This type of information can be quite helpful, so some surveys ask people both forced-choice and open-ended questions. Ultimately, the success of surveys depends on what information you are trying to gather. Scientifically surveyed data can be rich and provide speakers who plan well with much needed information as they prepare their speech.

Personal Interviews

Perhaps you do not have a contact person or do not have the time to create, implement, and analyze a scientifically valid survey instrument. This does not mean there is nothing you can do to gather more data on your audience. One final strategy you may employ is to personally interview potential audience members to allow you to gauge their interest in your topic and, perhaps, their actual opinion on the matter. If you know the person whom you interview, you also might get information on other potential audience members that can be quite useful—especially in a sales situation.

Interviews also have the added bonus of allowing you to get to know someone who will be in attendance at your talk. Knowing someone in the audience can help reduce tension and anxiety when you actually deliver your remarks. It also allows you to catch up with that person at the event before you talk to see if there is any other information he or she can relay to you.

Interviews are an intensely personal matter for several reasons. First, you are asking people to give time from their day to speak with you, and this in and of itself is a big commitment. Second, you are asking them to use that time to share their personal attitudes, beliefs, and ideas with you, so you should respect them for sharing that information, even if it might not be what you wanted or expected to hear. Finally, interviews occur in intimate settings, whether they are in person, over the phone, or even via Skype, so nonverbal behaviors that convey information regarding a person's personality will be available. This information must not be abused.

Summary

In any speaking situation, even those with no advance preparation time, audience analysis is a key component to a presenter's success. Information about the audience can help you tailor your message in a way that increases the likelihood of success. In this chapter, we have discussed audience analysis from several perspectives, all designed to illustrate how analyzing audience data can help you in crafting and delivering a successful speech. We covered different methods of audience analysis before the speech. We then provided strategies for audience analysis during the speech. Finally, we went over some specific ways of gathering information about an audience that might provide you with even more insight into their beliefs, attitudes, and personality. Audience analysis is the key to success in any speaking situation.

Key Terms

demographics   52

In COMM 1000/1003

We strongly encourage all students to conduct audience analysis research and incorporate your findings into your speeches. Questionnaires and surveys can be given in class by passing them out to your fellow COMM 1000 students or working with your professor on posting those surveys in Canvas. This is considered research, and a well-delivered questionnaire will count as one of the required sources. Please note that a one- to two-question survey or asking close-ended questions verbally in class are not "well-delivered questionnaires." Time and thought must go into these in order for them to count as true research. When adequately conducted, this type of audience analysis can be the difference in a good speech and a GREAT speech.

- Become familiar with three different types of supporting materials that can be used in a speech

- Understand the advantages and disadvantages of each type of supporting material

- Learn guidelines for using supporting materials for maximum effect

8
Supporting Materials

Introductions capture the audience's attention and conclusions leave the audience with something to remember, but the real action is in the body of your speech, where you provide materials to support the claims made in your presentation. These supporting materials are the key to successfully influencing an audience. Successfully incorporating strong supporting materials into your speech helps demonstrate your credibility on the subject and supplies the rationale behind why you are telling the audience what you are telling them. It is in finding the best evidence for your speech and connecting it through the reasoning process that you deliver a smooth and effective presentation.

In this chapter, we will explore some common supporting materials you might use for any speech, whether it is informative, persuasive, or delivered on a special occasion. First we will cover examples and how they can be used at different points in a speech. Then we will explain statistics and offer advice on how to effectively incorporate them into your presentation. Third we will explain testimony and its appropriate place in a speech. Finally, we will offer some guidelines for successfully incorporatng and using supporting materials in a presentation.

Examples

Examples can be useful as attention getters when beginning the speech, or they can help explain how data connects to the everyday experience of the audience. In this respect, good examples can enhance your credibility and help connect your audience with the topic by making seemingly abstract information relevant to their lives.

In fact, examples are one of the most common forms of supporting materials. We use examples in dialogue every day when talking with friends and family. We use them to make decisions in business and we use them in small group scenarios. They are the most ubiquitous and versatile form of supporting material available to speakers. Examples are instances we use to help our audience think of an entire category of objects or events. Examples can be used to help define or clarify concepts, draw attention to a particular feature of an experience, or elicit memories and emotions in our audience. Examples can be of a specific object or event, or can even include narratives that illustrate a common experience. Whether it's examples of television shows we enjoy, music we like, or athletes we think epitomize good models, we compare people and make judgments based in part upon examples of the best and the worst of a similar event, object, or scenario. One of the powers of examples is that they humanize information, grounding ideas to a concrete reality.

real example
an example that is factual

There are two types of examples, real and hypothetical, and they come in two forms, brief and extended. A real example is one that is factual, and you will often encounter real examples during the research process. Real examples can be employed as attention getters to open a speech, but can also help support claims within the body of your speech. If you use them for evidence, however, they should be coupled with other forms of information, thus enhancing their appeal. Using only one case or example to illustrate a point opens up the possibility of employing the reasoning fallacy of the hasty generalization.

hypothetical example
an example that is fictional

A hypothetical example differs from a real example in that it is not found during the research process. Hypothetical examples are fictional, though believable and relevant, stories that serve to make a point. Like real examples, hypothetical examples can be used to get the audience's attention at the start of the speech and as supporting evidence within a speech. It is even more important to supplement hypothetical examples used as evidence with other data; otherwise the claim you make can be easily dismissed as based upon a fabricated, unrealistic example. If you are using a hypothetical example, you should not present the example as real, and you should ensure that your example is germane to the point you are making.

brief example
an example that makes a very quick point and can be effective at any point in a speech

Both real and hypothetical examples can be brief or extended. A brief example makes a very quick point and can be effective at any point in a speech. These stories require little detail and focus on the connection between an aspect of the example and the argument or claim you are making. They are often only two or three sentences. Brief examples can be especially useful when you have a time limit for your presentation and need to find a way to connect with your audience and humanize your topic.

extended example
an example that takes time; the importance lies in the details

Extended examples require more information than brief examples. These stories take time, and the importance of them lies in the details. Extended examples can be used as attention getters, but they are more useful within the speech as a means to provide the audience with an opportunity to visualize what you are saying and hopefully remind them of what you are talking about. Extended examples can be quite interesting to an audience, but they can also be risky. The danger is that they can encourage speakers to go off on tangents and make it difficult to stay on point. It is also important as a speaker to carefully consider how much time it will take to deliver an extended example to the audience and whether that time is too much of the total presentation. Remember that the extended example is not the speech focus but rather a means to support your overall purpose.

Examples are powerful when used appropriately, but they cannot and should not be the crux of your entire argument. They help to humanize your argument, enhance your credibility, and connect the audience with the topic of your speech. Ultimately, however, examples alone will not win the day in your presentation.

Statistics

statistics
numbers that summarize and organize sets of numbers to make them easier to understand or visualize

Whereas examples provide color and a means to personalize information for an audience, statistics seemingly represent cold hard facts. Statistics summarize and organize sets of numbers to make them easier to understand or visualize. People generally "want the numbers" and believe numeric data are incontrovertible truths they cannot debate. This data gives your claims an aura of legitimacy and logical appeal. Like examples, statistics come in many forms and can be quite influential on an audience, but they also need to be carefully deployed because statistics can be manipulated, disputed, and used unethically. Perhaps the reason statistics are so powerful is that they surround our lives. Think how much of your academic life is statistically explained: your GPA, cost of tuition, cost of fees, enrollment numbers, open seats in classes, GPA to graduate with honors or get off probation, number of absences, and student loan calculations are just a few examples. Statistics provide an air of objectivity and certainty to an otherwise chaotic world, and so audiences tend to appreciate them when offered in support of an argument. Some of the most commonly used types of statistics include measures of central tendency (including the mean, median, and mode), the standard deviation, and percentages.

measures of
central tendency
statistics that
indicate where
the middle of a
distribution lies,
including the mean,
median, and mode

mean
the average of all
of the scores in a
distribution, which is
calculated by adding
all of the scores and
then dividing by
the total number of
scores

median
the middle number
in a distribution of
numbers

mode
the score that
appears most often
in a distribution of
numbers

One of the most common statistics used to quantify our experiences is the average, or mean. The average is calculated by adding up all the numbers in a specific group, then dividing that total by the amount of entries added together. We use averages to describe things such as unemployment, salary, temperature, crime rate, and even performance in sports. Averages provide a picture of the tendency of a group of like things, but they by no means indicate the certainty of an event's occurring. Just because a ballplayer has a batting average of .300 (meaning he gets a hit on average three out of every ten times), does not mean he will always get that many hits in that period of time. It just means that, over time, that is what you can expect to occur. Averages are just one type of statistic that we can use to explain numeric data to an audience, and it is not always the best piece of information.

Another way to make sense of a group of numbers is through the median, or the middle number of a group of numbers. To determine the median point, rank the numbers in the group from high to low, or low to high, and locate the middle number of that group. The median is the number in the middle. If the total number of numbers is odd, it is easy to ascertain. For instance, if you have eleven numbers you would select the sixth number, as there would be five numbers above and five numbers below it. In a case where there is an even number of numbers, you compute the median by combining the two middle numbers, and then dividing by two. The median can be better than the average in certain situations, such as when discussing real estate. For example, home sale prices are reported as both average sale prices and median sale prices. If there are a few homes that sell for much, much more than the typical home in an area, those homes would skew the average so that it is higher than someone would typically pay for a home in that area, whereas the median gives you a better idea of the typical price of a home. The median gives you an idea of the spread from low to high of a group of numbers. Medians are helpful at providing a more complete picture when offered along with the average of the same group of numbers, but one more statistic can aid even further in explaining a set of data to an audience.

The mode is the most frequently occurring number within a group of numbers. Modes explain both averages and medians by illustrating the most frequent score. Sometimes averages and medians can be skewed by outliers, and the mode helps paint a picture of where the most numbers occurred, thus showing whether the average and median were in the center or if they were changed because of outlying numbers. The example in Table 8.1 illustrates this point.

TABLE 8.1

Sold Houses in a Certain Metropolitan Area	
Property Number	Selling Price
1	$800,000
2	$770,000
3	$700,000
4	$350,000
5	$330,000
6	$330,000
7	$300,000
8	$275,000
9	$275,000
10	$275,000
11	$250,000
12	$100,000

Here are the measures of central tendency:

Mean = $396,250
Median = $315,000
Mode = $275,000

Note that the mean and median are similar, which indicates that the typical value in the neighborhood is close to $400,000. Unfortunately, this is not entirely accurate, because the mean and median have been skewed by three houses sold for way above average prices. Additionally, the mode of $275,000 is more than $100,000 less than the mean and median, demonstrating that most people paid below what the numbers indicate was typical.

One way to explain the spread of numbers in a group like the one we just explored is to calculate the **standard deviation**. The standard deviation is a measure of variability that shows how far apart the numbers are that create the average. The smaller the standard deviation, the closer the group of numbers is to the average, and thus the more accurate the average. A higher standard deviation indicates a group of numbers that are significantly spread out, and so the average becomes less useful.

Finally, many speakers use percentages or proportions to help audiences understand the data being presented. When comparing large numbers it is easier for audiences to visualize what 50% of a group looks like, rather than to think what 345 out of 690 looks like. Percentages are often useful when presenting demographic data or comparing the likelihood of two different events happening, such as comparing the likelihood of being in a car accident versus a plane crash.

No matter how you explain statistics, though, there are risks. You must use the most appropriate statistic for your topic and present that information as accurately and fairly as possible. Think of the example of the home prices. What if you constructed your argument using the mean and median as supporting materials? Someone could easily refute your argument by pointing to the mode and the standard deviation, thus making your statistics questionable and damaging your ability to connect with your audience. What if you tried to convince your audience that your hometown needed more police officers because crime had doubled in the previous year, and an audience member pointed out that the increase had been from two petty crimes to four petty crimes? While it might be true that the number of crimes doubled, it would not be especially fair to make your audience believe the danger is substantially higher and their lives are in far greater danger. There is one more type of supporting material in addition to statistics and examples, and we will discuss it next.

Testimony

Testimony, the third type of supporting material we will discuss, includes the words of other people. There are two types of testimony you can use in a speech: expert testimony and peer testimony. One of the powers of testimony is that it uses peoples' words, whether quoted or paraphrased, to lend support to an argument. It provides a perspective other than your own, and, like examples, serves to humanize your position.

The first type of testimony, **expert testimony**, can also be the most powerful. To be considered expert testimony, the information must come from someone who is an expert on the topic. This means the person has conducted extensive research on the topic, has significant experience with the topic, or holds a position that lends credibility to his or her ideas on the subject matter. Remember, however, that just because a person is an expert in one area does not make him or her an expert in every area. For example, consider a scientist who is an expert on the properties of physics. You would use his or her testimony or words to support an argument about the way things work in the natural world, but the scientist's ideas on constitutional law, for instance, would be no more expert than those of the average citizen.

It is also important to consider *how* the audience will view the person whose testimony you use. No matter the qualification of the person, if the audience does not see the person as credible, then that person will not be nearly as powerful as he or she could be. Experts need experience and knowledge about the topic as well as good character for the audience to see them as unbiased.

Not all testimony you use as supporting evidence comes from experts. It is also effective to use testimony from those in the same peer group as the audience. This helps them connect with the ideas you present in a more meaningful way because they identify with the person whose testimony you provide. **Peer testimony** requires no advanced degrees or experience with the topic, but it is important for the audience to identify with that peer. They also need to provide testimony relevant to the topic of the speech and the specific claim you are making. Peer testimony can be useful when you are explaining a similar group's opinion on your topic or showing how your audience might be affected by your topic. For example, you might use peer testimony to show how students are affected by increases in tuition.

standard deviation

a measure of variability that indicates how spread apart the numbers are in a distribution

testimony

using the words of other people as evidence

expert testimony

testimony from someone who has conducted extensive research on the topic, has significant experience with the topic, or holds a position that lends credibility to his or her ideas on the subject matter

peer testimony

testimony from someone who is in the same peer group as the audience, but who is not necessarily an expert on the topic

STEM Spotlight

When putting together a research proposal or project plan, support materials are critically important, especially in the STEM fields. Of the types of evidence that are discussed here that are usually used in speeches, it is likely you will be expected to rely on statistics and other quantitative data. Additionally, your proposal will likely need to include the following types of evidence to show that your proposal is feasible and will fully address your research problem:

- Formulas and calculations
- Measurements
- Materials specifications
- References
- Project timeline
- Budget
- Other relevant support materials

Expert and peer testimony can serve as powerful pieces of supporting material if they fit the topic and the situation. They also help connect you and your topic with the audience by enhancing emotional connections and logical assertions with perspectives other than your own. However, as with examples and statistics, testimony alone cannot be the sole evidence upon which you stake your claims. It is, after all, circumstantial evidence if it is used alone. In the next section, we will provide some guidelines for effectively incorporating supporting materials into your presentations.

Guidelines for Using Supporting Materials

During the research process you are certain to find more information and supporting materials than you will need in the speech itself. This is a good thing, but it can be frustrating when you decide what should go, what should stay, and where support is best used in the speech. So, when putting your speech together, carefully analyze what will assist you in getting your ideas across to the audience. In this section, we provide some helpful guidelines for doing just that.

1. **Be sure to have balance between your types of supporting materials.** As we have noted throughout the chapter, you cannot rely solely on any one of the three types of supporting materials to make your speech. Using all three types of supporting materials demonstrates a broad knowledge of the topic and its applicability to the audience, and also creates emotional and logical dimensions for your presentation.

2. **Only use supporting materials relevant to your topic and argument.** You may encounter information during the research process that is fascinating and interesting. This information may also be something you really want to share with your audience simply because of its "cool factor," but it has little to do with your topic. Do not include such data in your speech if it does not help you achieve the purpose of your speech. Use only supporting materials that connect to the claims you make within your speech.

3. **Make sure you stay focused when using examples.** As we mentioned earlier, an extended example can be risky, especially within speeches with tight time limits. Examples need to directly relate to the topic and help achieve identification with the audience, but you must also be able to quickly return from the example to the speech itself. In other words, it should not be a digression from the speech purpose but rather a piece of evidence in support of that purpose. When this happens, it allows you to stay focused on your goals. This is especially critical when using examples as attention getters, because if they are too long then you and your audience will quickly lose focus.

4. **Choose the type of testimony to use based upon the goal you are trying to achieve.** Not all testimony functions equally in a speech. If you want to personalize information to help an audience identify with the topic and with you as a speaker, then it is best to use peer testimony. On the other hand, if the testi-

mony is meant to provide credibility to the information you just provided or to support a claim you are making with objective information, then it is better to use expert testimony. You should never use peer testimony to justify a claim but rather use it to illustrate its applicability to the audience.

5. **Use supporting materials ethically.** Don't mislead the audience with your supporting materials, as this will alienate them and weaken your speech. The supporting material should be presented honestly, and you should not ignore statistics that weaken your argument or change information for the purpose of influencing the audience. Audiences actually respect honesty and openness, as these are qualities of a good speaker, and so you should be candid about any potential shortcomings with your information.

These are just a few guidelines to help you make judicious decisions regarding the placement and use of supporting materials within your speech. Many of your choices obviously depend upon the goals of your speech, the audience you will be speaking to, and the topic you are addressing.

Summary

Supporting materials are both the evidence for your claims and vehicles through which you can connect with an audience. As we illustrated in this chapter, there are three primary forms of supporting materials, each with a role to play in any speech. Good speakers balance their use of examples, statistics, and testimony when articulating a position to an audience.

Key Terms

brief example   60
expert testimony   62
extended example   60
hypothetical example   60
mean   61
measures of central tendency   60
median   61
mode   61
peer testimony   62
real example   60
standard deviation   62
statistics   60
testimony   62

In COMM 1000/1003

One of the most common questions we get in COMM 1000 is "Why don't I count as a source?" A source, by Google definition, is "a person, place or thing by which something comes or can be obtained." You should always use your own knowledge and expertise and add that into the speech in the form of narratives, testimony, or examples, but your own experience is not the process of "coming" across something or "obtaining" information. You need others to back up what you are saying, and that's where the required sources come into play. Having varied sources only makes your content stronger and that makes you, in the long run, a better speaker.

Chapter Objectives

- Understand the principles that serve as the foundation for any good outline

- Appreciate the difference between a preparation outline and a speaking outline

- Become familiar with other forms of speaking materials

Any good speech is carefully prepared and organized before its delivery. This organizational process begins with sifting through the information you gather when researching, but the structure of your speech really takes shape when you draft your outline. The development of an outline is not a one-time task but rather a process in which you create a full-sentence outline that illustrates the points you want to make and from which you practice your speech. As you practice, you become more familiar with the material and thus can pare it down to shorter phrases, which in turn constitutes your speaking outline.

In order to successfully use this process, it is important to understand the principles that guide the construction of a good outline. In this chapter, we will first cover the principles of outlining, and then discuss the characteristics of a preparation outline and how to turn that outline into a proper speaking outline. Despite the emphasis on outlining in this chapter, we recognize an outline is not the only type of speaking material you might use, and so the chapter concludes with a brief exploration of other types of speaking materials.

Outlining Principles

Outlining is a systematic method of organizing your ideas. This approach ensures that your argument is clear and that your information is in an appropriate place within the speech. There are three key tenets to outlining: subordination, coordination, and division. Each of these three principles helps you create an organized presentation that your audience can follow.

Subordination

All outlines work to create what is essentially a hierarchy of ideas through the use of symbols and indentations. This process of creating a hierarchy of ideas in which the most

subordination

process of creating a hierarchy of ideas in which the most general ideas appear first, followed by more specific ideas

general ideas appear first followed by more specific ideas is called subordination, and it is a key principle of outlining. In an outline, each level has a different symbol set, and those symbols correspond to items such as main points, subpoints, and sub-subpoints. The first or broadest level is a main point, and it is represented by a Roman numeral. The second, slightly more specific level is a subpoint, and it is represented by a capital letter. The third level, if needed, is even more specific than the second level, and is denoted by an Arabic numeral. The following shows what the system looks like:

> I. Main point
>   A. Subpoint
>   B. Subpoint
>   C. Subpoint
>   1. Sub-subpoint
>   2. Sub-subpoint
> II. Main point

Notice how indenting different levels creates the perception of a hierarchy of points. The main point is the most general and does not include specific evidence or data, but rather sets up an entire section of a speech that provides data and evidence in support of the main point. The subpoint is a more specific aspect of the main point and can include specific evidence or information in support of the main point. Sometimes this information can take several sentences of explanation, and in those cases another level of the outline, the sub-subpoint, is created.

Each time you move to a new level the information should support the level above it. So if you have a subpoint indicated by a capital letter and need to explain it further, you do not use another capital letter but rather move down a level to numbers so you can visually see that that explanation relates to the particular subpoint it is under. In essence, the deeper into the levels one goes, the more specific the information gets, but it always relates to the level under which it appears.

Coordination

coordination

all information on the same level has the same significance

The hierarchy created by an outline that adheres to subordinated points naturally creates coordination of information. By coordination we mean that all information on the same level has the same significance. In other words, you would not place a main point next to a capital letter or number because such a move would create a confusing speech. The same types of statements appear on the same level, and when you find yourself making a claim in a place where you should be providing data in the outline, it should indicate that you are at the wrong level of the outline and need to make a change. This coordination helps you and your audience stay on track and provides expected and relevant information when it is needed.

Division

division

principle that if a point is divided into subpoints, there must be two or more subpoints

The final principle of outlining we will discuss is the notion of division, and it is just as important as the ideas of subordination and coordination. If you are going to divide a point, such as a main point, into subpoints, you need to have two or more subpoints in order to do so. The same is said for dividing subpoints as well—you must have two sub-subpoints if you plan to create a new level for the outline. More succinctly: if you have a main point I, you must have a main point II, and if you have a subpoint A, you must have a subpoint B, and, of course, if you have a sub-subpoint 1, you must have a sub-subpoint 2.

The principle of division ensures that you give adequate attention to each line and claim you make in a speech. If you have too many claims and not enough evidence then the speech needs more attention to the supporting materials. Division ensures balance, explanation, and organization within the hierarchy of ideas and should not be discarded as unimportant.

Outlining helps you logically organize your ideas by adhering to the three principles of subordination, coordination, and division. Because of the structured nature of an outline and the use of these ideas, it is easy to see how an outline serves a speaker better than bullet points or random notes. It affords you the ability to lay the main points out and logically put the subpoints and sub-subpoints neatly into the hierarchy. Additionally, the earlier you start the outlining process, the better your speech will be, and the more you get into the practice of outlining, the more you will realize that it is a valuable tool, whether you are preparing a speech or writing a research paper.

Preparation Outline *1st type of outline

We have repeatedly noted that developing a speech is a creative and fluid process, and the development of an outline is no different. We mentioned a few moments ago that organizing your speech begins when you start gathering information but that it accelerates when you sit down to prepare an outline. The earlier you do this, the more time you have to make changes and work through different ways to deliver your material. The preparation outline is a tool that facilitates such changes in a smooth fashion by visually illustrating the information you collected and the arguments you wish to make.

Preparation outlines follow several rules. The first is that each symbol of the outline is followed by a full sentence. For example, we show a main point and subpoint:

    I. Main point stated as a full sentence
        A. Subpoint stated as a full sentence
        B. Subpoint stated as a full sentence
    II. Main point stated as a full sentence
        A. Subpoint stated as a full sentence
        B. Subpoint stated as a full sentence

Full sentences help demonstrate what you want to say and also allow you to make specific connections between points and evidence. Additionally, they allow you to practice your speech in its entirety, which, as you will see when we discuss how to create a speaking outline, is very helpful.

The second rule for preparation outlines is that there is only one sentence allowed per symbol. This rule has only one exception: when you directly quote a source that contains multiple sentences you include the entire quotation and source citation next to the same symbol. In doing this you can break a speech down to its component parts and ensure that your information appears where it should. This makes it easier to spot information that is out of place and to cut or move that information to another more appropriate location in the outline. If you find you cannot create a properly divided point, then this may indicate that the statement should be moved or discarded.

A third rule of preparation outlines pertains to in-text citations. Preparation outlines should contain proper citations for material drawn from sources. This enables you to cross-check the source and make sure you verbally attribute information when you share it with your audience. In your outline you should cite your source the same way you plan to cite the source verbally. Generally speaking, you will briefly cite a source and then provide the corresponding information.

Rule number four pertains to the difference between a preparation outline and an essay. Remember that a speech is not written like an essay even though it is typed into an outline. Instead, you should write the outline just as you actually plan to say the speech when you deliver it. When we write a formal essay we use different language, grammar, sentence structure, and even lengths of sentences. When you prepare and deliver a speech you should use language that is not too complex and with which you feel comfortable. Essays and speeches have different flows and different expectations. Remember that a speech is closer to a conversation in terms of language use than it is to an essay, so prepare your outlines with this in mind. If you choose to write a draft, this same rule applies because the ultimate product is to be spoken, not written.

A strong preparation outline is essential for preparing a successful presentation, but it is not the last outline you'll create. After practicing with the preparation outline and making any adjustments you deem necessary to organization and wording, you should begin to reduce it to a usable outline from which you will deliver your speech. This is the process of creating a speaking outline, which is the actual outline you will speak from when delivering your remarks.

Speaking Outline *2nd type of outline*

After you practice and become familiar with the material in your preparation outline, you prepare the speaking outline. The speaking outline is a truncated form of the preparation outline and does not have full sentences, unless you are citing a direct quotation from a source. There are several reasons to reduce the information and words on a preparation outline when developing the speaking outline:

1. If you speak from a preparation outline, it becomes a manuscript speech, and you are less likely to adapt to audience feedback.

2. Speaking from a preparation outline encourages reading to, and not conversing with, the audience, thus resulting in the perception that you are reading an essay instead of delivering a speech.

3. You are more likely to stare at the outline, thus dramatically reducing eye contact with the audience.

Healthcare Help

Outlining isn't just for presentations; it also can be a valuable tool for making sure that appointments with health practitioners are as successful as possible. Most medical appointments are relatively short, so it is important for you to come prepared. Before your appointment create an outline of what you want to discuss with your doctor, including:

- Symptoms and concerns
- Any lifestyle changes or plans
- Questions about treatment

If you're a medical practitioner, having an outline of topics to discuss with patients and a checklist (a simple type of outline) of things to check can help you make sure you do not overlook something simple that points to a serious condition. As Atul Gawande argues in *The Checklist Manifesto,* a simple checklist can help eliminate medical errors and reduce the number of deaths during surgery by more than a third.

Speaking outlines maintain several features of the preparation outline, so it is not as if you are developing a brand new outline from scratch. You still use the Roman numerals, capital letters, and numbers, and you still follow the principles of subordination, coordination, and division. This helps you clearly understand the hierarchal nature of your speech while delivering it and provides you with visual representations of the importance of information so that if you run short on time, you can quickly see what you can skip. In essence, the speaking outline is a shorthand version of the preparation outline. You should find the speaking outline much easier to prepare than the preparation outline. One important thing to remember is not to add anything new to the speaking outline— keep it close to the preparation outline in this respect because that is what you have been practicing with and know best.

The speaking outline also provides the opportunity to do a few things relevant to your presentation that you need not do in a preparation outline. For instance, you can add delivery cues for yourself based upon your practice with prior outlines. For instance, let's suppose you want to emphasize certain points during your speeches. On a speaking outline you can add a few reminders in the margin of your outline to give yourself a visual cue, such as a hand-drawn megaphone, or simply write in bold, "LOUDER!" Or suppose you want to make sure you slow down to explain a specific point. Again, you can use a visual cue, such as drawing a sign that says SLOW and coloring it yellow. The speaking outline is more flexible in this regard than a preparation outline, and you can modify it to meet your particular needs.

Other Forms of Speaking Materials

While we strongly recommend outlining a speech, we also recognize that there are several other strategies and approaches speakers can take when preparing their remarks. Two such approaches we will briefly discuss here are note cards and a teleprompter.

Some students like to use note cards, as they allow you to put a finite portion of your speech in one easy-to-find place. If you use note cards ensure that you do not run main points together on a card, but keep ideas separate. You should use Roman numerals, capital letters, and numbers to help you understand the hierarchy of your points. You also can put delivery cues on the cards. If you use note cards be sure to number them sequentially. It is very uncomfortable if you drop your cards and have to reorder them in front of your audience. Also, make sure you know if your professor limits the number of cards you may use. Note cards can be seen as less professional than having a speaking outline on regular sized paper, as you are constantly shifting between cards in front of the audience. If you use note cards, be sure to practice with them so they feel natural to you as you are speaking.

Another option for delivering prepared remarks is the electronic TelePrompter™. The teleprompter loads the draft of the speech word for word into its memory and scrolls slowly through the speech as you speak. The device is placed on a stand that can adjust to eye level. Teleprompters are very expensive and are used most often by politicians who do not have time to practice long speeches. As such, when speakers use teleprompters they deliver manuscript speeches and have little to no room for adapting to audience feedback or going off script. If you use a teleprompter, remember that technology can fail, and having a speaking outline or note cards prepared just in case is a smart thing to do.

To illustrate why it is important to have back-ups with you in case of technology failure, consider the case of Mary Fisher in 1992. Fisher was asked to speak about AIDS at the Republican National Convention that year and was afraid that the organizers of the convention, who did not want her to speak, would turn off her teleprompter. So, rather than back down, she prepared for the worst and went on stage with a copy of her speech in her pocket in case the teleprompter failed. Thankfully, it did not, but if it had she still would have been able to deliver her remarks.

Below is a sample outline for an informative speech.
Notice how it follows all the requirements for a strong preparation outline.

Sample Preparation Outline

Topic: Auburn University

General Purpose: To inform

Specific Purpose: To inform my audience about Auburn University

Organizational Pattern: Chronological

Introduction

I.   How many of you have ever been asked the question, why do you say War Eagle if your mascot is a Tiger? How many of you knew how to answer that question? (attention getter)

II. Auburn University is a world-renowned college with a vast history and many traditions. (thesis)

III. As a life-long Auburn fan and an Auburn alumna, I am familiar with much of Auburn lore. (credibility)

IV. As Auburn students, it's important to understand more about this great institution you are a part of. (relevancy)

V.   Today, my goal is to shed more light on three things about Auburn: it's past, present and future. (preview)

Body

I. Auburn's past is littered with colorful tales.

    A. The story behind War Eagle dates back to the late 1800s

        1. According to former Auburn Athletic Director David Housel as reported in The Gadsden Times, the battle cry came about when an Auburn professor who served in the Civil War was in attendance at an Auburn/Georgia Game and Auburn's eagle got lose. The crowd chanted "War Eagle" and it stuck.

        2. Housel goes on to say that no one knows the real story behind the legend.

        3. Of course we all know the correct answer to anyone's question about Auburn having two mascots is as follows: Aubie is our mascot; War Eagle our battle cry.

    B. Auburn University was not always the name of our illustrious school.

        1. The Auburn website states that Auburn University began as East Alabama Male College in 1856.

        2. It became known as the Agricultural and Mechanical College in 1872. In this era, women were first admitted.

        3. By 1899 its name had changed once again to Alabama Polytechnic Institute

        4. It wasn't until 1960 that Auburn University became Auburn University. Under this name, in 1964, Auburn's first African-American student was admitted.

Transition: Now that I've given you a brief glimpse into Auburn's past, let's move on to the present.

II. Today Auburn University is famous for two reasons: academics and athletics.

    A. According to a document from the Office of the Provost at Auburn University, Auburn students can choose from 118 majors.

        1. They range from anything like art to engineering, fisheries to finance, industrial design to apparel design, nursing to physics and many more in between.

        2. Auburn University has several famous alumni that represent our academic well. Names like Tim Cook, Octavia Spencer, Samuel Mockbee, Tim Dorsey and Cynthia Tucker are just a few.

    B. Auburn athletics is well-known throughout the country.

        1. Auburn men's and women's swimming and diving has won a total of 13 combined national titles.

        2. The Auburn Women's Softball team and Auburn Women's Soccer have been highly ranked the past few years.

        3. And who can forget Auburn football years like 2010 and 2013.

        4. Famous athletics include names like Cam Newton, Bo Jackson, Charles Barkley and Frank Thomas to name a few.

Transition: So now that we're up to speed, let' move into my final point on Auburn's future.

III. Auburn's future looks bright.

A. According to an Oct. 2016 article in The Auburn Plainsman, many construction plans are underway.

    1. More apartments are scheduled to be built on North College

    2. On campus, the RBD Library is undergoing a major renovation

    3. There are also talks of a multi-million dollar performing arts center.

B. And Tiger Fans should note several things:

    1. The Auburn men's basketball team had the no. 1 ranked recruiting class for 2017

    2. The Auburn softball program has its eye on the College World Series again

    3. And we all know Auburn football is chasing that third national championship.

Conclusion

I. I'd like to wrap things up with a reminder of what I've discussed the past few minutes. (signal)

II. Auburn University is an institution like no other. (re-state of the thesis)

III. I covered parts of Auburn's past, present and future in this speech today. (review)

IV. There's no other way to wrap this speech up than with a big WAR EAGLE, HEY! (memorable message)

Summary

In this chapter, we discussed the fundamental principles behind outlining: subordination, coordination, and division. We illustrated how these principles help you organize your speech throughout the development process. Then we explained how to construct strong preparation outlines and how to turn those into good speaking outlines after you practice. Finally, we covered two other ways in which you might prepare and deliver speeches: using note cards and using a teleprompter. We cannot stress enough the importance of organization in the speech development process, and a properly prepared an outline is one of most powerful tools you can use to ensure a successful presentation.

Key Terms

coordination 66
division 66
subordination 66

In COMM 1000/1003

When you are preparing your speeches, you need to give yourself adequate time to get everything done. Research, writing, putting things into outline format, figuring out your visual design and practicing take time. Many put the outline off until the last minute and find that they are unable to complete it in the necessary format or spend so much time on the outline that it leaves little to no time for practicing the speech itself. An outline is not busy work. A well-crafted outline ensures that all elements of an introduction, body, and conclusion are present in the speech. Give yourself several days to work through the process that delivering an effective speech entails. And don't cut corners when it comes to the speech outline.

- Learn how to properly format an introduction to a speech

- Discover how to connect segments of your speech in seamless manner

- Understand the different components of a speech conclusion

10
Introductions, Conclusions, and Connective Statements

The two most important moments of any speech are the introduction and the conclusion. They represent the only chance to make a first impression and the final opportunity to remind the audience about the key aspects of your speech. This is not to say that the body of the speech is unimportant, but rather to emphasize the importance of starting and finishing a speech strongly. This chapter addresses these two key parts of the speech and provides suggestions for how best to craft effective introductions and conclusions. It also provides some tips for connecting all the parts of the speech so the audience knows when you move between points.

To do this we first cover the structure of the introduction, followed by the structure of the conclusion. In doing so, we provide some guidelines for developing these two vital speech components. Finally, we discuss the use of connective statements and demonstrate how they can be deployed effectively to move between points within a speech.

Structure of the Introduction * 6 parts

Introductions follow a fairly standard approach, but despite the common elements contained in any good introduction it is important to remember that you can and should be creative in how you choose to style them. This creativity enhances the ability of an introduction to accomplish what it needs to, so do not view the goals of an introduction as a restrictive and boring set of rules. There are six goals that the introduction needs to accomplish within the introduction itself.

1. Get the Audience's Attention

The first thing that you need to do is to get the attention of the audience and make them want to listen to the speech. It is important to engage the audience early so they don't miss important information. Gaining the audience's attention may sound easy, but it involves effort. Simply stating a quotation or statistic is not enough; you need to connect that data to the speech itself so that the audience is dialed in to your topic right away.

There are numerous ways to grab the audience's attention, but you must carefully examine which strategy best suits your speech topic and your audience. For instance, providing a startling statistic or personal story might draw in an audience that is predisposed to disagree with you and what you plan to say. On the other hand, posing a rhetorical question or quoting someone famous might be a good way to gain the attention of an audience that might already agree with you. These are not hard and fast rules but rather ideas meant to get you to think about how best to make a first impression with an attention getter that is relevant to the speech topic and the audience.

One way to get an audience's attention is to ask a question. Speakers usually ask a rhetorical question, that is, a question that relates to the topic but does not require an answer from the audience. Suppose you were giving a speech about ways to live a healthy lifestyle. One way to start the speech is to ask the audience, "How many of you would like to live a long and healthy life?" Would anyone answer "no" to this? Highly unlikely. Rhetorical questions like these are not the only form of inquiry that can be used to start a speech and gain the audience's attention.

Another opening strategy is to ask the audience a question that requires a verbal answer. These questions help you gather data from the audience while also orienting them toward you and your topic. This question should be simple, and it is best if it's a yes/no type of inquiry. The more detailed the query, the less time you will have to speak because you will be busy listening to the audience's comments. The question also should not spark much of a debate, because that opens the opportunity for audience members to confront each other directly, which results in your losing control of the speaking situation. Remember that questions are a strategic way to get the audience's attention and not intended to open the floor to dialogue, debate, and discussion.

A third way to get the attention of the audience is with a famous quotation that aligns with your topic. For example, suppose you wanted to speak about community service. You might consider using someone else's words to begin your speech; perhaps President John F. Kennedy's words summarize your topic best: "Ask not what your country can do for you—ask what you can do for your country." Most everyone can attribute this statement to the former president. Regardless of whom you quote, whether the speaker is famous or not, the statement should be tied to the topic, or the audience may anticipate your speech going in another direction. You can easily focus the quotation by providing an explanation following it, and always be sure to verbally cite the person who made the statement you quoted.

A fourth way to creatively gain the audience's attention is through the use of startling statistics. Startling statistics surprise an audience and make them curious about what the data would mean to them. Suppose you had done research and found some unique information that provoked your interest. You might begin your speech by sharing that figure with your audience. Obviously, you would need to not only provide a source for these numbers but also cite that source. This not only helps get the audience's attention but enhances your credibility as well.

The fifth way to garner the attention of the audience is through a narrative or short story that relates to the topic. Humans are story-telling creatures. Stories make things real to us and organize our experiences into something that makes sense. The danger with using a story as an attention-getting device, though, is that stories sometimes take up too much time. Stories can be personal, fictitious, or factual, but they must be relevant to the topic of your speech.

Stories also present an opportunity to connect the introduction and conclusion by starting a story at the beginning of a speech but leaving its conclusion for the end of the speech. Suppose a student was giving a speech about how an education changed a woman's life for the better. The speech could begin with the story of hardship as a means to focus the audience on a theme. Then, at the conclusion, the speaker could finish the story with a happy ending, illustrating that despite the hardship, getting an education changed her life for the better.

The sixth potential strategy for gaining attention is one of the most common ones prescribed by people with little training in speech—it is also one of the riskiest ways to open a speech. Beginning a speech with a joke can be either effective or a disaster. Effective jokes, like the other attention getters we have discussed, must be appropriate for the audience and related to the topic of the speech. Just opening with a joke for the sake of a joke does not help the audience prepare for your message. Additionally, jokes should not be offensive or contain inappropriate language, because this sets a poor standard of expectations for the audience and damages your credibility. When you choose a joke to tell an audience—particularly an audience of people you do not know—you do so with the expectation that the audience will respond by laughing. But what if they do not? This would create a very awkward situation for you and it is not the way you want to begin your speech. For this reason, jokes should not be the first choice for an attention getter, despite what the general public may say.

2. Clearly State the Relevance of Your Topic

After you gain the audience's attention the important work of your speech begins. The human attention span is short, and so once you get the audience to focus on your speech you need to work to keep their attention. The first step in doing so is also the second thing you need do in your introduction: establish the relevance of your topic. Or, to put it another way, tell the audience why they should care about this topic. If you cannot justify the topic, then you must consider why you chose it. Most topics have real-world significance and can be justified with some research and consideration.

This process need not be a long explanation; in fact, it should be no more than a statement or two at the most. These statements, though, explicitly lay out what it is you will be addressing in your remarks and help focus the audience on a particular area of knowledge. Stating the topic also blends into the next task of an introduction: establishing your credibility on the topic.

3. Establish Your Credibility

Now that you have the audience's attention and have established the topic of your speech, you need to explain to them why they should listen to your comments about this topic. This answers the question, "Why am I qualified to speak on this topic?" There are two easy ways to answer this question. First, the topic may be one with which you have experience or expertise. For example, a mechanic delivering a talk on how to change the oil in a car has experience and expertise on this topic. All he or she needs to do to establish credibility is explain their vast experience with oil changes and cars. This type of experience, however, is not always easy to come by—especially when delivering a speech in class for an assignment. Even in these situations, though, you can establish your credibility. Just be careful not to exaggerate your knowledge and experience.

In classroom situations, you can establish credibility by noting the research you conducted on the topic. Let's say you have decided to deliver a speech on human trafficking. You do not have any experience with this activity and no first-hand knowledge, but you did a great deal of research on it for weeks leading up to the assignment. All you need to do is tell the audience about the time spent looking into human trafficking, and you have given them reason to listen to you. Establishing credibility is essential in an introduction because even if an audience gives you their attention and is interested in your topic, they will quickly move on to something else if they do not believe there is a reason to listen to your comments on the issue.

4. State Your Argument

Once you have focused the audience's attention firmly on your topic and convinced them you are qualified to speak on it, it is time to let them know what you intend to say about the topic. This means it is time to state your argument, or thesis, for them. This is the fourth part of an introduction. The thesis, or argument, is a carefully worded one-sentence summary of exactly what you will cover in your speech. You can see your thesis statement as the anchor for your speech because everything that follows it is related to it in some way. The claim you make and the focus you establish with this statement guide the rest of your speech. See Table 10.1 for some examples of thesis statements.

thesis
a carefully worded one-sentence summary of exactly what you will cover in your speech

TABLE 10.1

Thesis Statement Examples
Informative Speech Thesis Examples
• Dropbox is a great tool that will back up your files online and make them available from any Internet-connected device.
• Becoming a vegetarian benefits your health and the environment.
Persuasive Speech Thesis Examples
• Due to growing enrollment and limited space, the university should build a central parking deck for student use.
• Congress should work to develop a more equitable tax code.
Special Occasion Speech Thesis Examples
• George Smith was a loving father and a loyal friend who will be greatly missed.
• The winner of this year's Community Betterment Award has worked tirelessly to make sure that children have a safe place to do homework and play after school.

Connecting the rest of your speech to your argument helps ensure that your speech is sharply focused and does not go off on tangents. In short, it provides the destination of your speech—where you want the audience to be at the end of the presentation. As with any journey, knowing where you are going is nice, but knowing how you will get there is equally important, and so we will now turn to the next task of an introduction.

5. Preview Main Points

Once you tell the audience where you are headed, you need to explain how you plan to get there, and so the fifth element of an introduction is providing a preview of your main points. A preview can be one statement or a few, depending on how you wish to explain the roadmap of your speech to the audience. In either case it must contain all the main points you will cover in your speech in the order in which you plan to cover them (see Table 10.2). With a one-sentence preview, your main points appear as several different clauses within the sentence. For example, a student is going to give a speech about the historic Battle of the Bulge in World War II. The student could break down the speech into four points and have the following preview statement: "The Battle of the Bulge occurred in four primary segments, the German attack that created the bulge, the courageous stand of the 101st Airborne at Bastogne, General Patton's historical march to lend support at the bulge, and the clearing weather that made possible the allied air campaign." This lets the audience know there are four parts, or four main points, that will be covered in the speech. This roadmap makes it easier for the audience to comprehend and follow the speaker throughout the speech and also keeps the speaker sharply focused.

For novice speakers, the one-sentence approach to a preview may be a bit challenging. In that case a slower, but just as effective, method is using several statements. These statements usually begin with "First, I will explain…. Second, I will cover….Next, I will detail….Finally, we will explore. . ." These numeric indicators specifically indicate the order of main points and are helpful for both the speaker and the audience. This method obviously takes longer than a one-sentence approach, but it achieves the same end result. At this point the introduction is almost complete, save for one small, but important, task.

TABLE 10.2

Preview Statement Examples

- First, I will explain why public transportation is better for the environment. Second, I will tell you why using public transportation improves your community. Finally, I will describe how taking public transportation will help to improve your health.

- You should do three things to make sure you're ready next time an emergency strikes. First, build an emergency preparedness kit. Second, create a family emergency communication plan. Third, make sure your legal documents and insurance plans are up to date.

- You can take charge of your health by doing three simple things more often: move more, sleep more, and eat more nutritious foods.

- To save a life with CPR, remember to check your ABCs: airway, breathing, and circulation.

6. Transition to the Body

When you have established the topic and explained how you plan to approach it, all that remains is getting on with your speech. To do so, however, requires a subtle move to let the audience know you have finished introducing the topic and will now get into the details of your speech. This move is a transitional statement at the end of the introduction. A **transition** is a connecting statement that lets the audience know you are leaving one point and moving to another. If your preview statement and the transition are constructed properly, this should be apparent to the audience. See Table 10.3 for examples of transitional statements.

> **transition**
> connective statements that signal you are finished with one point and moving on to another

TABLE 10.3

Transitional Statement Examples

- To understand why a border collie is a great dog to have if you want a furry running partner, we need to begin by exploring the history of border collies.

- When you begin a new exercise regimen, it is important to start slowly.

- First, we need to understand the factors that led to the housing crisis.

- Let's start by learning about the need for organ donors in the United States.

One last thing to note about introductions: even though they are the first thing the audience hears, they are the last thing you write. The reason for this is that when constructing the body you may want to change the order of main points, thus impacting the preview and the transition. You also might want to use what you planned as an attention getter as data for a main point, especially if it is a statistic or quotation. So it is always best to prepare the body of the speech and the conclusion before constructing the introduction.

Transitions Between Main Points *3 types of transitions

Throughout your speech you will need to ensure that the audience follows your argument and understands when you are changing topics. Similar to travelers who use road signs to know when to change course and billboards to find places to eat and stay the night, speakers supply connective statements throughout their speech so that their audience knows they are shifting topics. Some of the most important connective statements in a speech are transitions between main points. Transitions between main points are easy for speakers to forget, but they are necessary for a successful presentation because they keep the speaker on track and aid the audience in understanding the direction the speech is going. A transition between main points could be accomplished in three ways: internal summaries, signposts, and internal previews.

Internal Summaries *type #1

internal summary
a statement that summarizes what you already have covered and precedes transitions

An **internal summary** reviews the point that you just covered and indicates to the audience that you are preparing to move to another point. Internal summaries serve to keep ideas well organized in the minds of both the audience and the speaker. They remind audiences about the important connections you made within a main point and also help push your argument along at the same time. For example, the blue, boldfaced portion of this statement is an internal summary a speaker might say: "I just discussed the second stage of wine-making, **which was testing with a hydrometer, adding chemicals and stirring, then allowing the wine to set for a period."**

Signposts *#2

signposts
key words that signal to the audience that you are moving from one part of the speech to another

Signposts are key words that signal to the audience that you are moving from one part of the speech to another. Signposts catch the audience's attention and, like traffic signs, help show the audience what is ahead and keep them on track while listening to your speech.

Signposts can help divide the speech into obvious parts for you and your audience. Some of the more common signposts are words such as "next," "additionally," "secondly," "third," and "finally."

Internal Previews *#3

internal preview
serves as an outline of what is to come next in a speech and is often combined with transition statements

Like the preview of main points at the end of the introduction, an internal preview provides a roadmap of what is ahead for the audience. An **internal preview** informs the audience of the elements of the next main point. For example, the blue, boldfaced portion of this statement is an internal preview: "Now that we have seen the initial stage of making wine, let's move into the second stage, **which includes taking tests with a hydrometer, adding some chemicals and stirring, then letting the wine sit for an extended period of time**." These are especially helpful when moving to a more complicated point because they foreshadow information for the audience.

Structuring the Conclusion

Once you have gone over everything in the speech body that you said you would do in the introduction, it is time to finish your speech. In finishing your speech, remember it is the last thing the audience will hear from you, thus increasing the likelihood they will remember it. Much like introductions, conclusions also have some essential elements: a signpost, a summary, and a clincher. In this section, we will discuss these three parts of a good conclusion.

Signal the Conclusion

After explaining your main points in detail and connecting them to your overall argument, you need to indicate to the audience that the conclusion is approaching. Just as you use a signpost to signal to the audience that you are moving from one point to another in a transition between main points, you should use another signpost to signal to your audience that you are beginning the conclusion. Signposts that signal you are about to conclude your speech include phrases such as "To summarize," "Finally," "To conclude," and "Let's wrap up." These simple statements clearly indicate to audiences that the conclusion is here and the speech is almost at an end. The signpost, however, is not the indicator that the speech is over, just that it is almost finished. There is still some work to do.

Provide a Summary

After the signpost, you need to revisit the main ideas and central argument of your presentation. There are two parts to this task: restate the thesis" and review the main points. In restating the main points, you want to remind the audience of the evidence and information you provided in the body of the speech. It is important that you do not include new information or cite new evidence at this point. The summary should recap the highlights of the speech and be as brief as possible. The summary also should be brief. It does not need to detail everything you just told the audience, but rather should generally summarize what you spent time talking about.

After summarizing the main points it is also important to remind your audience about the central argument or thesis of your speech. This is accomplished by briefly explaining how the main points substantiate the overall position you articulated in the presentation. In other words, explain how the roadmap got you and the audience to the destination. This restatement should not use the exact same words as the initial statement of your argument from the introduction, but should be similar to it. You also should create it so that if the audience remembers any one thing from your speech, it's the main argument.

Memorable Closer

Obviously, even though your argument is the most important part of your speech—it is, after all, why you spoke—you need more than that to end the presentation. The clincher, or the final statement of your speech, is an additional statement that follows the summary of your main points and argument. There are numerous forms of clinchers, and many are the same devices we shared as a means of getting the audience's attention. If you began the speech with a short story, you can finish the story at the end of the speech, giving a nice sense of fit and closure. You also may end with a famous quotation, personal reflection, or even a call to action for the audience. You do not have to revisit the same form of attention getter used in the introduction, but you might want to. No matter which route you choose to follow, it is important that you remind the audience why they listened in the first place.

clincher
the final statement of your speech

Summary

This chapter explored the requirements of introductions and conclusions within your speech and provided information on how to connect main points and move smoothly from one part of the speech to the next. These structural aspects of a speech are important, as they directly influence an audience's ability to follow your speech. Introductions get the audience's attention and establish a roadmap for the way you plan to cover a topic. Transitions between main points help audiences understand when new points will be covered and how they relate to your overall argument. The conclusion represents the last opportunity for you to emphasize the core components of your speech.

Key Terms

clincher   79
internal preview   78
internal summary   78
signposts   78
thesis   75
transition   77

In COMM 1000/1003

Many students comment that coming up with the opening line is one of the hardest parts of writing a speech. This chapter gives clear guidelines on incorporating effective attention-gaining statements, so it won't be repeated here. What is worth mentioning are common mistakes we see in the classroom in relation to attention getters.

Don't
1. **State your name** – we all know who you are by the time you give a speech

2. **State your topic** – this is important, but not as the opening line

3. **Make a general statement or use a well-known fact** – this adds nothing of interest

Introductory Speech Assignment

For this assignment, you will construct and present a short informative speech. You will be speaking on a topic very familiar to you: yourself.

I. Assignment objectives are:

    A. to introduce yourself to the class.

    B. to learn and practice the following principles of speech preparation:

        1. research and organization of information to fulfill the general and specific purpose of a speech;

        2. adequate development of a thesis statement; and

        3. clear organization of the body of a speech.

    C. to deliver the completed speech to an audience using effective and appropriate verbal and nonverbal communication that:

        1. catches and holds audience interest; and

        2. facilitates audience understanding.

II. Assignment requirements include:

    A. 3-4 minutes in length (minus 2 points for every 30 seconds over/under).

    B. a comparison of yourself and/or your life to something else (such as an object, movie, fictional character, or book).

    C. a clear, one sentence thesis statement.

        Examples of a thesis are: "My life experiences share some characteristics of the title character from the film *Rocky*," and "My personality is like a 1971 red Corvette convertible."

    D. two to three supporting main points that explain the relationship between you, your experience, and the chosen topic.

        For example, in a speech using the convertible example, a main point might be that you are a *flexible* or *adaptable* person. Your support would be that convertibles can adapt to both fair weather or foul weather.

    E. specific examples and explanations for each of your supporting main points.

        When choosing support for your main points, you may use any type of information that you think is best to draw your comparison. You need to illustrate how, for example, convertibles adapt to the weather, and HOW you have also adapted to a particular situation with specific examples.

    F. delivery from a speaking (keyword) outline written or typed on one side of a 4x6 note card.

    G. preparation materials turned in to your instructor, including copies of all articles, advertisements, etc., used as the basis of the speech.

- Understand the two different types of reasoning

- Learn the different forms of reasoning used in argument

- Identify the many different errors in reasoning that are common in arguments

11
Reasoning

Many believe that because we have reasons for doing or believing something, we have sound reasoning. Unfortunately, reasons are not the same as reasoning. Good reasoning is the foundation of any speech, and in this chapter we will explore how logically to organize ideas within a speech so that they maximize their ability to connect your message with the audience. We will also illustrate some common errors of reasoning, or fallacies, that creep into our justifications and attempts to persuade others, thus tricking us into believing someone's reasons are based on sound judgment.

We begin our discussion by differentiating between the two different types of reasoning: deductive and inductive. We then explore some common forms of reasoning used to make arguments every day. Finally, we will detail a number of common reasoning fallacies that infect our speech.

Types of Reasoning *2 types*

The reasoning process is different from providing reasons for something. It explains how the reasons you supply connect to the conclusion that you make, and there are generally two ways these connections can be accomplished. One of these, deductive reasoning, deals with providing structurally certain conclusions. The other, inductive reasoning, focuses more on probability.

Deductive Reasoning (#1)

Deductive reasoning uses specific premises to reach an unavoidable and certain conclusion. Deductive reasoning relies upon a formal structure that comes in three parts. That formal structure is a syllogism, which lays out claims that build upon each other to reach a conclusion.

deductive reasoning
an argument that reasons from known premises to an inevitable conclusion

3 types

The first part of the syllogism is the major premise that is the statement of a general truth or fact. After the major premise, a minor premise, or specific instance of the general truth in action, is provided. Taken together, the major and minor premises result in the third statement, the conclusion, which is the logical result of both the major and minor premises. Here is an example of perhaps the most famous syllogism:

Major premise:	All men are mortal.
Minor premise:	Socrates is a man.
Conclusion:	Socrates is mortal.

This syllogism illustrates that Socrates, the specific instance, is a manifestation of the major premise, man, and thus like all members of that group is mortal. This conclusion is both logical and certain, as the only way for this to fall apart would be for someone to prove that Socrates was not properly categorized as a man. This is an example of what is called a categorical syllogism, because it deals with minor premises belonging to a category established in the major premise. *(#1)*

A second form of syllogism that is also deductive in nature is the disjunctive syllogism. *(#2)* Rather than making claims about categorical membership, disjunctive syllogisms provide either-or scenarios. For instance:

Major premise:	This key will unlock either my house or my car.
Minor premise:	The key does not unlock my house.
Conclusion:	Therefore, this key unlocks my car.

Notice that this syllogism still deduces the proper conclusion by excluding one of two alternatives stated in the major premise. It is called disjunctive because the two aspects of the major premise are mutually exclusive and cannot coexist.

A third and final type of syllogism found in deductive reasoning is the conditional syllogism, *(#3)* which proposes "if-then" scenarios in the major premise. This is usually used for hypothetical situations or planning in the future. Let's look at an example:

Major premise:	If I take the bus home, then I will save money on transportation.
Minor premise:	I will take the bus home.
Conclusion:	Therefore, I will save money on transportation.

Here we see an alternative in a hypothetical situation eliminated in the minor premise. The "if-then" statement provided the conditions resulting from the stated action in the minor premise. When used correctly, each of the three syllogisms we discussed provides structurally certain conclusions. Unfortunately, few things in life are certain, so we deal more often in probabilities, and that is where inductive reasoning comes into play.

Inductive Reasoning *(#2) - types of reasoning*

Inductive reasoning is much different from deductive reasoning because it is based upon probabilities rather than absolutes. With inductive reasoning, you begin with particular pieces of evidence and use them to construct probable conclusions. This is the inverse of deductive reasoning, which begins with general certainties and applies them to specific cases.

One of the more common applications of inductive reasoning is the use of polling data to make assumptions about group behaviors. For example, if you know that 75% of students support a fee for a new recreation center on campus, and you are in a class with twenty students, then it is probable that five of them disagree with that position. This is not certain, because you might be in a class in which everyone supports, or does not support

categorical syllogism

a syllogism in which the argument is based on membership in a group

disjunctive syllogism

a syllogism in which the major premise includes two or more mutually exclusive alternatives

conditional syllogism

a syllogism in which the major premise contains a hypothetical condition and its outcome

inductive reasoning

an argument that comes to a probable, instead of an absolute, conclusion the fee, but it is likely given the evidence. With inductive reasoning, the more evidence we provide in support of a claim, the stronger the probability that the claim is accurate—but we can never be certain.

Both inductive and deductive reasoning are useful, but the far more commonly used reasoning process is inductive. Few things in life are certain; after all, we are not even certain the sun will rise tomorrow. We know it is highly probable, but we are not totally certain. In the next section, we will explore some specific argumentative structures that employ both deductive and inductive reasoning.

Forms of Reasoning – 4 forms

Whether you are delivering an informative or persuasive speech, you will always need to make strong connections between the information you provide and the claims you make. Properly employing solid reasoning enables your audience to understand the points you are making, while also bolstering your credibility with the audience. On the contrary, not using sound reasoning will cause the audience to disregard much of what you say and will damage your credibility. In this section, we will discuss four different reasoning forms: cause, example, analogy, and sign.

Reasoning by Cause – form #1

The first type of reasoning we will go over is by cause. **Reasoning by cause** occurs when you claim that one occurrence creates a specific effect. When making a claim such as this you must keep several things in mind. First, consider if the cause you present is necessary and sufficient for the effect to be produced. A **necessary cause** is one that must be present for the effect to happen, such as it must be lower than thirty-two degrees Fahrenheit for water to freeze. That temperature is necessary to produce freezing. A **sufficient cause** is one that can produce the effect in question, such as decapitation is sufficient to produce death. It is not necessary to produce death, as there are many causes that can produce death, but decapitation is sufficient for the effect to take place.

Causal reasoning is also one of the foundations for many superstitions we hold. In sports, athletes will often wear the same clothing or perform the same rituals during a game because they believe they have a causal relation to a positive outcome. There is little to no evidence to support these beliefs, yet they believe them nonetheless.

Reasoning by Example – form #2

Another way to reason is by example. This form of reasoning is quite common, as we often look for instances that help us make more general conclusions. When reasoning by example, you take a number of specific realities and arrive at an overall conclusion about them. For example:

Example one: My biology class was tough.

Example two: My chemistry class was hard.

Example three: My astronomy class was difficult.

Conclusion: Science classes present a real challenge to me.

When **reasoning by example**, the occurrences must be related. This argument, for instance, would not be as strong if we replaced biology with art, and chemistry with philosophy. The reason for this is that the examples then lose their relationship to each other. The more relevant examples you provide, the stronger the conclusion.

Reasoning by Analogy – form #3

Reasoning by analogy occurs when we use analogies to support a claim. An analogy is when you argue that what is true in one situation is true in another. Analogies differ from examples because they do not need to have more than one similar instance. Essentially, reasoning by analogy tries to argue for common elements between different cases. These analogies also can be either literal or figurative.

reasoning by cause
arguments that claim one event or factor produces an effect

necessary cause
a cause that must be present for an effect to happen

sufficient cause
a cause that can produce the effect in question

reasoning by example
the process of inferring general conclusions and making general claims from specific cases

reasoning by analogy
when you compare two similar cases in order to argue that what is true in one case is also true in the other

literal analogy
when the two cases being compared are classified the same way

Literal analogies take place when the two cases being compared are from the same classification. For example, you might argue that a certain crime prevention tactic effectively used at one school should be adopted at your school because the student population and campus environments are similar. This analogy takes a real occurrence in a similar classification and applies it to another real situation, trying to emphasize the commonalities between the two situations to argue for similar results in both cases.

figurative analogy
when the two cases being compared are from completely different classifications

Figurative analogies are different from literal analogies in that they compare cases from entirely different classifications. For example, an argument that a successful businessperson would make a good elected official is a figurative analogy. The reason it is figurative is because the business world and the political realm are two entirely different classifications, with very few similarities. Business is not policy making, but the figurative analogy seeks to make the comparison based on leadership experience in two different classifications. Just because the two examples are from different classifications, however, does not make the analogy false or even illogical—it requires you to be more explicit about the areas of comparison and reasons they are relevant. Both of these types of analogies are effective means of making a reasoned argument to an audience.

Reasoning by Sign - form #4

reasoning by sign
occurs when the presence of one thing indicates the presence of another

The final type of reasoning we will discuss is reasoning by sign, which occurs when the presence of one thing indicates the presence of another. The classic example of this type of reasoning is when you see smoke in the air, it is a sign there is a fire somewhere. Or, if you see footprints in newly fallen snow, it is a sign that someone has walked across the area since the snowfall ended.

Reasoning by sign can also be more than observation of simple natural occurrences, as it can apply to characteristics as well. For example, to run for president you must be at least thirty-five years old. Therefore, being president is a sign that the person in the office is at least thirty-five years old. Be careful with this type of reasoning, however, because the inverse when reasoning by sign is not always true: being thirty-five or older is not a sign that you are president.

As speakers, we must ensure that our reasoning is sound so it can have the desired impact on the audience. It is easy for speakers to err when reasoning, and some unethical speakers all too often employ reasoning fallacies to convince the audience to believe or do something. Additionally, as audience members, we have a responsibility to detect errors in reasoning so we can better assess the messages we receive. In the next section, we will examine several different examples of errors in reasoning, or reasoning fallacies.

Reasoning Fallacies

A fallacy is an error in reasoning. Some are easy to detect, yet others are more elusive to identify. In this section, we will cover ten of the more common reasoning fallacies that speakers use in presentations. You will also undoubtedly recognize that many of these fallacies are exhibited in advertisements and our interpersonal interactions.

Practical Politics

Many political ads rely on reasoning fallacies in an attempt to sway voter opinions on candidates or issues. As a voter, it is important for you to listen carefully to the types of reasoning being employed in political ads and beware of fallacies. Any time an ad tries to represent another candidate's position on an issue, you should take time to research the candidates to find out whether those representations are accurate. Whenever someone advocates for a policy, do some investigating on your own to make sure there is evidence to support that policy. As a politician, you have a responsibility to be ethical in your use of reasoning.

Ad Hominem

The first fallacy we will address is the ad hominem, which is attacking the opposing person's character instead of his or her argument. An ad hominem attack is simply name calling and does not address the ideas and reasoning of the attacked person. When we refute another person's position by calling him or her names or focusing on personal history when it is irrelevant, we employ an ad hominem attack. These types of attacks are unethical, inappropriate, and not grounded in logic, but unfortunately society uses them quite often.

Ad Vericundium

Another reasoning fallacy with a Latin name is the ad vericundium fallacy, which is an appeal to authority. This fallacy asserts that positional authority, such as being a parent or a boss, makes someone's argument correct and accurate. When a child asks a parent why he or she should take out the trash, and the parent responds "because I am your mother/father," the parent is using a reason based on an appeal to authority instead of giving a logical reason. Authority-based appeals can be made using parents, bosses, God, teachers, doctors, or any other position of authority as the reason that someone should do something. These do not assert logical reasons but rather assume that authority equals correctness. This is not to say that we should not follow instructions from people in authority, because refusing them can carry heavy consequences, but an argument based on an appeal to authority is not a logical argument and is not a good type of argument to use in your speech.

The Slippery Slope

Perhaps the most famous logical fallacy is that of the slippery slope. This fallacy relies on the belief that once a course of action is taken, other unavoidable events will inevitably occur. More succinctly, once we start down a path there is no turning back. You can think about a slippery slope as being similar to a domino effect—the speaker is arguing that once an initial event or action takes place, others will follow, just as pushing over the first domino can cause the others behind it to fall. These fallacies are often very subtle and seem to make sense, but they make unsupported assumptions about an end outcome based on an initial action. The slippery slope is a perverse version of a conditional syllogism in which there is a series of unsupported assumptions made with either explicit or implicit "if-then" statements. Politicians often make such cases to pressure public support for certain policies, but if we are more attuned to the structure of the slippery slope, then we can avoid being misled.

Non Sequitur

The next fallacy we will explain is yet another Latin term, non sequitur. Non sequitur means "not in sequence," and the fallacy thus refers to making an unjustified move from one idea to another. This is a very common fallacy, and some instances of it are harder to detect than others. Assuming that someone is wealthy because he or she owns expensive furniture or drives a nice car is an unwarranted jump from one idea to another. While it is possible that someone who has nice furniture or drives an expensive car is wealthy, it is also possible that someone inherited the furniture, is renting the car for a day, or bought an expensive-looking car by accruing a lot of debt while barely making ends meet. There is not enough data to make the assertion logical, and thus the conclusion does not follow from the observation. Think of all the times you may have made an unwarranted assumption about a person or an idea without enough evidence.

Straw Man

The fifth type of fallacy is that of the straw man, which happens when the speaker distorts the actual position of an opponent. In a straw man fallacy, the speaker misrepresents the opponent's position by oversimplifying that position, taking the opponent's comments out of context so that they don't represent the opponent's position at all, or representing an entire group's position with really bad arguments from one person in that group (who might be real or fictitious). The speaker then attacks this misrepresented position or one piece of problematic evidence, and then claims that the entire argument or position must be thrown out. However, even if one piece of evidence used in an argument is problematic, it does not necessarily mean that the entire argument is wrong. For example, some people who believe that warnings about climate change are a hoax might use an example of a single study that was found to have flawed data as evidence that the entire theory that the climate is changing is wrong, despite the mountains of evidence scientists around the world have collected indicating that climate change is a real, serious concern. Buying into a straw man argument is evidence of a lazy thinker who does not pay attention to the larger case being made.

Hasty Generalization

The hasty generalization is the next type of fallacy we will address, which refers to drawing conclusions about broad principles or categories based upon a small sample of evidence. Basing a decision about an entire group or category on just one or even a few examples of it is not a valid, logical argument, yet we do this all the time. Consider how many times you have tried one dish from a particular ethnic cuisine, or one movie from a specific genre, and did not enjoy it. Then, as a result of that experience, you refused to try anything from that cuisine or genre because you did not enjoy that one instance. These are examples of hasty generalization because you made a judgment about an entire large group or category based on a ridiculously small sample. Similarly, if you asked five students on your campus whether they think *The Daily Show* is the best show on TV, and then use this to claim that everyone on your campus thinks *The Daily Show* is the best show on TV, then you have used hasty generalization.

Either-Or

The seventh fallacy we will cover takes place when we assume there are only two alternatives, when in actuality there are more. This is called the either-or fallacy, and people sometimes use it to limit alternatives and force choices in a specific direction. These arguments, which are erroneous applications of a disjunctive syllogism, assume the audience must "either" do this, "or" do that. The argument proceeds to eliminate one of the two alternatives, leaving the audience to believe that the other action is the only one left, when really there are more possibilities to consider. For example, when then-President George W. Bush said, "Either you are with us, or you are with the terrorists" in his address to a joint session of Congress following the September 11 attacks, he was committing an either-or fallacy. Eventually, one of the two options that you present might be a good choice, but limiting the options to only two from the beginning is not the best manner in which to make a decision, and arguing that only two options exist is not a valid way to make an argument.

False Cause

The eighth fallacy is the false cause, which assumes that one event causes another unrelated event to occur. Remember earlier in the chapter, when we discussed reasoning by cause, we mentioned superstitions. Superstitions are the result of false cause, which is an error in the application of that reasoning form. This is why it is always important to seek a connection between an event and what the speaker believes causes the event. If evidence cannot support that there is a necessary or sufficient relationship between the two, then we determine that false cause has been applied.

The Red Herring

Ninth in our list of reasoning fallacies is the red herring, which happens when the speaker introduces irrelevant ideas to focus attention away from the real issue. This fallacy is very common on political news programs when a commentator questions a politician or candidate for office about prior actions or statements and the politician tries to avoid responding. This type of reasoning fallacy essentially tries to change the topic of discussion from one matter to another. When people cannot, or do not, want to respond to an argument, they will try to change the topic to more favorable ground by introducing a red herring to the discussion. In doing so they hope to avoid directly confronting what they have been asked. There is no logical connection between the red herring and the topic under discussion, but they can be introduced in a fashion that makes it seem like a connection is there.

Begging the Question

The tenth and final fallacy we will address is begging the question. We beg the question when we assume certain facts that have not been proven. These types of fallacies often are prefaced by statements such as "it begs the question," "it goes without saying," "everyone agrees," and "let's just say for the sake of argument." All of these phrases tell the audience to assume things to be true without offering proof of their accuracy. They are then followed with a series of other claims built from that false understanding until the end, when the audience agrees to the entire proposition without evidence supporting its foundation.

As speakers, you should carefully craft your messages to ensure that the reasoning supporting your claims is sound and fallacy-free. If audience members detect fallacious reasoning, then you will lose credibility. Even if the audience does not detect the fallacy, it is unethical to use a fallacy to gain agreement. As audience members, we should pay close attention not just to the evidence provided and the claims made but also to how the evidence and claims relate to each other. That is the fundamental characteristic of a good consumer of information.

Summary

In this chapter, we began moving from information gathering and organization to the way we articulate our claims and argument to the audience. Reasoning is both organizational, in that it helps direct us to the best way to connect our evidence with our claims, and inventional, because it helps demonstrate and enhance our personal credibility with the audience. We covered the two types of reasoning, deductive and inductive, as well as provided four forms of reasoning in arguments. We concluded with an exploration of the various ways reasoning can be corrupted and falsely applied.

Key Terms

In COMM 1000/1003

Do you know the number one reason why some students have fallacies in their speeches? They have not adequately prepared. When you know your topic and understand the intricacies related to the topic, you choose your words more carefully. When you don't give yourself enough time to conduct adequate research, you are so busy trying to meet the source requirement minimum that you don't adequately evaluate the information you are including in the speech. When you don't give yourself adequate time to practice, you may phrase statements in a way that won't ring true. In short, practice, and know the content. You will avoid fallacies every time if you observe these simple precautionary measures.

12
Informative Speaking

Now that we have covered the basics of research, organization, and how to make reasoned claims, we turn our attention to the first of three types of speeches you might find yourself delivering one day. We often equate speeches with political candidates making appeals to an audience, or perhaps a sermon on morality from a preacher, but not all speeches are designed to persuade a person. In fact, one of the most common types of speeches is an informative speech. Informative speeches are presentations in which speakers explain a topic to an audience without trying to convince them of anything. These speeches of explanation occur in a variety of formats, but the one you may be most familiar with is a classroom lecture by a teacher or instructor. These presentations are designed not to convince you to believe or do something but rather to explain something to you so you understand it. These are informative speeches.

Explanatory, or informative, speeches typically cover one of four broad topics and are often organized in one of several different ways to help the audience understand the subject in question. In this chapter, we will first discuss the four different types of informative speeches. Next, we will explain five of the most common ways to organize informative speeches. Finally, we will discuss the goals of an informative speech and provide some strategies for best delivering information to an audience.

Types of Informative Speeches – 4 types

There are four different topics you might explain to an audience, and these topics help differentiate between the four types of informative speeches. In this section, we will explain each of these four types of informative speeches. We will begin with speeches about objects, which are perhaps the most common informative speeches. Then we will discuss speeches about processes, which include things like recipes and installation directions. Third, we will cover speeches about events, such as vacations or historical occurrences. Finally, we will detail informative speeches about concepts, such as religious beliefs or laws.

Speeches about Objects - type #1

The first form of informative speeches we will discuss is that which addresses objects. A speech about an object concerns a tangible item such as a piece of sports equipment, a memento, a souvenir, a building, or even a country. These speeches are often found in the classroom and internal business meetings where new products are being developed. However, the term "object" can also refer to people. When you stand and introduce yourself at the start of a new class or at a company or church function, you are the topic being explained, and as something tangible, you are classified as an object for the purpose of identifying the type of informative speech you are delivering.

Informative speeches about objects can include any person, living or deceased, fictional or factual. For example, you might deliver a speech about Harriett Tubman, a prominent figure with the Underground Railroad during the mid-nineteenth century. You might also deliver a speech about the fictional character Sheldon Cooper, who appears on the television show *The Big Bang Theory*. All of these are people, and as such, they are considered objects.

Speeches about objects could also pertain to particular places. Suppose you visited the Statue of Liberty in New York City and wanted to inform your audience about the characteristics of this historic landmark. You could explain to your audience how to get there, tell them when the site is open, and highlight a few "must-see" places neighboring Ellis Island. Or, you might be tasked with explaining a larger space to an audience. For example, if your company is planning to introduce a product to a new market, you might be asked to explain the characteristics of that market to the senior staff. These could include demographic characteristics, economic prosperity, and geographical issues relevant to that new market. In either instance, you are delivering a speech about an object.

Speeches about Processes - type #2

Informative speeches are not always about objects. In fact, many times they are more of a "how-to" type of speech. The next form of informative speech is about a process. These speeches are generally easier to construct and deliver than other speeches, as they pertain to a sequence of events presented in chronological fashion. However, processes vary in terms of complexity.

A very simple process could be baking a cake or changing the tire on a car. In the latter example you would explain each stage of changing a tire, beginning with setting the parking brake, then moving on to blocking the wheels, loosening the lug nuts, jacking up the car, removing the flat tire and replacing the spare tire, tightening the lug nuts, lowering the jack, and checking the lug nuts again, before finally unblocking the wheels and releasing the brake. Each step depends upon the completion of the preceding one for the process to be completed correctly.

Informative speeches about processes can be more complicated as well. Consider a doctor explaining the treatment plan for patients suffering from cancer. This can include radiation schedules, chemotherapy plans, surgeries, and rehabilitation requirements. The process can be very complicated and confusing to patients, so doctors need to effectively explain how the recovery process will unfold. In business, marketing plans are also often complex initiatives with various components, and in order to move forward with those initiatives they need to be carefully explained in a step-by-step process to the staff responsible for their implementation.

Speeches about Events - type #3

The third type of informative speech includes those presentations about an event. Speeches about events can unfold in a variety of ways, but they focus on something that has happened, is happening, or might happen in the future. The central focus of informative speeches is to explain the characteristics of the event, and so it might take shape chronologically or topically.

You are probably familiar with informative speeches about events presented in chronological order from your time in history classes. History is the progression of events that already happened. For example, when history teachers and professors lecture about the World War II Battle of Pearl Harbor, they probably explain it in the chronological order in which the events happened. This makes sense and helps the audience of students understand how the battle unfolded. Even so, sometimes events are best presented in a topical format.

Consider the possibility of working for a company that is about to host a conference. During a conference many different things happen at the same time, and a large staff is responsible for administering the event. In this instance, someone will need to address the staff and explain what will simultaneously happen in different locations during the conference. For example, a wedding planner might talk about what needs to happen as the wedding ceremony unfolds and what needs to be done at the same time to set up for the reception that will take place immediately afterward in a separate location. This is not a chronologically sequenced presentation but rather one that is delivered around topics or locations.

Speeches about Concepts — type #4

The last type of informative speech covers concepts. Concept speeches are the most abstract of all the informative speech types, as they are about ideas and not concrete constructs. The speaker's task when delivering information about concepts is to take something abstract and ground it in reality through the use of real-life examples, illustrations, and vivid depictions. Concept speeches can be about religion, economics, politics, relationships, or any theory or idea that is not tangible.

Informative speeches about concepts can be about seemingly simple theories such as evolution or more complex philosophies like existentialism. It is important to remember that all products and tangible items we encounter once started out as an idea with no concrete dimensions, so try to think about these types of informative speeches as pertaining to the inception of an idea. If you have an idea for a new product, you first need to explain the concept of the product before getting approval to create it.

Of course, speeches explaining concepts also appear in non-business enterprises. For example, preachers in churches explain religious principles to their congregation by illustrating principles in action. Lawyers argue about the law, which is abstract, by applying it to particular real-life cases. All productions in the entertainment fields and advertising begin with conceptual frames and drawings. Speeches about concepts would explain these initial ideas before they ever become tangible, as once the topic is tangible it becomes a speech about an object.

Each of the four types of informative speeches can be about the same topic; they simply approach it in different ways. For example, if you want to speak about Buddhism, you could speak about Buddha as a person and describe his life, thus delivering a speech about an object. You could also focus on how to become a practitioner of Buddhism, thus delivering an informative speech about a process. The speech also could focus on a specific Buddhist ritual, thus coming at the topic from the angle of an event. Finally, it could be about the central beliefs of Buddhism, which is a speech about a concept. What matters is that your specific purpose statement clearly articulates which type of informative speech you plan to deliver. Once you determine the type of speech you are giving, you can then organize the body in a way that makes the most sense to the audience.

Organizational Patterns — 5 types

When explaining complex information to people who are unfamiliar with it, proper organization of your speech is essential. In the development of the speech, you must determine the most effective way to present complicated information to the audience. Sometimes it's as simple as laying out a sequence of steps, but often it is more complex. In this section, we will discuss five different ways to organize an informative speech. Treat these organizational patterns as tools in your speech toolkit that you can turn to at any time when they make the most sense. In short, let the information dictate the pattern; don't choose the pattern and then make your information fit it.

Chronological — type #1

The first organizational pattern we will present is chronological, which sequences events in the order in which they occur in time. This pattern illustrates to the audience not just what occurs at each step but also how the central focus of the speech is changed by each move forward. Take, for example, a speech about a medical treatment program. This is a fairly complicated subject; however, if the speaker explains what is involved at each treatment step, why it must go in that order, and how the patient will respond and feel after each step, then the topic becomes easier for an unfamiliar audience to follow.

You may believe that chronological patterns are restricted to informative process speeches, but in fact they are more versatile than that. For instance, they could also be used to organize speeches about objects, such as an airplane. A speech about airplanes could discuss their historical development and major moments of change in their appearance and use. Chronological organization is easily understood by an audience and can be used with many different speech topics, not just processes.

Cause-Effect - type #2

A specific form of the chronological organizational pattern involves causes and effects. The cause-effect pattern discusses one or more causes that result in a specific event. It is important when discussing this organizational strategy that you remember that just about everything has more than one cause, and so you must be careful when arguing that something caused something else. Now that the reminder is out of the way, let's talk about how to structure speeches like this.

Cause-effect speeches begin by explaining one or more things you claim cause a resulting event. For instance, a speech about a business plan for a company could have several different causes for the specific effect of monetary growth or loss. The causes could be a creative marketing plan for a new product, an expanded sales force, and more investment in product training. Each of these causes could then be linked to the specific effect of raising revenue for the company. Such an approach illustrates the complexity of multiple causes for one desired effect in a way an audience can follow. The cause-effect pattern is generally easy for the speaker to organize and easier for an unfamiliar audience to understand. The key element to a good cause-effect speech lies in making the connections between the causes and the effects explicit and obvious for the audience.

Problem-Solution - type #3

A third way to organize your speech involves focusing your explanation around a problem and its solution. As with the cause-effect pattern, it is important to make the link between the two explicit for the audience and also to focus on the past. We say focus on the past because with an informative speech such as this you are not proposing a specific solution to an existing problem but rather explaining how a past problem was solved. Doing this is what makes the speech informative and explanative, rather than a persuasive speech in which you try to convince an audience to enact a solution to an existing problem.

Teachers often employ problem-solution organization in their lectures and discussions with students. For example, when discussing the Civil Rights Movement they might set up their lecture by establishing all of the problems faced by African Americans in society during the 1960s. The teacher could then talk specifically about the nonviolent resistance of Martin Luther King Jr. and how it influenced the passage of legislation protecting the rights of the African American community. Such a speech is not persuasive but rather explains several problems and a way they were solved.

Spatial - type #4

Sometimes we cannot effectively explain something to an audience in a clear chronological sequence, so we need an organizational pattern that does not rely on time sequencing. Instead, spatial organization explains material to an audience by emphasizing how things are physically related to one another in a defined area or space. Here location, not time, creates the structure of points. Like time, however, spatial organization must follow a logical pattern in which the subject of each subsequent point is located near or adjacent to the location of the previous one.

Suppose a student wanted to deliver a speech about their native city of New Orleans and, after examining the city's geography, decided to organize the speech by regions of the city. The speech could have these spatial areas as its main points: the French Quarter, the Central Business District, the Downriver District, and the Uptown area. In each main point of the speech the prominent characteristics of each area would be explained. It would be important, however, to order the regions in a way that mirrors the way they are connected on a map.

Topical - type #5

The final organizational pattern we will discuss is topical, or categorical. In this pattern, you look at the particulars of the topic and find a theme for the topic in a certain category. This pattern often takes shape when you want to focus on a specific aspect of a topic, so that aspect becomes the organizing theme for the speech. Topical organization is also employed when the other organizational patterns do not seem to fit what you want to do.

If you wanted to explain different modes of dealing with interpersonal conflict to an audience you would most likely do so topically. In this speech, you would cover the five ways to handle conflict: withdraw, accommodate, force, compromise, and collaborate. Each one of these strategies represents a topic, or category, related to managing interpersonal conflict and is also logically linked. If the information was presented in this way, an audience would easily be able to follow the explanation of this complicated material.

Topical organization, however, is not restricted to speeches about concepts. You also might want to focus a speech about a person this way as well, as opposed to doing it chronologically. For instance, you could speak about comedian Bill Cosby topically by organizing the speech's main points around the categories of his family life, his comedic career, and his social activist activities. This is not chronological, but topical, and still allows the audience to follow along with your speech points.

When it comes to choosing an organizational pattern you should always remember not to be too rigid. There will be topics that will require you to combine some of these five patterns. Take the Bill Cosby example. The main points are ordered topically; however, the discussion of each of those main points might make the most sense if presented chronologically. This allows you to have an overarching organizational pattern for main points and also the flexibility to organize the subpoints of those main points differently so they make better sense.

Goals and Strategies for Informative Speeches

Each of the four types of informative speeches attempts to achieve a specific set of goals with an audience. Each also can employ particular strategies to achieve those goals, including determining the best organizational pattern for your speech purposes and integrating other tools into the presentation. In this final section, we provide a few strategies to help you maximize your ability to achieve the goals of each type of informative speech.

Tips for Informative Speeches about Objects

Many times it is difficult to precisely describe an object, and the less familiar your audience is with the object, the more description you will need to provide. This is why it is important to find out in advance how much your audience already knows about your speech topic. Doing so allows you to determine whether you need to bring a model of the object as a visual aid for your speech so the audience can actually see what it is you are talking about.

In the health field, doctors often find models useful when speaking to patients because medical conditions and procedures can be very complicated for those not trained in biology and anatomy to fully grasp. Let's use a dental procedure as an example. In any dentist's office, you will likely find a model of a mouth, or at least a poster with a picture of the mouth on it. When dentists try to explain

When you are teaching, each class period is basically an extended informative speech. As you develop your lesson plans, think carefully about which key ideas you want to focus on during your class period and which pattern of organization will be most effective for helping your students understand those concepts. To help enhance your students' understanding, try incorporating some of the following into your lesson plans:

- Live or video demonstrations
- Models or pictures of the objects
- Diagrams and idea maps that show how topics are related
- Activities that allow your students to apply and build on ideas
- Questions or assignments that allow you to check for understanding

Teacher Tips

to patients what is happening with their teeth, where cavities are, or where and how they need to brush better, they often need to pull out the model to show the patient. This allows the patient to have a visual representation and understand the complicated information the dentist provided them.

Tips for Informative Speeches about Processes

As we previously noted, process speeches consistently use a chronological sequence. These speeches are generally easy to understand, if logically presented, and are easy for the speaker to keep on track as one thing follows another. When one thing logically follows another it becomes important to detail for the audience when and how one stage progresses to another. For example, if you are developing a speech about the process of applying for a job, your speech will have several stages that build upon one another. First there is the research process of finding a job for which you wish to apply, after which you must prepare an application letter. With the letter, you must also prepare and submit a resume. In this presentation, you need to make sure the audience understands how each step relates and connects to the next.

By explaining the connections between main points, you do more than list things or provide directions to the audience. In essence, you are explaining the complexities of the process. Informative speeches about processes are more than recipes and lists of stages. They are explanations of each step and the dos and don'ts that come with each stage of the process. Take the time to explain the process and each of its steps to ensure that the audience understands it all.

Tips for Informative Speeches about Events

In many ways, events are more complicated than processes or even objects because they contain numerous elements upon which a speech can focus. So the primary tip in developing a clear and effective explanation of an event is to choose your focus and explain that focus to the audience early in the speech. This lets them know that you are not covering everything about the event but rather a specific aspect of it.

It is important that you also lay out the details of the event to the audience. Identify important people involved in the event that will appear in your speech. When covering what happened during the event, be sure to let your audience know how those occurrences will be covered. If you plan to cover the event spatially rather than chronologically or even topically, make sure your audience knows   this. Focus only on what you can adequately cover in the time you are allowed, and be sure your audience knows how you plan to discuss the event so they do not get confused.

Tips for Informative Speeches about Concepts

Concepts are abstract, so they hold particular challenges for speakers. Concept speeches need to take abstract ideas and relate them to the audience as clearly as possible. One of the most effective ways of doing this is through concrete and hypothetical examples. This is the same tool teachers use to explain new ideas to students. The apple falling on Newton's head, for example, is a tried and true way of explaining the abstract concept of gravity.

Before employing examples, however, make sure you clearly explain the concept. There will be times when your speech contains abstractions, but make sure those abstractions are followed with concrete examples that illustrate the concept at work. Whenever possible, draw these examples from things that will resonate with the particular audience to whom you are speaking.

Summary

Good informative speaking explains complex material to nonexperts in such a way that they can easily understand and learn the new material. As we discussed in this chapter, that new material can come in four different forms: objects, processes, events, and concepts. There are also several ways you can organize this information to effectively explain it to an audience, and here we covered five patterns of organization. Finally, we provided a few tips for developing effective informative speeches that explain objects, processes, events, and concepts to an audience.

In COMM 1000/1003

While the list of topics of past informative speeches for COMM 1000 could fill this book, here are a few that stand out because these were original ideas that turned into fantastic speeches.

1. The Mullet (yes, this is the hairstyle)

2. State of Wolves in America (the decline of wolf populations throughout history)

3. The Original Selfie (history of portraits in American art)

4. How Music Impacts One's Mood (the sound bytes used as a visual aid for this speech were highly effective)

5. Vinyl Records (why vinyl records went out of style and the re-emergence of vinyl)

Informative Speech Assignment

PURPOSE:
The purpose of the Informative Speech is to give the audience novel information about your topic. You can do this by describing a process, procedure, event or object, defining a term, system or idea, or explaining how something works or operates. The general idea is for you to create more knowledge and awareness of your subject matter.

TOPIC:
All topics must be cleared with your instructor. It is up to each instructor to determine how topics will be selected and what is and is not appropriate in his or her class. Your instructor may choose to add more topics to the banned topics list, so be sure you check with him/her on banned topic ideas.

When choosing your topic try to pick a subject that foremost interests you. Then, based on the information you read from your textbook about audience adaptation, try to make that subject interesting to your classmates. It's always a good idea to ask class members what they think about your topic—this gives you a better idea of their interest in it. Even if audience members don't seem to be interested in your topic, the ultimate power of making your speech engaging and interesting lies in your hands. Remember, the more you care about your topic the more likely the audience is going to be interested in it, even if they weren't before your speech.

DELIVERY:
You should be delivering your speeches from a keyword or speaking outline. Some instructors may require you to deliver your speech from notecards; others may ask that students use a sheet of paper to deliver the speech. Make sure you are clear on the number of notecards and/or sheets of paper you are allowed to use when delivering your speech based on what your instructor has told you.

ASSIGNMENT REQUIREMENTS:
1. The speech should be 4-6 minutes in length. (minus 2 points for every 15 seconds over/underthe time limit).
2. The topic is appropriate for the assigned general purpose
3. A minimum of four sources should be used to provide adequate supporting material
   - These sources must be cited in the delivery of the speech as well as on a reference page. You should also cite any additional sources you use.
   - Encyclopedias, dictionaries, Wikipedia, CDROMs and other general reference materials may not be used.
   - Only one source may come from the Internet.
   - At least one of the sources must carry a publication date within the last 12 months.
4. Two copies of your full-sentence outline (typed) must be submitted. If the outline is not typed,you will not receive credit for the outline. Most instructors require that you e-mail them one copy of the outline and bring another copy of the outline to class. If you fail to submit an outline then 20 points will be deducted from your speech grade. Please note that all outlines become part of the Department of Communication and Journalism's speech files.
5. A copy of the bibliography/reference should be attached to your outline. We use APA style forsource citation.
6. A PowerPoint Visual Aid

TIPS: Remember the following make for excellent types of supporting material:
- Definitions
- Examples
- Contrasts
- Comparisons
- Quotations

- Anecdotes
- Statistics

Make sure you review the grade sheet your instructor has posted for this assignment. It includes all the necessary elements of your speech and should serve as your guide/checklist to what you should include in your speech. Don't forget to pan out and show me your audience members before you begin speaking if you are in an online section.

13
Persuasive Speaking

We use persuasion in our personal and professional lives, and we are subjected to others' attempts to persuade us. At home we may try to convince someone to see a particular movie, eat at a specific restaurant, or watch a television show. At work we may negotiate salaries, try to motivate members of our team working on a project, or even get a boss to agree to let us leave work early. In today's world, no matter where we are or where we look there are advertisements trying to convince us to buy a product or believe a certain thing. Interstate highways are littered with billboards, hallways are filled with posters, and the average one-hour television show contains almost twenty minutes of advertising! Persuasion is all around us, and to be better at persuading others, as well as become more critical consumers of information, we must understand how it works.

In this chapter, we will cover the principles of the persuasive process and how to prepare and organize a persuasive speech. We will go over the persuasive process, paying particular attention to the role credibility plays in convincing an audience. Then we will cover the four different types of persuasive speeches you may be called upon to deliver. Third, we will explain the various ways those speeches can be organized. Finally, we will provide some tips for adjusting to different types of audiences during your speech.

The Persuasive Process - 4 stages

Persuasion is more complicated than it may appear on the surface. It takes time and occurs through a four-step process. Additionally, attempting to persuade someone does not guarantee success or an immediate response. Many times the effects of persuasion occur long after the persuasive message has been delivered, when the audience member encounters a situation that makes him or her think more about your persuasive appeals or has the opportunity to act upon that information. In this section, we will unpack the persuasive process and discuss its four stages in more detail.

Stage #1: Issue Awareness

issue awareness
first stage of the persuasion process in which you focus the audience's attention on the issue and show why the issue is important

The first step in persuasion is **issue awareness**. Audiences often have some knowledge of an issue before you speak to them about it, but it will vary how much they know as will how strongly they hold positions on the issue. Sometimes audiences have no knowledge about a particular issue until it is presented to them by a speaker. This is common when it comes to certain environmental or health issues that face a community.

To be effective in making an audience aware of the issue about which you are speaking, you need to know how familiar they are with the topic. Can you reasonably assume they know about the issue? How much do they know? Are they likely to share your opinion or disagree with you? These are important questions to consider when preparing to persuade an audience to believe or do something. Regardless, focus the audience's attention on the issue and make them aware of your feelings about why it is important to them. Only when an audience is aware that an issue exists can you move on to the next step of the persuasive process.

Stage #2: Comprehension

comprehension
stage of the persuasion process in which the audience understands the relevant components of the issue and the position that you want them to take

Once an audience is aware of a concern or issue, you need to make sure they comprehend both its relevant components and how you feel they should handle it. Thus the next step in the persuasive process is **comprehension**. Only when an audience comprehends the complexity of an issue and what the options are for responding to it can they make an informed decision about whether they will follow your advice.

Comprehension can be simple or complicated, depending on the familiarity the audience has with the topic. If they understand the issue, you need to spend time making sure they comprehend your position on it, but if they do not know much about the topic, then you must spend significant time educating them. When helping an audience comprehend a topic, do not give in to the temptation of telling only your side of the issue but rather give them as complete a picture as possible. This ethical approach creates good will with the audience and gives them the freedom to make an informed decision. However, just knowing that an issue exists or comprehending its components does not create persuasion; for that we move on to stage three.

Stage #3: Acceptance

acceptance
third step of the persuasion process in which the audience accepts that the issue is relevant to them

The third step in the persuasive process, **acceptance**, occurs when the audience accepts that the issue is relevant to them. This does not mean the audience members are going to agree with you or do what you desire, but they at least accept the accuracy of what you are saying and recognize how the issue pertains to their lives. This is important because if they do not accept the issue, then it will not be possible to persuade them. Just think, how likely is it that an audience will agree with, let alone consider, an issue that does not affect them in any meaningful way? Not very likely, thus making persuasion difficult at best, but most likely impossible.

Getting an audience to accept an issue's importance depends on whether you adequately explain the issue and how clearly you describe it. The audience must be able to comprehend an issue and see its connection to their own life in order to develop a position or change a position they may already hold. However, an audience can comprehend an issue and accept its importance to their lives but still disagree with you. That means there must be one more step in the persuasive process.

Stage #4: Integration

integration
the fourth step of the persuasive process in which the audience adopts the position that you want them to take

The final and most important stage of the persuasive process is **integration**. In this stage, the audience adopts the position that you want them to take. This occurs when audiences fully understand the issue, accept that it is relevant to their lives, and agree with your proposition regarding what to think or how to act. Your position becomes a part of the audience's personal philosophy and way of seeing the world. This change will vary among audience members, but ultimately, because you are seeking to change their understanding and feelings about something or someone, you bear significant ethical responsibilities.

The ability to achieve integration with persuasive speeches and messages depends upon several factors. The evidence, reasoning, and logic you present are obviously key to successfully influencing an audience, as is the audience's disposition toward the topic itself. The third component of persuasion is your credibility as a speaker. When an audience sees you as reputable, fair, and ethical, your ability to integrate your position into their own worldview will be enhanced. This aspect of persuasion is called credibility, and it comes in several forms, which we will detail next.

Types of Credibility

Credibility, or the ability of a person to inspire belief or trust in others, is an incredibly fluid concept. The degree to which we are credible varies based on who we speak with, what we speak about, and the way we speak about something. We can increase or decrease our level of credibility with our words or actions, thus making it something we must pay close attention to when delivering remarks to others. In persuasive speaking, it is essential that the audience see you as a credible source of information or your task of convincing them to do or believe as you ask will be almost impossible. In this section, we will explore three basic types of credibility.

> **credibility**
> the ability of a person to inspire belief or trust in others

Initial Credibility

The first form of credibility we will cover is initial credibility, which refers to the credibility that you have with the audience before you begin your speech. All of us carry a certain level of credibility on a topic going into a speech, but it varies depending on the topic and the audience. For instance, when giving a presentation in a classroom to fellow students you likely will have little initial credibility because they are unfamiliar with you and your experience. This presents a hurdle you must overcome if you want the audience to listen to you and believe what you say.

Initial credibility is not always zero for every speaker. In fact, the more experience speakers have with a subject, or the more recognizable their names, the more credibility an audience will give them before they even speak. Consider attending a presentation on fantasy novels by writer George R. R. Martin. You may recognize him as the mind behind *Game of Thrones*. These books are quite popular and successful, thus enhancing his initial credibility to speak on the topic. In your public speaking class, you and your classmates might even have some initial credibility based on classroom interactions and other conversations in class. Nonetheless, strong initial credibility does not guarantee success or even that the audience will continue to see the speaker as credible.

> **initial credibility**
> the credibility that you have with the audience before you begin your speech, based on your experience and the audience's prior knowledge about you

Derived Credibility

After the speech begins, whatever you say or do immediately influences your level of credibility, thus making it no longer initial. The form of credibility that manifests itself during your presentation is called derived credibility because it is the trustworthiness and believability you garner during the speech. After the speech begins, your level of credibility can either increase or decrease depending upon a number of different factors such as:

- your perceived level of preparation
- your delivery
- the organization of your points
- the quality of your evidence and information
- the way you speak to the audience, regardless of whether they agree with you

> **derived credibility**
> the form of credibility that manifests itself during your presentation

Derived credibility is very important because it helps you win over members of the audience who may be skeptical of your position or, in some cases, even opposed to it. It also helps strengthen the level of agreement among your supporters. Relying simply on initial credibility and not trying to maintain or improve your trustworthiness with an audience can lead to disastrous consequences because audiences see through it and interpret it as being disrespectful to them. For that reason alone, you should take care to develop and deliver the best speech possible.

Terminal Credibility

Once the speech concludes you will have a new level of credibility on the subject and with the audience, known as your terminal credibility. This level is the initial credibility you walked in with plus the credibility you derived during your remarks. Obviously, you hope you finish with more credibility than you began with due to your efforts within the speech. The level of trustworthiness you finish with is referred to as terminal credibility, and it also becomes your initial credibility the next time you speak to a similar audience about the same topic.

> **terminal credibility**
> the level of credibility that you have when your speech concludes which is the sum of your initial credibility and derived credibility

It is important to note that if you finish a speech and are less credible with an audience it is a significant challenge to recover that lost trustworthiness and believability. This can significantly hinder any future attempts at persuasion with that audience and possibly others as well. Suffice it to say, no matter what you plan to persuade an audience about, being perceived as credible is essential to your success. In the next section, we will discuss the different types of persuasive speeches and presentations you might find yourself delivering at some point. As we cover them, think about ways you might enhance your credibility in each situation.

Types of Persuasive Speeches

We are surrounded by persuasive messages that try to get us to believe something, feel something, or do something. There is so much information available today that you can find information to support almost any claim. There are four forms of persuasive speech we will cover in this section. Some persuasive speeches make claims about fact, others argue values, some suggest policies, and the final group refutes the positions of others.

Questions of Fact #1

Facts are not really the stubborn things people think they are. In actuality, facts are very hard to prove just ask a lawyer, judge, or jury. Trying to convince someone of a fact is simply an exercise in persuasion, not science. Typically, persuasive speeches of fact occur when the speaker argues that something did or did not happen. Whenever there is a question about the occurrence or existence of something, we see a persuasive message regarding a **question of fact**. Often, things we take for granted can be disputed. For instance, look at the lunar landing by Neil Armstrong and his crew. There are people who argue that this whole occurrence was faked, and they have data that supports their argument, thus calling this "fact" into question. Whether or not Lee Harvey Oswald acted alone in killing President Kennedy is another example of a question of fact.

question of fact
when a speaker seeks to persuade people about how to interpret facts

Facts are called into question more than we might realize. In court juries are asked to listen to two different interpretations of an event and to try to decide what the facts are. This is a very difficult task, especially when both sides know how to effectively research and wield information. So facts are not stubborn things; they are more often determinations of which interpretations are the most accurate. This leaves the door open to persuasion on questions of fact.

Questions of Value #2

Sometimes facts are not in dispute, but rather we wish to try and convince people to place value on a belief or object. This topic represents a second type of persuasive speech, one that deals with questions of value. People place value on almost everything. We value money, time, freedom, choice, family, friendship, and a whole host of other things, but when people try to get us to value something more than something else, or to value it more than we already do, they are providing an argument in response to a question of value.

question of value
a persuasive speech about the rightness or wrongness of an idea, action, or issue

Questions of value arise in a variety of different contexts. In sports, teams trade players, but in order to be persuaded to do so they need to be convinced that they are receiving value in return. In politics, pro-life and pro-choice supporters clash over differences of value. In business, companies must often answer questions of value when staff members receive contract offers from rival companies and they must ask themselves how much they value keeping that employee. As you can see, we place value on a great many things in life, and people try to convince us to value things in the same order and way they do, thus creating an opening for persuasive messages about the value of objects, people, and positions.

Questions of Policy #3

Another common area in which persuasion comes into play is in policy, or decisions on how to act in the future. While questions of fact in the courtroom deal most often with what has happened already, and values are how we feel now or in the moment, questions of policy refer to persuasive efforts about how we should act in the future. **Questions of policy** advocate a course of action. Again, these types of questions come up in many different settings, from home life to governmental affairs.

question of policy
when a speaker takes a position on whether an action should or should not be taken

Perhaps the most common place for persuasive speeches on questions of policy is in legislative bodies such as Congress or student government. These types of speeches question what should be done, such as where money should be allocated, what groups recognized, or what positions a group should announce on issues. These policies affect future activities in most instances, not past occurrences or present values.

Refutation

In some circumstances we are called upon to respond to the arguments made by another and attempt to defend our own positions. This is called refutation. These speeches try to disprove another's argument while also promoting your own. The topics can be facts, values, or policies. In order to be successful in refuting remarks by others, you will need to understand their argument and then address each of the points they raised while explaining the flaws in their position. This type of speech requires significant research and carefully planned responses.

refutation
response to potential opposition to your argument

What determines the type of persuasive speech you deliver is what you wish to accomplish. Also realize that you will likely use facts, refute other arguments, advocate for something to be done, or give your opinion on what you think is the best in any speech. Again, the type of speech is determined by your speech's goals. Your speech's goals also influence how you choose to organize your speech, and when advocating a position there are different organizational patterns to choose from than there are when explaining information to an audience. In the next section, we will cover those patterns available for advocacy speeches.

Persuasive Speech Organizational Patterns

There are four common ways to organize a persuasive speech that help maximize your ability to connect with and persuade an audience. Determining which one of these is best for you depends upon your topic and your goals, but all provide a clear way to lay out an argument for an audience in an easy-to-follow manner.

Problem-Solution

One of the more common times we present an argument is when proposing a solution to a problem we might encounter. The simplest way to organize this type of argument is in a problem-solution format. This organizational pattern typically has only two main points, but they are very detailed and explicitly connected to each other. The first main point presents the problem by explaining the issue in great detail. At this point, it is also important to explain to the audience how the problem affects them. Following the presentation of the problem, you provide a solution to the issue and explain what it entails. For example, a local homeless shelter is running low on money to provide services to disadvantaged people (problem), and you propose that they seek funds from the local government and wealthy donors (solution). In laying out the solution you need to explain how it will fix the problem you established in the first point. It is important to note, however, that most problems have a root cause that, if left unfixed, will cause the issue to reoccur, and this leads us to the second organizational pattern for persuasive arguments.

Problem-Cause-Solution

The second organizational pattern we will discuss simply adds a step to the prior problem-solution pattern. After presenting the problem in the first main point, you discuss the root cause of the problem in the second main point before moving on to offer your solution. Additionally, the solution you propose is not for the problem but for the cause of the problem, so that it never reoccurs. Suppose you have several potholes on your street that damage cars as they hit them. You take this problem to the local government, but rather than asking them to fill the potholes you point out that the potholes are there because the street was improperly sealed. You organize your argument so that you propose filling the potholes and resealing the road; that way the potholes will not come back. This is an effective example of using problem-cause-solution organization in persuasive appeal.

Comparative Advantages

In many cases, multiple solutions are offered to solve problems faced by individuals and communities. In these cases it becomes advantageous to organize your speech around a comparison of your solution with those proposed by other parties. This type of organizational pattern is called comparative advantage, and it can be used to

STEM Spotlight

Engineers often find themselves giving persuasive speeches as part of the solution validation phase of a project. During this phase you will be asked to present your proposed solution to clients and/or managers so they can learn about your solution, compare it with alternatives, and ask questions to identify potential problems. Your job is to persuade others that your solution is the best one, and you will need to have effective persuasion and communication skills as well as a firm understanding of the engineering concepts involved in your solution. At this stage, however, it is also important to listen carefully to your audience, consider their feedback, and be willing to discuss ways to adapt your solution so that it better addresses the problem and fits the constraints of the specific situation in which it will be implemented.

show how your solution is superior to the others. This type of organizational pattern can be especially effective in business settings in which you are competing with a rival company for an account. You can compare that company's product or service with yours and explain how yours is superior, thus making you look knowledgeable and helping the audience see the benefits of what you are proposing.

Monroe's Motivated Sequence

The fourth and final type of organizational pattern for a persuasive speech we will present is Monroe's Motivated Sequence. This pattern follows five steps, with each taking place in order within your presentation. Monroe's Motivated Sequence is most often found in advertising and business presentations, and it can often be easily identified within commercials.

The first step in the sequence is *attention*, during which you focus the audience on the issue you plan to address. This is done by tying the attention getter directly to your topic. The second step calls for you to establish a *need*, so the audience becomes aware of a problem or issue that needs to be addressed. This is a creative endeavor, as you must find a way to establish the need for the audience by illustrating your familiarity with their particular situation. The third step of the sequence is to present a way that *satisfies* the need. This solution fills the need you created in the audience. Simply presenting the solution does not guarantee they will adopt it, however, and so the fourth step of *visualization* uses colorful language and vivid imagery to encourage the audience to see themselves adopting your solution and fulfilling the need. The last step is the call to *action* and takes place during the conclusion of the speech, when you reiterate the desire for the audience to do as you propose.

Ultimately, you decide the organizational pattern by determining exactly what you want to accomplish in your speech. Persuasion is a mental process, and at times the audience will not react as you desire. That is why it is important for you to know what to do if you notice a negative reaction from the audience. In the final section, we will provide some suggestions on how to adapt to audience feedback during your presentation to help ensure that you stay on topic and retain the best possible chance at persuading your audience.

Adjusting to the Audience During the Speech

Just as credibility changes during a speech, so too does the audience's response to your presentation. Sometimes this is good, as they indicate enthusiasm and agreement with your position, but other times they can exhibit a lack of interest and even hostility as you lay out your argument. Knowing how to adapt to this feedback is an essential part of successful persuasive speaking. In this section, we will provide you with some tips for adapting to audience feedback.

Adapting to a Favorable Audience — *1st type of audience*

The ideal audience is one that looks upon you favorably. You may be able to adjust your delivery to garner even more support, so be sure to not do anything offensive that could jeopardize their support. If you notice nods of agreement with your statements, or clapping and cheering, capitalize on this good feeling by increasing the volume and tone of your voice. Mirroring their enthusiasm can help engender even stronger support for your position.

It might seem like engendering more support with an already favorable audience is unnecessary, but nothing could be further from the truth. It is imperative to maintain, and even increase, interest and enthusiasm for you and your position. When an audience sees your excitement, they will share it and take the message even further than the setting in which they heard you speak, thus giving your position even more reach than your speech. All of this can be created by adapting to and taking advantage of good feelings and a positive atmosphere created by a supportive audience.

Adapting to a Neutral Audience – 2nd type of audience

In many cases, you may be presenting to an audience that does not know you or what you are talking about, and we characterize these audiences as neutral. This audience has no position regarding you or your topic and thus could go either way, depending upon your speech. In this environment, you will again not want to be offensive, but will need to make a strong case, as you are asking them to choose among options. In these instances, you need to elaborate on the issue and connect it to your audience's life, demonstrating why they should care about it. Only then can you move forward to creating a persuasive call to action.

> If you work in sales, you will give persuasive speeches frequently to try to persuade clients to purchase your products or services. Sometimes you will be asked for bids and will be competing directly with others, while at other times you will cold-call potential customers to convince them they need something they might not have considered.
>
> If you are competing for an account:
> - Organize your presentation using comparative advantages.
> - Highlight the strengths of your product or service.
> - Address all of the key concerns your client identified in his or her request for proposals.
>
> If you are not in direct competition:
> - Organize your presentation using Monroe's Motivated Sequence or problem-cause-solution.
> - Tailor your presentation to your potential client. Do your research and make sure you can meet his or her needs before you ask for the appointment.
>
> Above all, tell the truth, even if it means admitting weakness from time to time. If you tell your client that your product will do something that it cannot, you will lose your credibility and the chance for future sales.

During your speech, you need to be prepared for several different audience reactions. They may appear confused, in which case you need to reframe what you are talking about to make it easier to understand. They may begin to demonstrate agreement, which you can then reference as you move forward with the speech. They also may appear uninterested, in which case you need to pause and find a way to bring them back. Neutral audiences can be the trickiest audiences you might address.

Adapting to a Hostile Audience – 3rd type of audience

There may be times when you are called upon to speak to an audience with an unfavorable disposition toward you and/or your topic. In fact, they might be outright hostile. In some ways this is easier than a neutral audience because you at least know in advance where they stand, making it easier to craft a message that might hit home. Establish common ground quickly with these types of audiences. Beginning from a place of agreement or familiarity will lessen their hostility and at least open the possibility that they will listen to what you have to say. In fact, even during the speech, when you notice disagreement or hostility in the audience, returning to these common issues can help dull that discontent in the audience.

You may also need to alter your delivery if the audience is not responding to you, as discontent can manifest itself not only in overt comments but also in disinterest and lack of attention. In these cases, try to change your style of speech to become more engaging, enthusiastic, and relaxed. Perhaps walking around the room or through the audience when speaking will help recapture the interest and attention of audience members. You also might pause from your speech to tell a story or reflect on the topic in a less structured manner. You might even consider asking for comments or questions just to break up the presentation.

In the real world, it is likely that when you are attempting to persuade an audience you will have a mix of attitudes toward you and your topic, including favorable, unfavorable, and neutral attitudes. Adjusting to the reactions of the audience can aid you in successfully persuading an audience.

Summary

Persuasion is a complicated process that does not always happen as quickly as we like. In fact, more often than not it takes time, evidence, and coherent arguments to convince an audience to go along with what you are advocating. In this chapter, we explained the four-step process of persuasion and the important role credibility plays in appealing to an audience. We also discussed how fluid credibility is and how it can change during a presentation. Next we covered the four different types of persuasive speeches and discussed the various ways they can be organized to maximize their ability to connect with an audience. Finally, we provided some suggestions for how to adapt to the different types of audiences you might encounter when delivering a persuasive message. All in all, persuasion is a complicated process and effectively creating a persuasive message takes time, evidence, and careful attention to the audience.

Key Terms

acceptance   106
comprehension   106
credibility   107
derived credibility   107
initial credibility   107
integration   106
issue awareness   106
question of fact   108
question of policy   108
question of value   108
refutation   109
terminal credibility   107

In COMM 1000/1003

While the list of topics of past persuasive speeches in COMM 1000 could fill this book, here are just a few that stand out because these were original ideas that turned into fantastic speeches.

1. Why all college students should learn to play a musical instrument regularly (the speech dealt with stress relief, a correlation between musical ability and higher exam scores and how music is good for your social life).

2. Overreliance on social media has a negative impact on relationships (the student used studies to try to prove how relationships suffer because of social media).

3. Genetically modified foods are not bad (using his experience as an ag major, this student presented evidence as to what genetically modified foods actually are and what they are not and how a growing population is putting demands on the world's food supply).

4. All students should work while in college (the student addressed the experience and preparation for career, the financial incentives of working, and the personal rewards that come from working while in school).

Persuasive Speech Assignment

PURPOSE:

The purpose of the Persuasive Speech is to identify a topic of interest to you and present the speech as a claim of fact, claim of value or claim of policy. Phrasing of the claim is essential in a persuasive speech, so clear language and accurate communication of the claim are essential to the success of this speech.

TOPIC:

All topics must be cleared with your instructor. It is up to each instructor to determine how topics will be selected and what is and is not appropriate in his or her class. Your instructor may choose to add more topics to the banned topic's list, so be sure you check with him/her on banned topic ideas. You must pick a topic in which at least two points of view exist. A general idea would be to focus on a public issue or subject you have a genuine interest in that has relevance to members of the class as well.

To ensure that you cover all aspects of the issue/topic, you will need to narrow your topic into points that you can reasonably discuss within the time limit. Consider both the audience's opinions as well as the range of issues surrounding the topic. It often works best when students narrow their topic to a specific issue related to a broader topic before they can make a convincing argument about it.

When choosing your topic try to pick a subject that foremost interests you. Then, based on the information you read from your textbook about audience adaptation, try to make that subject interesting to your classmates. It's always a good idea to ask class members what they think about your topic—this gives you a better idea of their interest in it. Even if audience members don't seem to be interested in your topic, the ultimate power of making your speech engaging and interesting lies in your hands. Remember, the more you care about your topic the more likely the audience is going to be interested in it, even if they weren't before your speech.

DELIVERY:

You should be delivering your speeches from a keyword or speaking outline. Some instructors may require you to deliver your speech from notecards; others may ask that students use a sheet of paper to deliver the speech. Make sure you are clear on the number of notecards and/or sheets of paper you are allowed to use when delivering your speech based on what your instructor has told you.

ASSIGNMENT REQUIREMENTS:

1. The speech should be 5-7 minutes in length. (minus 3 points for every 15 seconds over/under the time limit).
2. The topic is appropriate for the assigned general purpose
3. A minimum of five sources should be used to provide adequate supporting material
   - These sources must be cited in the delivery of the speech as well as on a reference page. You should
   - also cite any additional sources you use.
   - Encyclopedias, dictionaries, Wikipedia, CDROMs and other general reference materials may not be used.
   - Only two sources may come from the Internet.
   - At least one of the sources must carry a publication date within the last 12 months.
4. Two copies of your full-sentence outline (typed) must be submitted. If the outline is not typed, you will not receive credit for the outline. Most instructors require that you e-mail them one copy of the outline and bring another copy of the outline to class. If you fail to submit an outline then 20 points will be deducted from your speech grade. Please note that all outlines become part of the Department of Communication and Journalism's speech files.
5. A copy of the bibliography/reference should be attached to your outline. We use APA style for source citation.

6. A PowerPoint Visual Aid

TIPS: Remember the following make for excellent types of supporting material:
- Definitions
- Examples
- Contrasts
- Comparisons
- Quotations
- Anecdotes
- Statistics

Remember that persuasion usually occurs in small increments. You may not get everyone to commit themselves to your cause, but you might be able to convince them to take a smaller step toward your ultimate goal.

At this point in the semester you have received feedback about your other speeches. Please note that because you have had the opportunity to hone your skills in two previous speeches, more is expected from you for this speech and you will be graded accordingly.

Make sure you review the grade sheet your instructor has posted for this assignment. It includes all the necessary elements of your speech and should serve as your guide/checklist to what you should include in your speech. Don't forget to pan out and show me your audience before you begin speaking if you are in an online section.

- Become familiar with the different types of commemorative speeches

- Understand how commemorative speeches differ from informative and persuasive speeches

- Learn some general guidelines for creating and delivering a commemorative address

14
Commemorative Speeches

You will hear a great many informative and persuasive speeches in your lifetime, but some of the more memorable presentations you encounter will be of neither type. Instead, you will be more likely to remember the creative and colorful commemorative speeches than you will the informative speech about the state of your company's finances or the persuasive speech designed to get you to vote for a candidate. These commemorative speeches are the third general category of presentations, and they contain characteristics that make them quite distinct from informative and persuasive remarks.

In this chapter, we will first explain the different types of commemorative speeches, paying particular attention to the contexts in which they occur. We will then detail how these speeches differ from informative and persuasive speeches before concluding the chapter with some helpful suggestions for creating and delivering a good commemorative address. As you will see, these speeches contain room for creativity and can be some of the most enjoyable speeches to write and deliver.

Types of Commemorative Speeches

Many different occasions call for a celebratory speech. These speeches are called commemorative because they commemorate, or celebrate, a person, event, object, or even an idea. In this section, we will identify and discuss five different forms of commemorative address with which you might be familiar. The first, and saddest, is a eulogy, which occurs when someone passes away. The second form of commemorative address is a toast, which is reserved for happier occasions. The next two take place when someone presents or receives an award. A fifth type is a speech of introduction. Finally, we will detail a specific form of commemorative address you will hear in the not-too-distant future: a graduation address.

Eulogies

eulogy
a speech that pays tribute to the life of the deceased

The first type of commemorative address we will discuss is a eulogy. Eulogies are emotional speeches; however, that emotion need not be one of sadness. As we indicated in the definition above, commemorative speeches are celebratory, not depressing, and so eulogies should be a celebration of a person's life, not a moment to focus on his or her death.

If you are called upon to deliver a eulogy you will most likely have a few days to prepare your remarks. These types of speeches should focus on major events and accomplishments in the life of the deceased. Since these speeches are celebratory and happy, you might also consider telling a humorous story about the deceased person. It is imperative, however, that you do not appear to mock the person but rather emphasize a positive quality he or she exemplified during life. This story helps to establish a common bond between you, the audience, and the dearly departed person.

Although eulogies are intensely personal and emotional speeches, you should take care to talk about the person in such a way that the audience feels involved. You should refrain from telling "inside jokes" that people in the audience would not understand or appreciate. The speech is as much a moment of emotional release for you as it is for them. In fact, eulogies are best understood as communal celebrations of a life and not personal retrospectives about another individual. They should emphasize the qualities of the person by telling specific stories from his or her life that illustrate those aspects. You are, in essence, creating a way to remember another person.

Toasts

In contrast to eulogies, one of the more entertaining and enjoyable commemorative speech events involves giving a toast. The most common occasion when toasts are used is a wedding. If you are the maid of honor or best man at a wedding, you will likely give a toast for the bride and groom. Like eulogies, wedding toasts are personal in nature and are celebrations of the union of two people. Of course, toasts occur at other times as well, such as at holidays and dinner parties, but the same general expectations apply. Usually you will know that you will be delivering a toast well in advance, so you will have plenty of time to prepare your remarks for the occasion.

There are certain characteristics and expectations common to all toasts. First, the person making the toast should talk about the person being toasted by connecting that person to the occasion and the audience. Often this is accomplished by telling a brief anecdote about the person you are toasting. In all toasts it is important to name the people being celebrated or honored and discuss the qualities that make them deserving of a toast. Remember that these events are celebratory in nature and should never be confused with roasts, during which the honoree is mocked. Toasts also are usually quite short, rarely going beyond two or three minutes.

Presenting an Award

Toasts are not the only way we commemorate the achievements of others; sometimes we present them with awards. Like toasts, presentations of awards are usually short because you, as the presenter, are not the focal point of the event. The important person is the one you are introducing. When presenting an award, there are certain goals you need to accomplish before handing over the microphone to the award recipient.

It is important to know if the winner of the award has been announced in advance or if you are the first to make the person aware of the award. If the award is announced in advance, then it is acceptable to talk about the individual by name, but if the awardee is not known to the audience then you should reserve the name until the very end of your remarks to maintain a sense of excitement and anticipation.

Regardless of whether you say the name of the honoree or conceal it to the end, when presenting an award you still need to do several things. First, talk about the award itself. If it is named after someone be sure to discuss who the individual was and why the award is named after him or her. Explain the qualities required to win the award and how the winner fits those characteristics. This connects the award recipient with the award itself, thus commemorating the recipient and the occasion. These remarks, however, differ from those you should prepare when receiving an award.

Receiving an Award

As we mentioned a moment ago when discussing speeches that present an award, sometimes honorees know they are getting an award and sometimes they do not. In either instance, usually (though not always) there is an indication that you might receive an award and should be prepared to speak. Based on contemporary practice, you might think that this type of commemorative address is a simple laundry list of "thank yous," but you would be mistaken. There are, in fact, certain expectations in a good award acceptance speech, and they begin with a level of humility.

Of course, expressing gratitude for receiving the award is important, and mentioning a few people who made your winning possible is always a nice thing to do, but it is not the only thing you should do. In fact, in accepting an award you should also express knowledge about the award itself and convey an appreciation of the qualities it celebrates. Thus, award acceptance speeches should exhibit gratitude and also an understanding of the award and what it commemorates. Doing this connects you to the award in a way the audience appreciates and wants to celebrate.

Graduation Addresses

Commencement, or graduation, is an important milestone in anyone's life, and that is why graduation ceremonies come paired with several different speeches celebrating the importance of the moment. School principals, presidents, keynote speakers, and class valedictorians often deliver remarks at these ceremonies. Should you be in a position to give a commencement address, there are several things you should keep in mind.

First, these speeches should be between five and seven minutes because there are many other elements to a graduation and you do not want to delay the ceremony with an unnecessarily long presentation. Additionally, these speeches should celebrate the achievements of the entire graduating class, not just yourself, so you should refer to common experiences and not personal achievements while in school. These speeches are also more forward looking than eulogies, or even toasts, and should contain some discussion of what will come for everyone after graduation. In this respect, commencement addresses are hopeful regarding the future. Finally, commencement addresses should thank those who made graduation possible.

> **Tips for giving a graduation speech**
>
> - speech should be between 5 and 7 minutes
> - celebrate the entire graduating class, not just yourself
> - look to the future and be hopeful
> - thank those people who made graduation possible

Whether it is a commencement address, eulogy, toast, or award ceremony, all commemorative speeches require that you tie the occasion to the audience. They also call for a positive tone; after all, commemorative speeches are celebrations of milestones or achievements. As they are celebratory in nature, such speeches are different from informative and persuasive speeches, and in the next section we will detail those differences.

Characteristics of Commemorative Speeches

All speeches have certain common requirements. For example, they need to be organized, keep the audience in mind, and rely on a balance of emotion, logic, and credibility in order to be successful. There are certain elements that make speeches different. Informative speeches, for instance, are designed to convey information to an audience, while persuasive speeches attempt to move an audience to a particular belief or action. Commemorative speeches seek neither of these goals but rather wield information in order to celebrate an event, person, object, or idea. This section of the chapter will illustrate what makes commemorative speeches different from informative and persuasive speeches.

Language Differences

One of the most significant differences between commemorative speeches and other forms of speech is that they rely on more colorful and ornate language. In an informative speech you fulfill the role of teacher by helping an audience understand a complicated subject. In a commemorative speech you draw an audience's attention with emotional and colorful language, not information. As you are well aware, there are many ways to say something, and the occasion and audience often dictate the best way to do it. Look at a couple of examples:

Basic: "Today we graduate."

Commemorative: "Today, we celebrate four years of tireless effort that allows us to open the next chapter in our lives."

Basic: "Today we celebrate Larry's retirement."

Commemorative: "Today we recognize Larry for his thirty years of service, the countless students he taught, and the lives he changed."

Notice in each example how the language makes the event more meaningful by being more elaborate and descriptive. This is a hallmark of any commemorative speech, whether it is a toast, a eulogy, or an award acceptance.

Emotional Quality

In using ornate language you tap into the second unique quality of commemorative speaking: the audience's emotions. How could someone not be emotional at someone's death or the celebration of a commencement? These are important events in our lives. Language provides a way to express that meaning to ourselves and others, so a commemorative address is by its very nature emotional. The emotions you express, however, must also be shared by the audience, so it is important to keep their feelings about the event in the forefront of your mind when developing a speech.

The Importance of Context

All speeches must pay attention to audience and context, but the degree to which this is necessary is heightened for commemorative speeches. Connecting the occasion to the audience through the values being celebrated is the core element of any commemorative speech. Yes, knowing and adapting to an audience is necessary in informative and persuasive speeches, but in commemorative speaking the context, or occasion, is the focus of the speech, which is not something to which you adapt.

Less Rigid Organization

One thing you should note when constructing a commemorative speech is that there are no set organizational patterns as there are with an informative or persuasive speech. When celebrating a person or commemorating an event it does not make sense to have previews or set patterns for addressing a problem. In fact, the best way to arrange main points in a commemorative speech is topically. Make sure the topics connect to the values you are honoring in the individual or event. This topical arrangement provides commemorative addresses with a less rigid structure.

Just because they are less rigid, though, does not mean that commemorative speeches have no required elements. Commemorative addresses still entail getting the attention of the audience and signaling that the end of the speech is near, but they do not contain summaries and have little cited material. They also still necessitate an engaging delivery and depend more than other speeches on the speaker's tone and delivery to emotionally connect with the audience. Simply put, if you are celebrating something your delivery and demeanor should convey excitement to the audience.

As you can see, commemorative speeches have some similarities and some differences from informative and persuasive speeches. In this final section, we will provide guidelines to help you construct commemorative speeches.

Guidelines for Commemorative Speeches

Due to their unique nature, commemorative speeches require careful attention, often in shorter periods of time than persuasive or informative speeches. After all, we are usually given plenty of advance notice when we are asked to help nonexperts learn about something or give persuasive speeches, especially in a business setting.

Commemorative speeches come with some, but often not much, time to get your thoughts in order before presenting to an audience. To help you prepare, we will provide three guidelines for constructing commemorative speeches.

1. Connect the Audience to the Event

It is crucial for a commemorative speech to use language to connect the audience to the event. Examples of ways to accomplish this include:

- Note the reason why everyone is there together.
- Note the significance of the event.
- Note how you connect to the event, and then how the audience does as well.
- Tell stories that exemplify the values being celebrated.

Practical Politics

When working in politics, you will be called on to give numerous speeches, and many of these will be ceremonial speeches. Here are a few examples of ceremonial speeches you might be asked to give:

- Speeches to pay tribute to those who are honored on holidays (Memorial Day, Labor Day, Mother's Day, etc.)
- Speeches to commemorate the opening of new buildings, monuments, memorials, parks, and other public spaces
- Commencement addresses at high schools, colleges, and universities
- Toasts at dinners and receptions that honor special guests
- Speeches to present awards traditionally handed out by those in the office you hold
- Eulogies for other public figures
- Speeches when receiving honors or awards from organizations

Each of these strategies helps the audience members understand why they are gathered at the event and situates the actual gathering as the most important element of the occasion.

2. Use Descriptive Language

Commemorative speaking turns the speaker into an artist who creates a visual image of an important event. The best way to do this is by using colorful, vivid, and ornate language. Commemorative speeches do not happen every day, and so you should not use everyday language when delivering them. Rather, take the time to detail what the occasion means, why it means what it does, and why people should celebrate. This takes time and creativity, so be sure to think through exactly what feeling you want to convey and use language that does exactly that.

3. Consider the Audience

Finally, you need to consider the expectations of the audience. If you are speaking at commencement, then graduation should be the center of your speech, as that is what the audience expects to hear about. Sometimes speakers use these events to push their personal agendas, addressing politics and other topics not relevant to the occasion, but that is not what the audience is there for. This is not to say that a speaker could not exhort the audience, especially the graduates, to be involved in their cause, but that should be held to a minimum. Instead, focus on the moment and the values embedded within it that are being celebrated.

Summary

In this chapter, we identified various elements that make commemorative speaking the third form of address. We detailed five different types of commemorative speeches that you may encounter and provided tips for how to approach developing each of them. We also elaborated on the differences and similarities between commemorative, persuasive, and informative speaking. Lastly, we provided some guidelines for developing and delivering commemorative speeches.

Key Terms

eulogy   118

15
Presentation Aids

In many respects speeches are no longer what they used to be. Sure, they still have the same general formats, structures, and purposes, but the manner in which people deliver them has changed substantially in recent years. Until recently speakers would stand in front of an audience and detail their main points. If the speech was complicated, then the audience just had to pay really close attention. Today, however, speakers have ways that they can use to take complicated materials and make them more understandable. These presentation aids fundamentally transformed professions in which speaking is an essential part of the job, such as teaching. Today's advanced digital and multimedia platforms provide great assistance to speakers, but they must be used properly.

In this chapter, we will address presentation aids, or as they are more commonly called, visual aids, and explain how to properly use them in your speech. We will first go over traditional types of aids before moving on to more advanced technological types. Finally, we will provide guidelines for implementing and using these aids within your speech so that they help, rather than hurt, your presentation.

Traditional Aids

Presentation aids come in a variety of different forms, but each has its purpose. Today we focus more on PowerPoint™, Prezi™, Keynote™, and other digital means for aiding a presentation; however, much of what appears in these platforms is merely a digital representation of basic traditional presentation aids. In this section, we will discuss five of these traditional aids, which have been used for many years. We call them traditional presentation aids because they do not necessarily appear in electronic forms. For instance, for many years transparencies were used by both professors and students when providing information such as graphs of data. Transparencies may be moving toward extinction, but graphs are not. So here we will explain the traditional ways of visually depicting complicated information so that you may then incorporate them into a multimedia presentation.

Models

model
a three-dimensional representation of an actual object

The first type of traditional aid we will go over is a model, which is a three-dimensional representation of an actual object. To be effective, models need to be made to scale so that the audience gets an idea of what they are looking at and how it might function in its actual environment. Science teachers often use a scale model of human organs, such as the brain or heart. Museums also contain models of prehistoric settings; while students at science fairs create models of the solar system, with the sun in the center and the planets represented in their proper positions. These visual representations show how things are represented in space while allowing the audience to see them in a reasonable size. It would be very hard, for example, for a speaker to use a model of the heart at its actual size when speaking to an audience of fifty, so they create a model to scale to enable everyone to see it.

Charts

chart
visual depiction of summaries of numeric data

Models are not the only traditional form of presentation aid useful to speakers. A more common example is a chart, such as a frequency table. Charts allow you to visually depict summaries of numeric data for an audience. For example, if a manager is briefing his superiors on how productive different geographic regions have been in terms of sales, he might construct a chart that depicts sales for each region of the country and rank them from highest to lowest earnings. Charts help audiences quickly identify key points about data that would normally take a longer time to explain.

Graphs

graph
a type of chart that illustrates numeric data by using a visual diagram

One specific type of chart that speakers often rely on is a graph. Graphs help illustrate how numerical data relate to one another. Statistics are helpful if the audience can understand them, and graphs illustrate the impact and relationship of numerical information. Graphs also come in many forms, and you should choose the one that best illustrates your information to the audience in an uncomplicated way.

line graph
a graph that uses lines drawn along two axes that show growth, loss, or flat developments over time

Let's briefly examine the three types of graphs that are most commonly used as presentation aids. First there are line graphs, which use lines drawn along two axes to show growth, loss, or flat developments over time (see Figure 15.1)

FIGURE 15.1

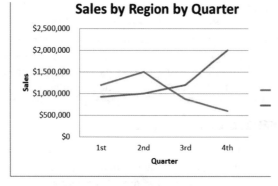

bar graph
a graph which shows two axes and bars going either horizontally or vertically to represent total achievement

Next there are bar graphs, which also show two axes, but the bars run either horizontally or vertically to represent total achievement. For example, the vertical axis can be years, while the horizontal axis represents profit for a business in millions of dollars. The bars extend up for each year to the total profit achieved in that year (see Figure 15.2).

FIGURE 15.2

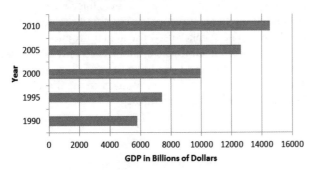

The third type of graph is a **histogram**, which is similar in appearance to a bar graph. A histogram is a visual representation of a frequency table in which the categories are placed on the horizontal axis, while vertical bars are used to represent the number (or frequency) of individuals that fit into that category. Histograms are usually used when data is continuous, so the categories on the horizontal axis represent an interval of scores that make up that category. For example, you might use a histogram to represent the grades that were earned on the first speech in class. Grade categories (A, B, C, etc.) would be shown on the horizontal axis, and the height of the vertical bar would represent the number of people who earned a specific grade (see Figure 15.3).

histogram
a visual representation of a frequency table in which the categories are placed on the horizontal axis and vertical bars are used to represent the number (or frequency) of individuals that fit into that category

FIGURE 15.3

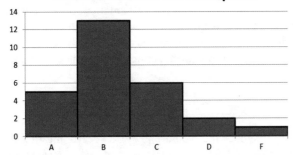

Finally, we have **pie graphs**, which are circles that are "sliced" apart to represent percentages of the total "pie" for particular groups or categories (see Figure 15.4).

pie graph
a graph that shows circles that are "sliced" apart to represent percentages of the total "pie" for particular groups or categories

FIGURE 15.4

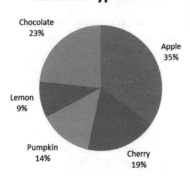

There are several types of graphs from which you may choose, and you should select the one that best represents your point.

Objects

object
the thing being discussed, not a model or representation of that thing

The fourth type of traditional presentation aid we will detail is an object. An **object** differs from a model in that it is the actual thing being discussed and not a representation of it constructed to scale. Objects are useful presentation aids for speakers who seek to demonstrate something to an audience. Think about the now-infamous infomercials for the cleaning product called a Sham Wow™. The speaker used the actual product in a demonstration for the audience while explaining how and why it operated. Objects should be used only when they are of a reasonable and accessible size, as you do not want to carry around large bulky items. There are also some types of objects that you are not allowed to bring into a classroom, including weapons, alcohol, illegal substances, and live animals. In those instances you should simply use a model or a picture.

Photographs

photograph
a picture of the object about which you are speaking

The fifth and last type of traditional presentation aid is a **photograph**. Today's digital cameras and cellular phones allow you instant access to an image. There is a vast assortment of photographs available on the Internet. Photos allow the audience to experience the event, action, or person in a real-life context. They can also generate an emotional response from the audience, thus enhancing your appeal.

Traditional speaking aids have been around for a while, but with technological advances, speakers now have a variety of options available. In the next section, we will discuss how technology has enhanced our delivery options with presentation aids.

Technological Aids

Technology has enhanced our ability to make presentations and changed the manner in which we can use traditional presentation aids. Now we can provide video and audio technology with our presentation, thus making it even more dynamic. It is important to remember, however, that these technological tools, although exciting and attractive, do not substitute for, and should not overshadow, your speech. In this section, we will discuss how video and audio can enhance a speech, as well as provide you with tips for constructing effective slideshow presentations using PowerPoint™, Keynote™, Prezi™, or other similar programs.

Video

Video can be very effective in short bursts, but you must remember that you are giving a speech and that the video is an aid, not your entire speech. Frankly, the video should not be a large part of your presentation. Prerecorded videos, YouTube clips, or other such videos should be used to help an audience understand a point you are making, not just to fill the time. They also require that you explain where the video came from and how it is relevant to the point under discussion. Without the explanation the audience will feel that the video clip was used simply to add time, and they will not understand its connection to the speech topic.

There are numerous times when a brief video clip would help to enhance a speech. In a demonstration speech a presenter may use a video explaining how to use a particular tool or accomplish a specific task. In persuasive speaking, videos may be helpful to enhance testimonial evidence by allowing the audience to see the people as they endorse a product. Regardless of what you are trying to accomplish by showing the video, do not comment while the video is playing; let the audience focus their attention on the medium. If you need to explain something happening in the video, pause it to do so. This ensures that the audience stays focused on the message and not the presentation aid.

Business Basics

It is common for business professionals to deliver presentations and hold meetings via Web conference technology such as WebEx, Adobe Connect, or other videoconferencing software. In many businesses, especially sales organizations, this allows professionals to work from home part or all of the time, which cuts down on office and travel costs and allows them to interact with several clients in several locations in a single day. When using a conferencing tool such as WebEx you should follow the same guidelines you would if you were using PowerPoint™ for an in-person presentation. However, you will need to be deliberate about soliciting verbal feedback and using effective animations to draw attention to particular parts of your slides, especially in online presentations in which you are not using a webcam.

Audio

In addition to video, audio can also be a good supplement to a speech, but, like video, it has some limitations. Audio clips allow an audience to hear expert and peer testimony straight from the source, rather than paraphrased or quoted by you. Audio can also help provide sound effects that illustrate key sounds in a speech that you cannot deliver on your own. For example, an engineer could explain how to identify when a machine is stalling due to a malfunctioning piece of equipment by providing the particular sound it makes.

Audio is, however, not usually used on its own. In fact, you should always ask yourself if the audio clip you intend to play for the audience helps them understand something more clearly. If it does, then you are using it appropriately, but if it does not, then you should not incorporate it into your presentation. In any event, technologies such as audio and video can be combined with the more traditional presentation aids we discussed earlier.

Slideshow Presentations

In the last twenty years presentation software has been readily available for students, professors, and professionals to use when delivering remarks. You can now choose from PowerPoint™, Keynote™, Prezi™, and several other platforms to create a dynamic and colorful slideshow.

We first discuss a mistake that many novices make when creating slideshows: wordiness. In essence, placing too many words on slides turns them into giant note cards that are then read to and by the audience. This design is unprofessional and defeats the purpose of visual aids by distracting the audience from your speech. Remember that these are *presentation aids*, not your entire presentation. Professors are often guilty of this approach. Think of teachers you might have had who put their entire lecture on PowerPoint slides. We would wager you paid more attention to writing down what was on the slide than listening to and understanding what the instructors were saying. Salespeople are also often guilty of putting too much information on slides for sales presentations.

Embedding Video and Audio

You may want to embed video or audio into your speech. Embedding a video allows you to save the video directly in your slideshow program so that you do not have to link to an external Web site, such as YouTube, to show the video clip. Most presentation software programs allow you to do this, but you should practice to make sure it works the way you want. This is especially important if you will be using a different computer during your presentation, since there are occasional compatibility problems among operating systems or software. Another option for displaying video is to link directly to the URL on an overhead slide. The problem with this approach is that the Internet might be down, which would mean you would not be able to access the link. Whenever possible, it is a good idea to embed the video in the slide and include the URL in the notes field so that you have a backup option for showing the video.

Color Schemes

Slideshow presentation programs have a myriad of color selections from which you may choose. It is important to be aware, however, that not all color schemes go well together. Color can help your audience focus on a specific item on the slide, and it can also contribute to the mood or emotional dimensions of your speech. There are three significant areas for which you choose color applications on slides: background, borders, and lettering. It is important that the lettering be visible, so do not choose the same or similar color for the background and borders. If you are using a dark background, use light-colored text, and vice versa.

One simple color scheme to use is black and white, but these colors do not generate much energy. Certain topics lend themselves to a particular color palette. For example, a speech about breast cancer might use pink, while one about communism might use red. Whichever color pattern you use, realize that what you see on your computer monitor may not look the same as what you will see in a classroom on a giant overhead monitor. To avoid this potentially catastrophic problem, test your color pattern in advance.

Animation

Many slideshow programs now allow for rudimentary forms of animation. Animation can be clever, but it can also be distracting and even cause headaches and nervousness in your audience. Having spinning pinwheels and stars fading in and out may be creative, but do not assume that it makes your speech better. If you use animation, make sure it is fleeting and does not run throughout your speech. For example, you might have a key word quickly fly into place or use animation to highlight a specific part of a diagram. After it has served its purpose, you should disengage the animation and focus upon the remaining portion of your speech. If used correctly, animation can help bring something to the audience's attention, but it can also distract from your speech.

Dos and Don'ts of Slideshow Usage

Constructing a slideshow can seem like you are writing a whole new presentation. Developing the slides can become a distraction when preparing to speak because it is a uniquely creative endeavor that taps into our desire to invent things. Table 15.1 provides a list of dos and dont's for creating a slideshow.

TABLE 15.1

Dos and Don'ts of Slideshow Usage	
Do	**Don't**
• Prepare slides carefully	• Use if unnecessary
• Make sure slides are of the proper size	• Speak to the aid
• Practice with your slides	• Look too much at the aid
• Ensure slides are visually pleasing	• Trust technology
• Have a backup plan	• Use slides as note cards
• Ensure slides are relevant	• Use as an outline
• Refer to slides when discussing them	• Depend upon them too much

As you can see, regardless of their format, presentation aids can assist you with your speech's success if used properly. In the final section, we will provide you with some basic guidelines to consider when preparing presentation aids. Realize that each speaking situation has its own opportunities and challenges, so what works in one speech does not automatically work in another.

Guidelines for Using Presentation Aids

There are several things you should think about when considering presentation aids. First, they should be used to help you accomplish the goals of your speech. They should help the audience understand complicated evidence, testimony, or arguments. They should not be used as a form of window dressing, nor should they be a distraction to you or the audience.

The type of presentation aid you use depends on what your topic is and what you want your audience to retain. Research has shown that presentation aids help the audience remember certain aspects of your speech but not the whole thing. Besides, you want the content of your speech, not the actual aids you used, to be the takeaway for an audience.

The next thing to consider is how to deliver a speech with presentation aids. When speaking, your focus should always be your audience; do not turn and talk to the aid. Speak to the audience as if the aid were not there, and if you need to mention it to the audience, then do so when discussing the points you wish to make. Remove each aid you use as soon as you are finished so that your audience is not distracted. One helpful way to do this with slideshows is to insert blank slides at points where you know the aid is not needed. This is much better than placing an unnecessary visual in view of the audience.

Finally, practice your speech with the presentation aids. You need to appear comfortable handling them and transitioning between slides, and to do this requires practice. This also creates the impression that the aids are extensions of you and your content and not a distinctly separate element of the talk.

Summary

Presentation aids help speeches become memorable and dynamic, thus increasing the chances that your message will come across to an audience. They come in many forms, and the nature of your speech should dictate which aids are the most applicable to your presentation. In this chapter we reviewed the different types of visual aids, from the traditional forms to the contemporary digital slideshow. Regardless, the same general principle applies: presentation aids help the audience follow and understand, but they are not the speech itself.

Key Terms

bar graph   124
charts   124
graphs   124
histogram   125
line graph   124
model   124
object   126
photograph   126
pie graph   125

In COMM 1000/1003

When you deliver a PPT presentation you need to remember the slide design principle your instructor covered in class that is known as assertion-evidence design. This approach ensures that your visual aid focuses on the "visual" aspects related to your topic. As a quick review, each slide of your PPT presentation should include a sentence headline at the topic and a corresponding image. Do not include bullet points or additional explanations using "words" on the PPT. Your verbal explanations are all that are needed to explain and reinforce the image on each slide. Using assertion-evidence design does require more time and thought and makes for a much more appealing and effective visual aid to accompany your speech.

- Learn the characteristics of language

- Familiarize yourself with the structure of language

- Recognize different language devices used in speech

16
Language

There are many things that separate humans from the rest of the animal kingdom, but none is more unique and powerful than language. This is not to say that birds, insects, reptiles, fish, and mammals do not communicate, but they cannot communicate abstract ideas. Human beings alone are uniquely capable of creating meaning in their surroundings through the use of a complex system of symbols we call language. Language is also the primary building block of any speech, whether it is informative, persuasive, or commemorative.

In this chapter, we will give some insight into language and how it influences people every day. First we will discuss the particular characteristics of language and then cover how language is structured. Third, we will explore some language devices that creatively use words to help craft appealing messages. Finally, we will provide basic guidelines for how to use language in your speeches.

Language Characteristics

Not every noise people make constitutes language. In fact, there are several characteristics that define language. In this section, we will discuss four characteristics that define language and explain how language functions differently in spoken and written forms. Each of these components creates both inherent difficulties and opportunities when connecting with and influencing people around us.

Arbitrary

The first characteristic of language to note is that it is arbitrary. By arbitrary we mean that words, which are merely symbols, have no real relationship to what they represent. For example, the word textbook has no real relationship with the physical or electronic manifestation it represents; it only has the meaning and relationship that we assign to it in everyday usage. We assign meaning by using language to

arbitrary
symbols used to represent things that are not intrinsically connected to those things

create labels for things, but those labels have no inherent tie to the object they represent. This arbitrary nature of language helps explain how different cultures can have different words representing the same thing.

Ambiguous

ambiguous
language that does not have precise, concrete meanings

In addition to being arbitrary, language is also ambiguous. The ambiguity of language refers to the fact that words do not have precise or exact meanings and can be used in a variety of different capacities. Take the word "viral," for instance. In one context viral could mean a virus, or illness, that someone may contract. In another it could mean an Internet video that became immensely popular in a short period of time. Other words that exhibit this type of flexibility include "cool," "hot," "chill," and even "love." Language's ambiguous quality is what often leads to misunderstandings between people; one person uses a word to mean one thing, while the receiver interprets it in a different way.

Abstract

abstract
words are not concrete or tangible items; they are only representations

The third characteristic of language is that it is abstract. Language cannot be touched, no matter how hard you might try to touch it. It is intangible and thus abstract. Even more fascinating is that some words are more abstract than others when they refer to less specific things. For example, "animal" is more abstract than "canine," which is more abstract than "golden retriever." The more precise the language, the less chance for misunderstandings to occur. This shows how language can be more concrete or more abstract, depending on the labels you choose to use.

FIGURE 16.1

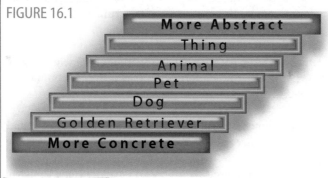

Hierarchical

hierarchical
language that is structured according to more or less, higher or lower

As humans, we all seek to create order in the world around us, and the primary means by which we do this is through language. Language allows us to order things from top to bottom, more to less, or larger to smaller. This ordering process illustrates the fourth quality of language: it is hierarchical. This means that language creates structure and value through ordering things along a continuum. Think of how college is structured. You begin as a freshman, then move up to sophomore status, after which you grow into a junior, until finally you enter your senior year. This is framed as a progression upward, but there is no physical direction there except that which we provide through language. The structure creates new levels with higher value above the older ones, creating an artificial hierarchy. We do the same with main points in a speech by ordering them from least important or powerful to most important or powerful. In fact, outlining is itself an exercise in creating a hierarchy. Figure 16.1 shows an example of hierarchical language.

Spoken vs. Written Language

Even though we use language in both oral and written forms, it functions differently in each. There are two key elements that differentiate language in these two contexts. The first is that spoken language is irreversible; once you say something you cannot "unsay" it. We can apologize or even try to refute our own statements, but the fact remains that we did say the words, and those words had an impact on anyone who was listening. On the other hand, when writing something on paper or even on a computer screen, you can erase it or destroy it before sending it to a recipient, thus making it as if it were never written in the first place.

The second difference between spoken and written language is that spoken language is less formal than written language; we do not speak the way we write. When speaking, we use more pedestrian, or colloquial words, including slang. Additionally, we use contractions, whereas when writing an essay we do not use this shorthand method of message construction. Keep this in mind when writing a speech, because if you end up speaking the way you write, your language will come across as awkward to the audience.

Now that we have identified the key components of language and illustrated how it functions differently in oral and written media, we can get down to how language can be structured for maximum impact on an audience.

Structuring Language

Language, as you can tell from its characteristics, is a flexible thing that we can adjust, shift, and essentially "play with" to create impressions for our audience. Following are several different ways we can structure the language we use to create impressions that influence an audience. In this section, we will discuss four ways to structure words in a speech to create memorable lines and creative representations of our argument.

Repetition

The first way to structure language is through repetition, which involves repeating words and phrases. One of the more well-known examples of repetition occurred in Dr. Martin Luther King Jr.'s famous "I Have a Dream" speech, in which the title phrase is repeated over and over in one section. Anytime you repeat a word or phrase it improves the chances that the audience will pay attention and remember what you said. Repetition is, therefore, a useful tool for highlighting key moments and ideas within a speech. Repetition also creates a certain rhythm to your delivery.

repetition
repeating words and phrases

Alliteration

Alliteration, or repeating the same consonant or vowel sound at the beginning of subsequent words, is another tool you can employ to enhance your speech. Here are some examples of alliteration at work:

> "Bitter batter befuddles the brain."
>
> "Time, talents, and treasure"
>
> "Peace, prosperity, and progress"

alliteration
repeating the same consonant or vowel sound at the beginning of subsequent words

The use of the same consonant structure to start subsequent words makes the phrase much more appealing to the ear, but you must also make sure the words you use relate to each other in more ways than sound.

Parallelism

The third structure of language we will explain is parallelism, or similarly structuring related words, phrases, or clauses of speech. Parallelism places related concepts in a pattern that helps highlight the qualities they all have in common. Here are some examples:

parallelism
similarly structuring related words, phrases, or clauses of speech

> "My hobbies are boating, hiking, and fishing."
>
> "Who we are is who we were, and everything we will become."
>
> "Love is patient, love is kind. It does not envy, it does not boast, it is not proud."

In each example the qualities and items listed relate to each other in the same way. In the first example, all three hobbies are described using present participle verbs (verbs that end in *-ing*). In the second example, *we* is repeatedly followed by a different tense of the verb *to be* (*are, were, will become*). In the third example, the first two phrases are identical except for the last word; similarly, the last three phrases end with a different word but are otherwise nearly identical. Parallelism adds a poetic element to your language, makes your message more memorable, and helps the audience pay close attention to the key elements of the message.

Antithesis

antithesis
when two ideas that sharply contrast with one another are put side by side in a parallel structure

The last type of structure we will discuss is antithesis, which is when two ideas that sharply contrast with one another are put side by side in a parallel structure. This is a highly involved and creative way to illustrate a point by means of the careful construction of a sentence. One of the more famous quotations by a president is an example of antithesis. That was John F. Kennedy's famous declaration that citizens should "Ask not what your country can do for you, but what you can do for your country." Here he takes two seemingly opposite ideas and contrasts them to make a point. Here are some other examples of antithesis:

> "As the jet soared higher in the air the moods of the passengers sank."
>
> "We can all learn together, or we can all fail individually."

Antithesis is very useful in pointing out how two ideas contrast with one another, and it is a very creative way to deliver a message to an audience. It forces them to think about the relationship between the parts of the statement in order to discern what it means.

These types of language structures are not the only creative capabilities of language. In fact, there are several other language devices worthy of note that you can use within your speeches.

Language Devices

There are many different forms that language can take, and what words you choose to use will determine whether your speech is boring or memorable. These linguistic devices can be as creative as the grammatical structures we just covered or as simple as choosing the right word. In this section, we will focus on the latter and explore four linguistic devices that can help you create an interesting and appealing message.

Similes

simile
linguistic device that compares two things through the use of "like" or "as"

The first linguistic device we will discuss is the simile, which compares two things in a way that allows each to maintain its own respective properties while still making a connection between them. Similes are generally identified by the use of either "like" or "as." Here are some examples:

> "He sweats like a horse."
>
> "She is as happy as a lark."
>
> "Your smile is like a sunrise."

In similes both terms being compared are present in the statement. You know they are compared in certain respects, but not all, through the appearance of "like" and "as." Similes are useful, but they are not the only way to compare objects for an audience.

Metaphors

metaphor
linguistic device that allows for comparisons between two objects by highlighting qualities of each object in explicit comparison

Metaphors are another linguistic device that allows comparisons between two objects. The difference between metaphors and similes can best be explained by stating that all similes are metaphors, but not all metaphors are similes. (Yes, that last sentence was another example of antithesis.) Take the prior examples, for instance. They are metaphoric because they highlight qualities of each object in their explicit comparison. However, not all metaphors are so exact and explicit in their comparisons. In fact, most metaphors do not function that way. Let's briefly explore metaphors that do not qualify as similes.

synecdoche
using one part of something to represent the whole thing

Synecdoche: The first type of metaphor we will explain is a synecdoche, which is when we use one part of something to represent the whole thing. An example of synecdoche is the statement "We watched a number of sails pass through the strait." The sail is not the entire boat or ship but rather a part of the ship being used to reference the entire ship. Synecdoches do not explicitly use "like" or "as," but rather, like most metaphors, make the implicit connection between the two objects.

Metonymy: The next metaphor is called a metonymy, which involves using a tangible object to represent an otherwise intangible thing. Metonymies occur when you hear things like hard work being called "blood, sweat, and tears," or love being called someone's "heart." In both applications a tangible object becomes a metaphor for the intangible concept. This helps make a description more vivid and concrete.

Archetypal: Archetypal metaphors transcend culture, as they relate to common human experiences. Things such as seasons, disease, and light and dark are often used as archetypal metaphors. Think about how the forces of "light and darkness" are used to represent "good and evil," how some sports teams have players they refer to as "clubhouse cancers," or how senior citizens are sometimes characterized as in the "twilight of their days." Each of these metaphors uses common human experiences to describe another object, thus making them archetypal metaphors.

Mixed: The final type of metaphor is a mixed metaphor, in which you combine two objects that have no logical connection with each other. Mixed metaphors are common in everyday language. We often hear sayings such as "He is a wolf in sheep's clothing" and "You could have knocked me over with a feather." These are mixed because the idea of being stunned and a feather's weight have no logical connection in most contexts, nor do animals like wolves and sheep have any relationship to clothing or disguise. Mixed metaphors can add color to your speech, but be careful; the more you mix them, the greater the chance the audience will not see the connection.

Narratives

Metaphors and similes use words and phrases to construct their meaning, but some other language devices use more than that to create impressions with an audience. One such extended language device is that of the narrative, which essentially is a story. Narrative theory suggests that all human beings are story-telling animals, and so everything we say is a story. We tell stories when we give speeches, and we use other stories as examples in our speeches. The thing about stories, though, is that they have a beginning, middle, and end, so you should never leave the audience without finishing a narrative you began. Narratives are powerful tools because, as the speaker, you control what happens in your story and you can tell it in a way that maximizes its ability to connect with your argument and your audience. One especially effective way to use narrative in your speech is to use a bookend story. When using a bookend story the speaker tells the first part of a story as an attention getter in the introduction of the speech and then finishes the story at the end of the conclusion.

Guidelines for Using Language

As we have illustrated in this chapter, language is a powerful tool for any speaker, and it can be deployed in a variety of different ways. Thanks to its ability to move an audience, there are several things you must keep in mind as you develop your speech.

1. **Avoid profanity:** Profanity refers to language that is vulgar and irreverent. Profanity gets you nowhere in a speech and will likely insult and offend your audience, and drive them away from you. Profanity also makes you sound less educated and coarse. In short, avoid it.

2. **Avoid hate speech:** Hate speech involves attacking a person or group of people based on their gender, ethnicity, religion, sexual orientation, social actions, or any other category that indicates applications of a negative, unwarranted stereotype. Sometimes people use this unethical behavior to incite violence against an individual or group. Be aware that your school very well may have a policy prohibiting hate speech. Whether or not such a policy exists on your campus, you should never use hate speech.

3. **Overuse of metaphors:** Do not overuse metaphors. They can add color, be pleasing to the audience, and even help explain things to your audience, but their overuse can cause you to look like a bad poet and thus distract your audience and even hurt your credibility.

4. **Use vivid language when telling a story:** Telling an interesting and vivid story can enhance your speech. Using vivid language paints a picture and makes it easier for the audience to comprehend your story and its relationship to your speech.

metonymy
using a tangible object to represent an otherwise intangible thing

archetypal metaphor
metaphor that uses common human experiences to describe another object

mixed metaphor
metaphor that compares two objects that have no logical connection with each other

narrative
a story

bookend story
a narrative in which the speaker tells the first part of a story as an attention getter in the introduction of the speech and then finishes the story in the closer at the end of the conclusion

profanity
language that is vulgar and irreverent

hate speech
attacking a person or group of people based upon their gender, ethnicity, religion, sexual orientation, social actions, or any other category that indicates applications of a negative, unwarranted stereotype

5. **Use language with which you are familiar:** We have all heard people try to use words and phrases that sounded awkward or meant something the speaker did not believe they meant. Before choosing to use a word be sure you are comfortable with it, know its definition, and can pronounce it correctly. If you don't adhere to this recommendation, you will sound awkward and the audience will notice, thus taking the focus off your message and onto your misuse of language.

6. **Use inclusive language:** It is certainly fine to use "I" language when needed, but if you can use "us" and "we," then this will help to generate good will with the audience by making the audience feel included in the speech. Moreover, you should make sure that your language includes all members of your audience. Many words and phrases that are commonly used imply unwarranted assumptions that particular jobs are only an appropriate choice for either men or women, or that all members of the audience have the same sexual orientation. If you are giving a speech about law enforcement and use the term "policeman," you are ignoring and excluding all of the women who also work as police officers. If you talk about women trying to find "Mr. Right" or men trying to find a girlfriend, you exclude and ignore everyone in the LGBT community. When giving a speech, use inclusive language to help your entire audience connect with your topic and to show respect for all members of your audience. Table 16.1 gives examples of exclusive and inclusive terms.

TABLE 16.1

Inclusive Language	
Terms that Exclude	**Terms that Include**
Policeman	Police officer
Mailman	Mail carrier
Stewardess	Flight attendant
Congressman	Representative, congressperson
Mankind	Humanity
Boyfriends, girlfriends	Significant others
Fireman	Firefighter

7. **Use active voice:** Active voice is much more energetic than passive voice. You can easily identify passive voice by looking for forms of the verb *to be* immediately before an action verb. It takes care and effort to eliminate passive voice, but it is well worth it and creates a much more exciting speech. Here is an example of passive voice: "As his speed picked up while going downhill his brakes were slammed on." Now note the difference when put into active voice: "He slammed on the brakes when he began to pick up speed while going downhill."

8. **Avoid wordiness:** Wordiness occurs when you use too many words to make a point. You should be as concise as possible, ensuring that you do not leave out content. Wordiness can lead to rambling and can cause the audience to drift away. Wordiness also can hurt your delivery and cause you to get off track or even lose your place in the speech.

9. **Adapt your language to your audience:** When choosing your words, keep your audience in mind. If you are speaking to an audience of experts, you can use words and jargon that are commonly known in that field, and using such language will help to show that you are a member of that group of experts. However, if you are speaking to an audience of nonexperts, you should use simpler language that the audience will understand easily.

Summary

Language is something that makes human beings unique in this world. The symbol system used to convey meaning and ideas to one another is a powerful tool for speaking. Language is both powerful and dangerous because it is arbitrary, ambiguous, abstract, and grounded in hierarchy. In this chapter, we discussed how using language in the oral tradition differs from the written form. In either context, however, the different structures and linguistic devices we explored in the chapter are useful for creatively and artfully constructing memorable messages for an audience. We also provided some quick and useful tips to consider when deciding how to say something to an audience in the best possible way.

Key Terms

abstract   132
alliteration   133
ambiguous   132
antithesis   134
arbitrary   131
archetypal metaphors   135
bookend story   135
hate speech   135
hierarchal   132

metaphors   134
metonymy   135
mixed metaphor   135
narrative   135
parallelism   133
profanity   135
repetition   133
simile   134
synecdoche   134

In COMM 1000/1003

Please remember you are in a classroom, which means things you might say to close friends or family members won't come across in the same way to a room full of mere acquaintances. There's something about being in a classroom environment that makes certain topics or the phrasing of certain words uncomfortable for the audience. Remember those times in middle school when your entire grade had to gather for talks about things like "hygiene" or the "differences in boys and girls"? Remember how awkward and uncomfortable those moments were for everyone? Remember all the nervous laughter surrounding those topics? It doesn't change in college. While the only off-limits topics were addressed in an earlier chapter, keep in mind that being in a classroom will have an impact on how an audience responds to your topic in general and that some topics aren't great for a classroom environment

- Understand the different modes of delivery

- Learn the verbal and nonverbal aspects of speech delivery

- Acquaint yourself with some tips for good speech delivery

17
Delivery

When people think about the difference between a good speech and a bad speech, they focus almost exclusively on one aspect: delivery. Delivery is the most visual element of any speech, but it also conveys the least amount of concrete information. For that reason we spent significant time explaining ways to construct your argument before wading into instruction on delivery. Now, however, it is time to turn our attention toward delivery.

In this chapter, we will discuss four different modes of speech delivery, each of which is unique in its own right. Then we will cover verbal delivery, which involves anything related to the delivery of the speech's content via words to the audience, and physical delivery, which has to do with visual aspects of speech delivery. Finally, we will provide you with some tips for a successful delivery.

Modes of Delivery

All speeches are not created, nor are they delivered, the same. In fact, there are four primary means through which a person may deliver a speech. Each one comes with a different set of challenges and benefits, and the choice of whether to use one or another is largely dependent upon the context in which you will speak. In this section, we will explore each of these four delivery types.

Memorized Speeches

The first form of speech delivery we will discuss is also the one that engenders the most fear for novice speakers; it also happens to be the least commonly found speech in society today. Memorized speech delivery is when the speaker has no notes and has, instead, committed the entire speech to memory. This was a common practice in Ancient Greece and Rome, but today it is not employed very often. In fact, it is so rare that we strongly urge you not to memorize your speech.

memorized speech
when a speaker commits an entire speech to memory and delivers with no notes in front of him/her

There are a couple of very good reasons for this recommendation. The first is that you might forget what you are supposed to say. With no notes to rely on, this would cause you to freeze and create a very uncomfortable situation for you and your audience. The second reason we advocate against memorizing your speech is that, unless you are trained in how to deliver it properly, a memorized speech will sound unnatural and awkward. Memorized speeches also force you to focus on content and do not allow for natural delivery, so you increase the chances of appearing stiff in front of your audience. Finally, memorized speeches leave no room for adapting to audience feedback, which we already emphasized as an important element of a successful speech.

Manuscript Speeches

manuscript speech

when a speaker has an entire speech written out word-for-word in front of him/her as he/she speaks

The second type of speech is a manuscript speech. Manuscript speeches are written out word for word in an essay format. This approach is actually more common today than memorized speeches. Politicians deliver manuscript speeches though a TelePrompter™, a machine that allows them to read the speech as it scrolls up the screen in front of them. Likewise, news anchors typically speak using a TelePrompter™. Manuscript speaking may sound seductively simple at first, but it is harder than it sounds. Speakers usually have to be trained to sound natural when using a TelePrompter™ or a written manuscript, and it usually takes a lot of practice to become comfortable doing so.

There are several advantages to manuscript speaking. Manuscript speaking allows you to plan exactly what you will say and exactly how long it will take, and there are some occasions in which precise language is especially important. For example, when the President of the United States delivers the State of the Union address, he (or, someday, she) is setting a policy agenda for the year ahead. Even though the speech is delivered to a joint session of Congress, it is also watched by people around the world and analyzed by the media for weeks afterward. In this case a precisely planned message is important, since even a few misspoken words could have dire consequences. Likewise, when giving the news, anchors must be certain that everything they say is correct and that all of their stories can be delivered in an exact amount of time, so using a manuscript is necessary.

However, there are some disadvantages to manuscript speaking. Like memorized speaking, manuscript speaking requires careful training and preparation. It is not as if you can simply write a draft and then read it to an audience. As you may remember from our discussion about language, there are significant differences in linguistic style between written and spoken messages, and manuscript speaking requires that you learn to write in a spoken style. Even when speaking off a manuscript, you should sound natural and conversational, and that is hard to do when reading what amounts to an essay. Manuscript delivery also reduces your ability to maintain eye contact with your audience and to use gestures and movement effectively, and this is an essential part of strong delivery.

Impromptu Speech

impromptu speech

a presentation done with little or no preparation

The next style of delivery is an impromptu speech. Impromptu speaking can also be a scary experience, because this is when you are asked to speak to an audience with, at best, a few moments to prepare remarks. This often happens in the classroom when the professor calls on someone to talk about something from the readings or elaborate on a topic that emerged in class discussion. The lack of preparation time requires you to plan what you will say while you are speaking, which can be nerve-wracking for many people. On the plus side, however, you do not have to do any research, as there is no time to properly conduct it, and you are more likely to make eye contact with your audience, since you do not have a manuscript that draws your attention.

Extemporaneous Speeches

extemporaneous speech

a speech delivered with notes but without the entire speech in front of the speaker

The last mode of delivery involves elements of each of the others we have just covered. An extemporaneous speech is a practiced, polished speech that makes use of a speaking outline to properly deliver remarks to an audience. Extemporaneous delivery is the most natural sounding of all the delivery styles because it lacks the pressure of memory or the cadence of a written essay. Extemporaneous delivery also allows you to make eye contact with the audience and adapt to their feedback during your presentation. It is, by all measures, a combination of the best of each of the other delivery styles.

No matter which delivery style you choose or are asked to use when delivering a presentation, it takes practice and experience to develop your own natural speaking rhythm. Rest assured that anyone can have competent delivery if they prepare, practice, and are familiar with their outline. To practice delivery, though, means understanding the verbal and nonverbal elements of delivering a speech.

Components of Delivery

Delivery can be divided best into two elements: verbal delivery, or elements of speaking that deal with voice, and physical delivery, or elements of speaking that deal with the body. In this section, we will address how each of these are two important dimensions of your delivery functions.

Verbal Delivery

Your voice is the conduit through which your spoken messages travel to an audience. Your voice, though, is not a simple thing but rather a series of interrelated elements. You must understand and pay attention to each of these elements as you practice and ultimately deliver your speech. In this section, we will talk about eight of those aspects.

1. **Pronunciation:** What a word should sound like when it is spoken is its pronunciation. When you mispronounce words it damages your credibility with the audience and makes the speech sound like it was just recently developed and that you did not practice it.

2. **Articulation:** This is the process of physically producing the sound that makes the word. Common articulation errors occur when we run words together. Articulation errors are so common that they seem like they are actually how the words should sound. In fact, this happens because in casual conversation articulation errors are not seen as a big problem as long as everyone understands what was said. However, in formal conversation, such as in business settings and speeches, they should be avoided. Like mispronunciations, improper articulation will damage your credibility with the audience. Here are some common articulation errors:

   > "You all" becomes "y'all"
   >
   > "I do not know" becomes "I dunno"
   >
   > "You bet" becomes "you betcha"

3. **Volume:** The third thing to consider is the volume of your voice. This concerns how loud your voice is. You should speak with enough volume so that the person farthest away from you can easily hear you without straining to discern what you are saying. If you think there are some people who cannot hear you, consider pausing your presentation and simply asking them if they can hear you. In many situations microphones are available that can help you augment the volume of your voice, but be sure you do not come across as too loud.

4. **Pitch:** The pitch is how high or low your voice sounds, along with the rise and fall of your voice. Some people have deep voices, while others have higher voices. To determine your pitch and understand how you sound, consider recording your voice and listening to yourself.

5. **Rhythm:** Rhythm is the pattern of movement, or cadence, of your voice. Most of us have a natural cadence to our voice and have a pattern in the way we speak. When we're nervous, though, we sometimes begin to speak in a repetitive pattern that gives our voice a sing-song quality, does not reflect the meaning of what we are saying, and sounds unnatural. When giving a speech, be careful to not let your voice fall into an unnatural, repetitive pattern that distracts the audience from your message.

6. **Rate:** The next aspect is the rate, or speed, at which you speak. Some people, and some geographic regions, have different rates of speech than other people or geographic regions. Again, recording yourself and calculating the rate of speech is a great way to monitor your pace. Speaking too fast can make it hard

verbal delivery
elements of speaking that deal with voice

physical delivery
elements of speaking that deal with the body

pronunciation
the accepted standard of how a word sounds when spoken

articulation
physically producing the sound needed to convey the word

for people to follow, and speaking too slowly can come across as condescending, so be careful to maintain a pace of between 125 and 150 words per minute.

7. **Tone:** Tone refers to the variable level of your voice. Tone is important, as it helps convey emotions and interest. If you have low variance in tone, otherwise referred to as a monotone voice, your audience may quickly lose interest, as it appears as though you yourself are not interested in the topic or the audience. Conversely, getting too excited can also be a distraction.

8. **Vocalized pauses:** Vocalized pauses occur when speakers feel the need to utter some sort of sound but do not have anything to say. Vocalized pauses are also sometimes referred to as filler words. These sounds come in many forms, all of which you may recognize: "ah," "uh," "umm," and "y'know." They are not a problem if held to a minimum as they are quite natural, but too many will distract the audience, hurt your credibility, and likely increase your anxiety.

Your voice is a very important element of your delivery, but it is only half of the delivery equation. Your body is also an essential part of delivery, and we will next explore the facets of physical delivery.

Physical Delivery

Many people do not realize that the body also sends signals to the audience while you are speaking. There are five components of physical delivery that we will cover, and each plays an important role in effective delivery. Understand that these all have a purpose and a time to be emphasized during the speech, but only through practice and experience will you get a proper feel for your own physical delivery style.

1. **Apparel:** The first thing we will discuss is your appearance. Consider the occasion when you speak, as more formal dress is required for weddings and funerals than for classroom speeches. You should, at a minimum, ensure that what you wear is neat, pressed, and not torn or stained. Your hair should be well groomed, and you should avoid wearing headgear of any kind, as it looks unprofessional. Also remember that if you are giving a business presentation you represent more than yourself; you also represent your employer and should do so with care and respect. If you do not know what kind of dress code the occasion calls for, remember that it is better to overdress than to underdress.

2. **Posture:** Your posture refers to how your body is positioned when speaking to an audience. If you are standing, be sure that you stand straight and have your feet in a relaxed and natural pose. It should not look as if you are squaring off with the audience. You also should not lean on the podium, although it is acceptable to place your hands on the podium as long you do not use it for support. Standing or sitting straight conveys confidence and respect, while a slack posture creates the impression that you are uninterested and uncomfortable with the situation.

3. **Facial expressions:** Facial expressions are important from the first moment you stand behind the lectern to speak through the moment you finish. Your facial expression should reflect the emotions associated with what you are saying. In most situations, it is appropriate to smile before you begin a speech, which will help to create good will with the audience and help you appear happy to be there with them. However, you should consider the occasion. If you are about to deliver a eulogy, talk about a tragedy, or deliver bad news, a smile would be inappropriate. Be sure that your facial expressions mirror the tone of your speech and the occasion, as people will know your true feelings through how your face looks during the speech.

4. **Eye contact:** As the saying goes, the eyes are the windows to the soul. Maintaining eye contact with the audience is essential for establishing a rapport with them, but it is also one of the most stressful aspects of delivery for novice speakers. Good eye contact does not require that you keep your eyes continuously trained on the audience but rather that the majority of your time is spent focusing on them. After all, you will need to consult your notes from time to time. One of the best ways to reduce the stress of looking out over a huge crowd is to change the way you see the process. Instead of staring at the entire audience, make eye contact with each individual member for a few moments at a time, thus treating the speech like multiple individual conversations instead of a lecture to a large group. Make sure that you include your

entire audience and make eye contact with each person for at least a few seconds. Be careful not to stare at one person through your entire speech, as that is uncomfortable for everyone, but also be careful not to scan the audience so quickly that you do not connect with anyone.

5. **Gestures:** Gestures are the movement of your hands and arms, and they can accentuate points that you wish to emphasize. If done improperly, they can also be distracting to your audience. Speakers often wonder what they should do with their hands when speaking, and thankfully, your hands can be useful during a presentation. Gestures should be used to emphasize important ideas and to help illustrate the relationships between ideas. These should be natural, not contrived, and in order to make this happen, you should practice incorporating them into your speech while standing in front of a mirror or in front of others.

Functions of Physical Delivery

The physical, or nonverbal, dimensions of delivery can serve many purposes during a presentation. Learning what these functions are and the most opportune times to use them during your speech helps you integrate physical and verbal elements of delivery with the content of your speech. This is the recipe for a dynamic and effective speech: good delivery that complements well-ordered points. In this part of the chapter, we will briefly discuss the five functions served by physical delivery.

1. **Repeating:** Gestures and facial expressions can repeat the message you just stated. For example, you may call an audience member by name and then point at the person. This helps you make sure the audience understands the content of the message by using gestures to repeat that content in a different manner.

2. **Accenting:** Accenting gestures emphasize message content through action. You may accent a point by raising or pumping your fist in the air as in a spirit of triumph, or you may tap on the lectern as you make strong statements. These simple actions can let your audience know that this is an important moment in the speech.

3. **Complementing:** Gestures and facial expressions can also complement, or mirror, content in a speech. Examples of complementing are shrugging your shoulders when you say, "I don't know" or smiling when you say something amusing. This helps the speech appear natural and not forced or planned, and makes you look comfortable in the situation with the audience.

4. **Substituting:** Nonverbal acts can substitute for verbal statements, which means that you give a nonverbal message that has no corollary in the speech itself. If you wave or smile at the start of the speech, but do not say "hello," then the waving and smiling substitute for the verbalized greeting.

5. **Regulating:** Nonverbal behaviors that regulate act as controls for the flow of the communication situation. They indicate when other people should respond or when you have finished speaking. You may, for example, use a question to the audience at the start of your speech and expect a few responses before moving on. To indicate this you could lean back in your chair or raise your eyebrows and look at members of the audience. In situations in which you are a member of the audience, you may raise your hand, indicating you wish to ask a question. These behaviors regulate whose turn it is to speak.

repeat
when physical actions restate verbal messages

accent
nonverbal behaviors that augment a verbal message

complement
when the action demonstrates the message contained in the verbal content

substitute
physical actions that take the place of verbal messages

regulate
nonverbal actions that help govern the course of a speech or interaction

All of these nonverbal behaviors can aid you in having a successful speech presentation. Ultimately, however, delivery and content must seamlessly merge into a coherent and natural whole for you to give a successful presentation. In this final section, we will offer some tips for successfully integrating delivery into your speech.

Tips for Good Delivery

There are three tips we can offer you to help develop your skill at delivering a speech. Each one involves time and a change in the typical mind-set regarding speaking, so do not consider these to be "magic bullets" but rather ways to help you as you gain more public speaking experience.

STEM Spotlight

When presenting a proposed research project or solution you can enhance your credibility or diminish the likelihood it will be accepted through your delivery. While strong delivery cannot make a bad proposal effective, poor delivery can make an effective solution look questionable. Make sure that you practice your delivery before you give your presentation. Dress in a way that enhances your credibility in the situation in which you are speaking, whether the situation calls for a lab coat, business casual, or a business suit. Watch your audience for nonverbal feedback and adjust your rate, gestures, and language as needed to make sure that your audience understands your ideas. The best plans in the world are useless if you cannot effectively communicate them to others!

1. **Practice your delivery:** Use whatever advance time you have to practice both the content of your speech and how you deliver it. You should practice at least three times a day, if not more, as the more you work at the speech the more natural it will feel. Also keep in mind that when you practice your speech you might go through it a little slower or faster than when you actually give the speech, so time yourself accordingly. In the next chapter we will discuss some specific practice strategies, but for now just understand that the more you practice speaking, the better your speech will become.

2. **Discover your own speaking rhythm:** As you write and then practice your speech, remember that it should have a different rhythm than a written message. Everyone speaks at a different pace and with different pitch and tone. Speak in a way that feels natural and not forced, and as you find that rhythm, look to repeat it with each speech you develop. Write outlines and manuscripts that reflect that speaking rhythm.

3. **Put delivery cues on your outline:** On your speaking outline you can draw signs like the ones you see used on highways that should help remind you when you should employ certain delivery techniques within your presentation. You can put in cues for physical as well as verbal delivery, but remember not to read those cues when giving the speech.

Summary

Delivery is a seemingly daunting task for novice speakers. In fact, many believe it to be the "be all, end all" of speaking. Good delivery, however, comes from practice and involves integrating verbal and nonverbal actions with the content of your message. There are verbal and nonverbal elements of delivery, and both are important to pay attention to when delivering remarks to an audience. In this chapter, we discussed the various elements of these two parts of delivery and provided you with tips for finding your own effective and natural delivery style.

Key Terms

accent   143
articulation   141
complement   143
extemporaneous speech   140
impromptu speech   140
manuscript speech   140
memorized speech   139
physical delivery   141
pronunciation   141
regulate   143
repeat   143
substitute   143
verbal delivery   141

In COMM 1000/1003

"I won't read the speech. I just need to have my speech written out word-for-word with me when I deliver because it makes me more comfortable." AH, words spoken by public speaking scholars throughout time immemorial. You may not plan to read, but it sure is easy to start looking down and before you know it you are reading much more than you intended. And once you start looking down, it becomes harder and harder to look up. Do yourself a favor, learn to deliver from a keyword outline. Your future self will thank you!

18
Practice

Good content and an understanding of delivery are essential for any successful speech; however, the backbone of strong presentation skills lies in practicing your speech in advance. Public speaking is a skill and not a talent. Talents are individual aptitudes that people are born with; they cannot be learned. Skills are abilities individuals develop over time and are things any person can learn. Public speaking is one of those capabilities people can learn to do very well, but it takes time, dedication, and, most importantly, practice.

In this chapter, we will help you understand the importance of creating effective practice sessions. We will then discuss the stages of practice before finally presenting you with some tips for creating effective practice sessions.

Quality and Quantity

All speakers need to practice, but some need more time than others. Those with speech anxiety issues need more practice time than those who are not as apprehensive. Due to this variance, you should focus more on the quality rather than the quantity of time you spend practicing. There is, after all, no prescribed number of times you should practice your speech to guarantee success. In this section, we will discuss some different types of practice sessions you can use when preparing to give an address. Understand, however, that you should try to make use of all of these and not rely solely on one.

Mirror, Mirror

The first type of practice session involves delivering your speech in front of a mirror. At first this may feel a bit awkward, but that will dissipate with time and experience. Note the expression on your face and how you use gestures and other aspects of physical delivery as you give the speech. Remember from our discussion of delivery in the preceding chapter that using your hands should look natural.

The mirror is also a good way to review your appearance. Even though there is no one watching you when you practice in front of a mirror you should dress the way you will when you give your speech. The mirror practice session not only reflects you but should also be reflective of your speaking situation. Some people practice in front of a mirror quite a bit, while others do so less often. It is a good way to reduce anxiety and get comfortable with the speech.

Friends and Family, Gather 'Round

If you are comfortable speaking in front of the mirror and have a speech that you feel is ready for public consumption but not quite where it needs to be for the actual presentation, consider asking friends and family to listen to you practice your speech. Make sure when you do this that you tell the practice audience what you are doing and what type of feedback, if any, you hope to receive from them. This focused direction allows you to maximize your returns from this type of practice session.

Practicing in front of an audience helps you with anxiety and speech development as well as helps you get a more accurate idea of how long it will take to deliver your speech. When friends, family, and colleagues listen to you at this point, they will be generally supportive, and thus be a good test audience that creates a reduced level of anxiety for you as a speaker. Additionally, when you provide them with specific items on which you want feedback, they can help you polish your message and delivery. Listen to their feedback and make adjustments if you agree with their assessments. If you disagree, talk about it with them and determine whether the changes need to be made. Ultimately, you are not required to act upon their feedback, but at least you have managed to get a sample audience's perspective on your presentation and should know what to expect when "showtime" arrives.

Lights, Camera, Practice!

A final practice session worth noting can actually be done with or without an audience. As you get more and more comfortable with your speech, consider video recording a practice session of it and then watching the video for things you could improve or adjust. Seeing yourself speak is a powerful, if somewhat initially awkward, tool for improving your organization and delivery. The key to effectively using a video to make adjustments is to focus on both delivery and content. Many people look at a video and only examine their physical delivery, but that misses some of the most important parts of the speech.

It also may be helpful to review the video from the mind set of someone who might be in the audience. Ask yourself if you covered the points that the audience would consider important. This can be especially helpful in advance of a sales presentation, because you will know who the audience is and can watch the speech to see if your message hits home the way you want it to. Practice, however, does not solely involve giving a finished speech. There are several stages of practice, and in the next section we will explore those stages in detail.

Stages of Practice

Developing a speech should happen concurrently with practicing it. You can, and should, practice portions of the speech as you create and draft them to make sure they flow and fit the way you design them to. As you finish more of the speech, more and more things need to be practiced, so paying attention to the stage of development you are in will help you polish pieces of the speech as they are created.

Early Stages: Organization

After you start to put your research into a speech format, you should begin to consider practicing elements of the presentation. In these early stages of practice you should focus on organization and adjusting the outline of the speech. Keep in mind that what you have written and organized at this point is a draft and is not set in stone. There may be better ways to organize this information, and once you say it aloud it may not sound as good as when you wrote it. When you have gathered all of your information, lay it out, assess it, and see which method of organization works best to help you accomplish your goals and make an impact on the audience. Then practice each section you create out loud to see how it sounds.

Middle Stages: Feedback

In the second stage of practice, you should begin to get feedback. This should be feedback on both the outline or manuscript and your delivery. In both cases, you will need to bounce off elements of your speech on a willing and helpful audience. This is why you might be given time for a peer workshop during class, but if not, you should set aside time to work with others to obtain this feedback. There are certain questions that you can ask this audience to get useful feedback:

- Have I adequately established the significance of this topic? Does my speech make you care more about this topic?
- Were the main points clear and organized in a logical fashion?
- Were there parts of the speech that were confusing or hard to understand?
- Did I cite enough sources? Did the sources that I used add to my credibility during this speech?
- Did I leave anything out?
- Are there areas in which I need to elaborate more?
- What can I do to improve my delivery?

Each of these focused questions will help you get valuable feedback for developing your speech.

Final Stages: Refining Your Speech

The last stage of practice is when you refine and polish your speech. This usually takes place very close to the time of the actual presentation, and so it is more about shaping and cleaning things up than it is about major organizational adjustments. This is also when you practice extemporaneous delivery, ensuring that you are not reading your speech. While doing this you should focus on things such as eye contact, making natural gestures, and using facial expressions. By this time you should be comfortable with just glancing at your outline.

In terms of assessing the balance of the speech, there are several general guidelines to which you should adhere. The body, where most of your information resides, should constitute about 65–75% of the total speech. The introduction and conclusion should each be about 10–15% of the total speech time. Each main point in the body of the speech should take about the same amount of time to get through. If you deviate too much from this allocation your speech will come across as unbalanced, so during the final stages of practice you can and should make sure you are close to this type of time allocation within your speech.

Tips for Good Practice Sessions

There are several common-sense things you can do to help create successful practice sessions. In this section, we will provide you with five suggestions for helping you create strong practice sessions as you work on your speeches.

1. **Practice orally:** Sometimes novice speakers believe they get just as much help from reading a speech to themselves as they would from orally practicing the speech. Nothing could be further from the truth. Practice means doing the activity you are expected to perform, but without the pressure of evaluation. Reading a draft to yourself does not help you with delivery, nor does it help you hear the words as they will sound. To this end, every time you practice you should do so out loud.

2. **Provide questions to the practice audience:** When you get to a point that you want feedback from an audience, help them help you by providing them with a few brief questions that focus on areas in which you want them to give you feedback. If the speech is for a class, consider giving them a critique sheet to fill out. This ensures the practice audience will address your areas of concern. This will maximize these practice sessions and ensure you get more feedback than "I liked it" or "It could've been better."

3. **Practice with a stopwatch:** In many speaking situations, you will be given a set amount of time to deliver your remarks. This puts added emphasis on practice sessions because you need to time yourself to make sure you stay within the allotted time for your remarks. Practicing with a stopwatch or a timer will help you mark how long your speech takes to deliver. This can then be used to adjust the lengths of areas of

the speech if necessary. If you don't use a timer, then you run the risk of rambling on well beyond your time or, worse, not going long enough and looking underprepared.

4. **Keep it simple:** It is possible to overprepare, and when you do this for an extemporaneous speech it comes across as memorized. This makes you sound over-rehearsed, even wooden. Remember that generally speaking, the best speeches are simple speeches. Even complicated material can be presented in an understandable manner.

5. **Keep the audience in the forefront of your mind:** When you practice, the focus is always on yourself, because you are trying to create and deliver an effective speech. It thus becomes easy to forget that the goal is not to have the spotlight on you but rather for you to achieve the specific purpose of informing, persuading, or helping an audience to celebrate. Whoever the audience is for your speech, keep them in mind and try to practice with an eye toward how you believe they will respond to parts of your speech as you deliver them. Don't forget who you are trying to reach, even when you practice.

Summary

Practice does not always make perfect, but it does help you achieve success when you speak to an audience. Practice is, essentially, a low-pressure way to gain speaking experience so that when the time comes you are prepared to do well. It is not about how much you practice but how well you use your practice time, so we provided several different ways that you can practice your speech. We also detailed different stages of practice during the speech development process. Remember, the more experience with speaking you get, the better you will become.

In COMM 1000/1003

We all know the saying: practice makes perfect. Well, forget that. You aren't practicing in order to reach perfection. You are practicing in order to be familiar with your content and to help decrease your nervousness before a speech. Too many individuals state that practice makes them more nervous. While it is true that preparation anxiety is a real phenomenon, it only enhances the need to practice. If you are nervous while practicing, you are most certainly going to be nervous for the real thing. If for no other reason remember this: practice makes for a good grade.

19
Group Presentations

In many professions, you will find yourself working in teams, and those teams will often be asked to deliver their findings or project results to an audience. When this happens you will present as part of a group, not as an individual. These types of presentations may be informative, as in a corporate board report, or they may be persuasive, such as sales teams trying to persuade a client to purchase a particular product. Regardless of the type or topic of the presentation, there are certain elements of a group presentation that differ from individual performances.

In this final chapter, we will explain the requirements and expectations of group presentations. First we will cover the two types of formats for group presentations. Second, we will explore different roles for individuals in groups. Finally, we will provide some guidelines for being a good group member.

Group Presentation Formats

A common mistake that novice group speakers make is not seeing the presentation as one speech. Instead they see a group presentation as a loose connection between multiple individual performances. For instance, if there are five speakers in the group they often make the mistake of seeing the group presentation as five distinct speeches rather than one whole performance. This error is often made early in the development of a presentation and comes from not clearly establishing the most appropriate format for the presentation. To better equip you in making this determination early, and thus avoiding the error of a loose connection between participants, we will explain the two effective formats for group presentations: the bookend approach and the panel approach.

In the bookend group presentation approach the first speaker is also the last speaker. This speaker's responsibility is to introduce the topic and provide an overview of which

bookend group presentation
a group presentation in which the first speaker is also the last speaker, providing both the introduction and conclusion for the group

group members will explain each component and why they will do so. The "why" helps explain each individual's credibility regarding their topic. For example, suppose Kris, Jarrod, Liz, and Brian are giving a presentation proposing a parking shuttle system to and from campus. They are going to use the problem-cause-solution organizational pattern for the body of the presentation. Kris will introduce the topic and the qualifications of each group member and then conclude by introducing Jarrod, who will speak next. Jarrod will detail the problem, and when he is finished he will introduce Liz, noting that she will discuss the cause of the problem. When she finishes discussing the cause, Liz will transition to Brian by explaining that he will provide a solution that addresses the cause of the problem. After Brian presents the solution, Kris will deliver a conclusion that summarizes the group's talk.

There are several benefits to the bookend approach for a group presentation. The bookend approach gives a nice sense of closure by having the same person begin and end the presentation. It also gives the performance continuity by having each speaker connect his or her topic with the next. Additionally, the bookend approach allows for a degree of individuality in performances by giving each person a specific focus to develop on his or her own and then connect to the other parts developed by the group. It is important, however, that the individual aspects of each presenter do not overshadow the need to have a fluid presentation. Be sure to have clear transitions between speakers and have all speakers work together as they develop the individual components of the presentation. Keep in mind that in a group presentation every speaker is still required to provide evidence, cite sources, and use logic, just as they would in an individual speech.

panel group presentation

a group presentation in which individual speakers present their ideas on a single topic or a subset of a topic

The panel group presentation approach is another common approach for giving a group presentation, and it is structured differently from the bookend model. Panel presentations occur in both formal and informal settings and are most appropriate when audience interaction is expected or encouraged. Panel presentations are individual performances, but all cover the same topic in different ways. Each member of a panel may present his or her ideas on a single topic, or each may have a specific subset of a topic. Panel speakers may agree or disagree with one another, and sometimes even challenge other speakers on their content or positions. To handle transitions between speakers, panels need to have a person play the role of moderator.

moderators

a person that acts as the coordinator of the discussion flow and ensures a civil, organized, and complete delivery of information to the audience

Moderators are unique participants in a group presentation using the panel approach. First, they should be objective and should not present their own opinions, ideas, or thoughts on the topic or speaker presentations. Second, they introduce the entire panel at the start, establish the order of speakers, and transition between speakers when each individual completes his or her remarks. It is important that panelists and the moderator talk before the panel convenes so that there is no miscommunication when the performance is delivered to the actual audience. Moderators also serve the important role of handling interactions between speakers and the audience. They indicate when individuals may ask questions and let the speakers know when they reach the end of their allotted time to talk. Ultimately, their task is to maintain an orderly presentation and keep the interaction on topic. It should be obvious that the panel approach does not have as much structure as the bookend approach, but it has the advantage of being more interactive and covering more material than the bookend model.

Group Roles

In covering the two forms of group or team presentations we explained the two speaking roles used in each approach: moderator and speaker. Good team presentations begin well before they are convened to address the audience. Members of a team need to be aware of the different roles and responsibilities that occur in the development process. In this section, we will cover the three broad types of roles that people fill in small groups when developing a team presentation.

Task Roles

Task roles refer to the parts people play that move a group toward a goal, and these are performed by all members of the group at one time or another in the development process. When developing a presentation, a group needs to accomplish several important tasks, and although everyone may not be involved in each task, every person will help in some way with some tasks. For people to accomplish important tasks to the best of their ability, it is important for the group to identify the strengths and expertise of all members before proceeding. This allows the group to assign members to develop the parts of the presentation with which they are most qualified to help. Table 19.1 gives some examples of group task roles.

TABLE 19.1

Examples of Group Task Roles
▪ **Meeting facilitator:** organizes the information and tasks during the meeting, keeps group members on track during meetings, makes sure that everyone gets to contribute during meetings
▪ **Logistics coordinator:** schedules meeting times and locations, sends out reminder e-mails
▪ **Note taker:** takes notes during meetings, sends minutes to group after meetings, keeps records that the group can refer to when needed
▪ **Compiler:** takes all of the components prepared by individual group members and compiles those components into an initial draft of the group presentation

There are multiple tasks a group needs to accomplish when preparing a presentation. The first two are identifying the information they plan to present and then assigning people to gather relevant research and information. Once the data has been collected, the presentation needs to be outlined and organized. This should not be done individually unless the format will be in a panel, and so several members of the group should review, edit, and revise the presentation outline. When this is done, the speaking roles should be assigned and practice should commence. Each of these stages involves tasks for people to perform, from research to revision, but task roles are not the only roles necessary for a successful group presentation.

Maintenance Roles

In the United States, task roles receive the highest degree of emphasis, but relational dimensions of the group are also important, and maintaining functioning relationships between group members is essential. Without good working relationships between group members, tasks may not be completed well, or at all, because time will be spent dealing with disputes and conflicts between members instead of achieving the group's goal of developing a presentation. To succeed, a group needs to take a collaborative approach, not create a combative or competitive environment in which people constantly angle to do what they want regardless of the needs of the group.

Maintenance of good relationships involves having people who help the group stay loose and supportive. This can sometimes involve joking, attending social events together, or participating in other activities that help group members bond and get to know each other's personalities. If all a group does is focus on the task, then stress will mount and potentially become an obstacle to developing a successful presentation. On the other hand, too much joking and emphasis on relationships also can contribute to an atmosphere in which constructive criticism is never delivered, and the presentation suffers just as much as when no emphasis is placed on maintenance roles. The responsibility to balance the needs of the group falls to the leader.

Leadership Roles and Styles

Every group has a leader, the person who keeps the group focused, motivated, and on task. Every leader also needs followers, and those followers need to buy into the vision and plan advocated by the leader. It is important to know that different groups call for different leadership approaches, and group members also need to learn and appreciate how leaders go about fulfilling their responsibilities.

At a minimum, all leaders need to do three things. First and foremost, they must demonstrate competence on the issue or task the group is setting out to accomplish. When it comes to developing presentations, the person putting together the remarks may not be the person with the highest position in the organization but rather the person who knows the issue or how to prepare a presentation best. Knowing the topic or task is one key part of a well-functioning group, and a core characteristic of a good leader.

Secondly, leaders need to accept responsibility for both their actions and those of their group. As President Harry Truman once said, "The buck stops here" when it comes to leadership. It is the leader's duty to identify things that are not going well and to provide a way to fix problems. If things do not go well, leaders must understand that they played a role in that poor performance, but if things go well, they participated in the success as well. A leader knows and accepts the fact that a group succeeds or fails as a team.

Finally, leaders must satisfy the expectations of the group. These expectations should be clear at the outset of the project. Group members often have both task and maintenance expectations of their leaders, and it is important for leaders to fulfill both responsibilities. The manner in which group leaders go about this can vary.

Leadership Styles

autocratic leadership

a style of leadership in which a leader tells group members what they should do

Typically speaking, leadership styles can be broken down into three different categories, each of which can be effective depending on the group. The first style is autocratic leadership, in which a leader tells group members what they should do. There is little emphasis on maintenance tasks and relationships between group members with an autocratic leader, and more of a focus on accomplishing the task at hand. When projects are under a deadline and there is not much time, this style can be very effective, but if used in all group situations, then group members sour on the leader and do not end up working well together. This can have a serious and negative impact on a presentation by a group.

laissez-faire leadership

a style of leadership in which the leader provides little direction on the task and makes little effort to develop or maintain relationships between group members

On the other end of the spectrum of leadership styles is laissez-faire leadership, in which the leader provides little direction on the task and makes little effort to develop or maintain relationships between group members. This approach would potentially work in a panel format for a group presentation, but it would not be nearly as effective for a group that needed to develop a coherent presentation for a bookend-style talk.

democratic leadership

a style of leadership in which a leader finds a balance between task and maintenance dimensions in a group

The third style is democratic leadership, and in this model you find a balanced emphasis on task and maintenance dimensions in a group. When there is time for collaboration and discussion in planning the presentation, a democratic style can be very effective at allowing members to feel part of the project, but the leader must also reserve some degree of freedom in making decisions. However, when there is a firm deadline and time is limited, the democratic style may not be very effective, as the group can spend too much time deliberating and not enough time working.

Leadership Tasks

Some people often wish to be a group's leader so that they can control their own contributions to the group, but this is not a viable or successful approach to selecting a leader for a group. There are, however, two visions for what task leaders are responsible for in groups: vital functions and leader-as-completer.

vital functions approach

a leadership approach that calls upon group leaders to perform tasks others in the group either cannot or are not qualified to perform

The vital functions approach to leadership calls upon group leaders to perform tasks others in the group either cannot or are not qualified to perform. Sometimes these responsibilities involve a person's access to certain information or skills they have that others do not. In this approach, the leader fulfills a gap that the group needs but cannot fill without the leader.

leader-as-completer approach

a leadership approach in which the leader is the person responsible for completing tasks that are not finished or undertaken by other group members

The leader-as-completer approach functions somewhat differently than the vital functions model. In this model the leader is the person responsible for completing tasks that are not finished or even undertaken by other group members. For instance, in academic departments many chairpersons decide to teach the required courses that the other faculty did not volunteer to teach, thus completing the offering of necessary courses in a given semester. In this approach, leaders are often somewhat experienced with a variety of different tasks that the group needs to perform, so they can step in when needed.

No matter which approach leaders take or what type of leadership style they use, good leadership is necessary for a group to function well. However, a leader cannot be successful without good group members. In the next section, we will discuss how you can be a good team member.

Being a Good Team Member

Being a good team member has several characteristics. The first of these involves the ability to listen to several messages at the same time. To be an effective member of any group, you need to be able to listen to the leader of that group and offer feedback and ideas whenever appropriate. Additionally, you have a responsibility to listen to other group members when they offer ideas and comments related to the task or group as a whole. Finally, you need to listen to the audience at the presentation to make sure you can help the group adapt to feedback during and after the performance. Remember that listening means paying attention to these other people, because only if you do so will they do the same for you when it is your turn to offer ideas.

Listening can be hard, because it often means suppressing our desire to comment in favor of hearing someone else out. Therefore, remember that one of the strengths of any group is that there is a multiplicity of ideas and opinions, and only through hearing them out completely can you identify the best way to accomplish the task and still maintain positive relationships between members. Be patient with others, even if you disagree with them, and give their thoughts fair and unbiased attention. Realize that just because someone might not want to do something in the same way you would doesn't mean that it is not a viable approach; there are usually several ways to accomplish something. A good idea for facilitating and developing good listening skills is to take detailed and accurate notes to which you may refer at a later time. Even if the group has an assigned note-taker, take notes anyway for your own reference.

Just as you have the group obligation to listen attentively and in an unbiased manner to the ideas and opinions of others, group members also have the obligation to extend that same courtesy to you. Group sessions usually have brainstorming sessions, so if you have an idea, present it to the rest of the group members. Good groups function on the principle of civility, which means all have a responsibility both to pay attention to each other and to assert their own ideas about the task at hand (see Table 19.2 for examples of productive and disruptive behaviors).

A second characteristic of high-performing groups is the ability to identify the skill sets for each member and assign tasks that take advantage of those skills. People come to groups with differing talents and abilities, which is often what makes groups stronger than individuals. Some people are good analysts, some are better at researching, some better at organizing presentations, some at keeping records, and others at actually delivering the remarks. Determine your best set of skills and offer to work on tasks that fit your talents. Beware, however, that asking for the assignment does not mean that you will get it, so don't be afraid to go out of you comfort zone and try something new. After all, you may discover that you have strengths you did not know you had!

TABLE 19.2

Productive vs. Disruptive Behaviors	
Productive Behaviors	**Disruptive Behaviors**
▪ Listen carefully to others ▪ Ask for clarification when needed ▪ Make connections between others' ideas ▪ Provide constructive feedback ▪ Arrive at meetings on time ▪ Distribute agendas and meeting minutes ▪ Identify and utilize individual strengths	▪ Attack others or their ideas ▪ Bring up unrelated topics ▪ Arrive late or miss meetings ▪ Dominate the conversation during meetings ▪ Fail to complete your components of the project ▪ Be inflexible and unavailable ▪ Speak rudely to others

A third characteristic of a good group member involves helping facilitate efficient and productive meetings. As group members work on their tasks, it is important to stay in contact with each other. These meetings can occur via conference calls, in person, or even through Skype, but each group member should be aware of what is going on elsewhere in the group. This allows people to offer assistance if necessary and also to get feedback on their part of the project to help make the presentation more seamless. That is why frequent meetings are often necessary; each group member needs to know what the others are doing to avoid redundancy and wasted effort as well as to ensure that the material is consistent.

These meetings are run best when there is an agenda provided to group members in advance. This allows everyone to bring information relevant to what will be discussed and to know roughly how long the meeting will take. Agendas serve important task functions and are often the responsibility of a group leader to both produce and disseminate among the group members.

Another obligation for group members is to meet deadlines. Group tasks often rely and depend upon one another, so when one is delayed, all are delayed. It is both unprofessional and unethical to have others waiting on you. This behavior is also rude and can cause tension and feelings of resentment and distrust, ultimately damaging the harmony of the entire group. If you do fall behind and do not believe you will make a deadline, be sure to let your group know immediately so they can see if they can assist you in completing the task on time.

All group members are also expected to be present for all meetings. Anyone can have a conflict that requires their absence, but this should be avoided if possible. Missing meetings is rude and can result in negative feelings, as someone else may have to do your job in addition to his or her own.

Attendance is also essential when the group plans to practice the presentation, and being a good group member means being there for the practice sessions, even if you do not have a speaking role. Groups must practice together to ensure a smooth delivery, because if any one speaker does something different or unexpected, the whole presentation will become disjointed. Remember that a group presentation is not a set of individual speeches but rather one speech with several speakers. Speakers should polish their individual portions of the address before meeting with other group members but also be open to changes and adjustments when the group practices together. A group presentation is more than just the sum of its parts.

During the practice sessions, group members should critique one another's performance, assessing all aspects of content and delivery, and provide helpful feedback to make the presentation more successful. If possible, implement the feedback immediately. Also realize that if you provide feedback others may disagree, and ultimately it is up to each speaker what to cover. Feedback can be very useful if given in the right manner. Never criticize the person but rather note how the project or presentation can be improved.

Group presentations require more effort because of the need for multiple people with divergent skills, abilities, ideas, and opinions to work together. Many hands, when it comes to group presentations, do not make light work. In many instances when you might deliver a group presentation it will be followed by a question and answer, or Q&A, session in which the audience becomes involved. We will cover this part of the presentation in the next section of the chapter.

Group Discussion and Q&A Sessions

After all, the information has been presented to the audience, they may be given the opportunity to offer feedback and ask questions. This practice is most common in the panel format of group presentations, but it is not unrealistic for it to happen in bookend-style talks as well. This part of the presentation can be stressful for members of the group, so think about it as a conversation rather than an interrogation; this will help reduce your anxiety. Here are some other tips for handling Q&A sessions:

First, you should always allow audience members sufficient time to ask their questions or offer their comments. In doing so you should never interrupt them when they are making their point, as this will only irritate them. If the person's points are not easily discerned and his or her statements seem unclear, ask for clarification. Whatever you do or say, remain polite. Even if an audience member becomes agitated, you should "keep your cool," as you have the obligation to the rest of the audience and to your group to do so. Just because an audience member is emotional does not mean that you have to behave in the same manner.

It is also a good idea to take notes when a person asks a question or makes a comment, especially if the comments are somewhat long. You may learn some things from the audience and might want to consider those points in a later presentation. Taking notes also signifies that you value the feedback that you get from the audience and that you paid careful attention to them when they spoke.

It is also important to be comfortable with the fact that you do not know everything and may even be stumped by a question from the audience. This is not a bad thing, as delivering a presentation is not a quiz show and you will not be eliminated for not knowing the answer. In fact, it is far worse to lie or make up an answer than to state the honest truth. The audience does not expect you to always know everything. There is nothing wrong with saying, "I do not know the answer to that question, but I will find out and get back with you. Make sure I have your contact information before we leave here." Audiences usually respect this answer.

Summary

In this chapter, we have discussed several aspects of group presentations. We went over the two different formats and the main tasks and roles that emerge in groups, paying particular attention to both leadership and how to be a good team member. Group projects and presentations can be rewarding, and you may discover skills of which you were unaware, but they are not easy. In fact, group presentations often take a lot more work and effort than individual presentations because of the constant interaction between different people.

Key Terms

autocratic leadership   154
bookend group presentation   151
democratic leadership   154
laissez-faire leadership   154
leader-as-completer approach   154
moderator   152
panel group presentation   152
vital function approach   154

Group Assignment

PURPOSE:

The purpose of the speech evaluation assignment is three-fold. First, it will provide you with examples of speeches before you begin on the more lengthy and challenging assignments of informative and persuasive speaking. Second, it will allow for group work, which research has indicated is one of the most productive activities in classroom settings if participants put forth the effort to make it so. Third, it requires students to answer questions about delivery, audience adaptation, structure, etc. in an effort to deepen understanding about the core principles related to public speaking.

INSTRUCTIONS:

Your instructor will randomly assign all students to groups of 4–6. At the beginning of class two speeches on the same topic will be viewed by the entire class. Your group will then proceed to answer questions about these speeches both in writing and in a question/answer session with instructor. The speeches will be available for further review on Panopto.

REQUIREMENTS:

- Typed, well-composed responses that thoroughly encompass the details related to the questions posed. Each group will turn in one response through Canvas by the date assigned on the syllabus.

- A 15–20 minute question/answer session with the instructor. The date for this session will be assigned by the instructor. The session will be based off the written responses of the group. All group members are expected to verbally participate.

- Each group member must be an active participant. Any group member absent, without a valid university approved excuse, on the class days assigned for this assignment will lose a letter grade for each day not in attendance.

- A peer evaluation must be completed by each group member. These evaluations are intended to ensure that any group member not actively contributing, or perhaps hindering group efforts, can be docked points based on group input.

Group Assignment Evaluation Questions

Directions: Answer the following questions in detail. Use terminology from the textbook and examples from lectures or discussions in class to support your ideas. All answers must be typed.

1. How does the introduction's organization differ in the two speeches? What is the impact that the introduction from the "good" speech has versus the lack of impact from the "mediocre" speech?

2. Explain how the delivery in each speech impacts the credibility of the speaker? What, if any, are specific instances that your group observed that damaged the credibility of the speaker?

3. What role does audience analysis play in each speech? What, if anything, does being audience-centered add to the "good" presentation? What, if anything, does the lack of being audience-centered detract from the "mediocre" presentation?

4. What are the differences in how the visual aids are presented in the speech? Which speech has a stronger impact because of the visual aid and why?

5. What are some differences in content that your group observed in these two speeches? What are specific examples of supporting material that made the speech stand out (either good or bad)?

6. What are the differences in the conclusion of the two speeches? Which speech ends with a stronger memorable message and why?

7. What letter grade would your group assign to the "mediocre" speech and why? What letter grade would your group assign to the "good" speech and why?

Key Terms

A

abstract	words are not concrete or tangible items; they are only representations
accent	nonverbal behaviors that augment a verbal message
acceptance	third step of the persuasion process in which the audience accepts that the issue is relevant to them
alliteration	repeating the same consonant or vowel sound at the beginning of subsequent words
ambiguous	language that does not have precise, concrete meanings
antithesis	when two ideas that sharply contrast with one another are put side by side in a parallel structure
arbitrary	symbols used to represent things that are not intrinsically connected to those things
archetypal metaphors	metaphors that use common human experiences to describe another object
articulation	physically producing the sound needed to convey the word
artistic proof	constructed by the speaker for the occasion; concerns ethos, pathos, and logos
autocratic leadership	a style of leadership in which a leader tells group members what they should do
awareness	first stage of the persuasion process in which you focus the audience's attention on the issue and show why the issue is important

B

bar graph	a graph that shows two axes and bars going either horizontally or vertically to represent total achievement
bias	an unfair preference or distortion of information
bookend group presentation	a group presentation in which the first speaker is also the last speaker, providing both the introduction and conclusion for the group
bookend story	a narrative in which the speaker tells the first part of a story as an attention getter in the introduction of his/her speech and then finishes the story in the closer at the end of the conclusion
Boolean operators	using words such as "and," "but," and "or" when typing in search terms to focus the results
brainstorm	to create a list of possible topics and keep adding to this list as you think of new ideas
brief example	an example that makes a very quick point and can be effective at any point in a speech

C

categorical syllogism	a syllogism in which the argument is based on membership in a group
channel	the media through which an encoded message is transmitted from a source to a receiver
chart	visual depictions of summaries of numeric data
clincher	the final statement of your speech
communication apprehension	the fear or anxiety associated with real or anticipated communication with another or others
complement	when the action demonstrates the message contained in the verbal content
comprehension	stage of the persuasion process in which the audience understands the relevant components of the issue and the position that you want them to take
concept map	also known as a mind map, a visual representation of the potential areas that you could cover in your speech
conditional syllogism	a syllogism in which the major premise contains a hypothetical condition and its outcome
coordination	all information on the same level has the same significance
credibility	the ability of a person to inspire belief or trust in others

D

dais	a table at which people sit in the front of the room

decoding	process of drawing meaning from the symbols that were used to encode a message
deductive reasoning	an argument that reasons from known premises to an inevitable conclusion
democratic leadership	a style of leadership in which a leader finds a balanced emphasis on task and maintenance dimensions in a group
demographics	categories of definable characteristics of groups of people, such as age, race, religion, socioeconomic status, education level, and sexual orientation
derived credibility	the form of credibility that manifests itself during your presentation
disjunctive syllogism	a syllogism in which the major premise includes two or more mutually exclusive alternatives
division	principle that if a point is divided into subpoints, there must be two or more subpoints

E

encoding	taking an abstract notion and providing it with meaning through the application of symbols
environment	the context in which the communication process takes place
ethics	involve morals and the specific moral choices to be made by a person
ethos	the credibility of the speaker
eulogy	a speech that pays tribute to the life of the deceased
expert testimony	testimony from someone who has conducted extensive research on the topic, has significant experience with the topic, or holds a position that lends credibility to their ideas on the subject matter
extemporaneous speech	a speech delivered with notes but without the entire speech in front of the speaker
extended example	an example that takes time, and the importance lies in the details

F

feedback	the receiver's response to a message that is sent to the sender
figurative analogy	when the two cases being compared are from completely different classifications

G

general purpose statement	a brief statement representing what you aim to do with the speech; there are three types
global plagiarism	taking an entire piece of work and saying that it is your own
graph	a type of chart that illustrates numeric data by using a visual diagram

H

hate speech	attacking a person or group of people based upon their gender, ethnicity, religion, sexual orientation, social actions, or any other category that indicates applications of a negative, unwarranted stereotype
hierarchical	language that is structured according to more or less, higher or lower
histogram	a visual representation of a frequency table in which the categories are placed on the horizontal axis and vertical bars are used to represent the number (or frequency) of individuals that fit into that category
hypothetical example	an example that is fictional

I

impromptu speech	a presentation done with little or no preparation
inartistic proofs	all the evidence, data, and documents that exist outside of the speaker and the audience, but nevertheless can aid in persuasion
incremental plagiarism	using part of someone else's work and not citing it as a source
inductive reasoning	an argument that comes to a probable, instead of an absolute, conclusion
initial credibility	the credibility that you have with the audience before you begin your speech that is based on your experience and the audience's prior knowledge about you
integration	the fourth step of the persuasive process in which the audience adopts the position that you want them to take

interactive model of communication	communication theory that views communication as a two-way process that includes feedback and the environment
internal summary	a statement that summarizes what you have already covered and precedes transitions
internal preview	serves as an outline of what is to come next in a speech and is often combined with transition statements
issue awareness	first stage of the persuasion process, in which you focus the audience's attention on the issue and show why the issue is important

L

laissez-faire leadership	a style of leadership in which the leader provides little direction on the task and makes little effort to develop or maintain relationships between group members
leader-as-completer approach	a leadership approach in which the leader is the person who is responsible for completing tasks that are not finished or undertaken by other group members
lectern	the stand behind which people speak and on which they place their notes
linear model of communication	theory that views communication as a one-way process in which a source conveys an encoded message through a channel to a receiver, who then decodes that message
line graph	a graph that uses lines drawn along two axes that show growth, loss, or flat developments over time
literal analogy	when the two cases being compared are classified the same way
logos	the logical dimension of the appeal

M

manuscript speech	when a speaker has an entire speech written out word-for-word in front of him/her as he/she speaks
mean	the average of all of the scores in a distribution, which is calculated by adding all of the scores and then dividing by the total number of scores
measures of central tendency	statistics that indicate where the middle of a distribution lies, including the mean, median, and mode
median	the middle number in a distribution of numbers
memorized speech	when a speaker commits an entire speech to memory and delivers it with no notes in front of him/her
message	the content or idea that the source tries to convey to the audience
metaphor	linguistic device that allows for comparisons between two objects by highlighting qualities of each object in explicit comparison
metonymy	using a tangible object to represent an otherwise intangible thing
mixed metaphor	metaphors that compare two objects that have no logical connection with each other
mode	the score that appears most often in a distribution of numbers
model	a three-dimensional representation of an actual object
moderator	a person who acts as the coordinator of the discussion flow and ensures a civil, organized, and complete delivery of information to the audience

N

narrative	a story
necessary cause	a cause that must be present for an effect to happen
noise	anything that can change the message after the source encodes and sends it

O

object	the thing being discussed, not a model or representation of that thing

P

panel group presentation	a group presentation in which individual speakers present their ideas on a single topic or a subset of a topic
parallelism	similarly structuring related words, phrases, or clauses of speech
patchworking	a speaker or writer takes original source material and changes a few words in it, but not enough to consider it a paraphrase, all the while not citing the original source material

patchwork plagiarism	taking ideas from more than one piece of work and putting them together into a new piece of work, and then presenting them as original work without giving due credit to the sources
pathos	the emotional dimensions of the appeal that can influence an audience's disposition toward the topic, speaker, or occasion
peer testimony	testimony from someone who is in the same peer group as the audience but who is not necessarily an expert on the topic
phobias	a persistent, irrational fear of a specific object, activity, or situation that leads to a compelling desire to avoid
physical delivery	elements of speaking that deal with the body
physical location	the immediate environment in which the speaker will be speaking
photograph	a picture of the object about which you are speaking
pie graph	a graph that shows circles that are "sliced" apart to represent percentages of the total "pie" for particular groups or categories
plagiarism	taking the intellectual achievements of another person and presenting them as one's own
podium	a raised platform on which the speaker stands
profanity	language which is vulgar and irreverent
pronunciation	the accepted standard of how a word sounds when spoken

Q

question of fact	when a speaker seeks to persuade people about how to interpret facts
question of policy	when a speaker takes a position on whether an action should or should not be taken
question of value	a persuasive speech about the rightness or wrongness of an idea, action, or issue

R

real example	an example that is factual
reasoning by analogy	when you compare two similar cases to argue that what is true in one case is also true in the other
reasoning by cause	arguments that claim one event or factor produces an effect
reasoning by example	the process of inferring general conclusions and making general claims from specific cases
reasoning by sign	occurs when the presence of one thing indicates the presence of another
receiver	the person or audience that a message is being transmitted to
refutation	response to potential opposition to your argument
regulate	nonverbal actions that help govern the course of a speech or interaction
repeat	when physical actions restate verbal messages
repetition	repeating words and phrases

S

self-fulfilling prophecy	convincing yourself that something is going to happen before it does, thus leading to the occurrence of what you originally expected
signposts	key words that signal to the audience that you are moving from one part of the speech to another
simile	linguistic device that compares two things through the use of "like" or "as"
source	the person responsible for inventing the idea on which they intend to speak and crafting that idea to an audience
speaking tool	devices that assist speakers, such as microphones, podiums, lecterns, and lighting
specific purpose statement	a narrower version of the general purpose statement that identifies what you will talk about, what you will say about it, and what you hope the audience will take away from the speech
standard deviation	a measure of variability that indicates how spread apart the numbers in a distribution are
statistics	numbers that summarize and organize sets of numbers to make them easier to understand or visualize

subordination	process of creating a hierarchy of ideas in which the most general ideas appear first, followed by more specific ideas
substitute	physical actions that take the place of verbal messages
sufficient cause	a cause that can produce the effect in question
synecdoche	using one part of something to represent the whole thing
systematic desensitization	the process in which people are slowly introduced to their fear so that each time they overcome the fear, the intensity is decreased

T

terminal credibility	the level of credibility that you have when your speech concludes and that is the sum of your initial credibility and derived credibility
testimony	using the words of other people as evidence
thesis	a carefully worded one-sentence encapsulation of exactly what you will cover in your speech
transactional model of communication	the theory that views communication as a constant process in which all parties simultaneously play the roles of sender and receiver
transition	connective statements that signal you are finished with one point and moving on to another

V

verbal delivery	elements of speaking that deal with voice
vital function approach	a leadership approach that calls upon group leaders to perform tasks others in the group either cannot or are not qualified to perform
Voice Over Internet Protocol (VOIP)	allows for voice and images to be sent live over the Web to another person

Index

Grade Calculation Form – Fall and Spring Semesters

Participation   _____ X .10 = _____

Introductory Speech   90   X .05 = 4.5

Group Assignment   90   X .10 = 9

Informative Speech   62   X .20 = 12.4

Persuasive Speech   84   X .30 = 25.2

Final Exam   91.8   X .25 = 22.95

Grade Calculation Form – Summer Semester

Participation   _____ X .10 = _____

Group Assignment   _____ X .10 = _____

Informative Speech   _____ X .25 = _____

Persuasive Speech   _____ X .30 = _____

Final Exam   _____ X .25 = _____